MW00933624

The Magic
of
Dreams

Tootsie,

Much love and
happiness.

Love,

Denny

12/20/2014

The Magic of Dreams

An American Diplomat's Journey

Eleanor Lopes Akahloun

Copyright © 2014 by Eleanor Lopes Akahloun.

Library of Congress Control Number:		2014917631
ISBN:	Hardcover	978-1-4990-7931-9
	Softcover	978-1-4990-7932-6
	eBook	978-1-4990-7930-2

All rights reserved. No part of this book may be reproduced or transmitted in any form or by any means, electronic or mechanical, including photocopying, recording, or by any information storage and retrieval system, without permission in writing from the copyright owner.

Any people depicted in stock imagery provided by Thinkstock are models, and such images are being used for illustrative purposes only.
Certain stock imagery © Thinkstock.

This book was printed in the United States of America.

Rev. date: 11/20/2014

To order additional copies of this book, contact:
Xlibris
1-888-795-4274
www.Xlibris.com
Orders@Xlibris.com
541088

CONTENTS

Part Three

DEDICATION

In memory of my grandparents and their generation who taught me how to courageously overcome adversity.

For my loving parents who both allowed me to pursue my dreams.

For my late husband and children who give immeasurable meaning to my existence on earth.

And for the Cape Verdean diaspora, so that they remember the fortitude of our ancestors and the value of our rich cultural heritage.

No matter what you are doing, keep the undercurrent of happiness, the secret river of joy, flowing beneath the sands of various thoughts and the rocky soils of hard trials.

—Paramhansa Yogananda

Walk with the dreamers, the believers, the courageous, the cheerful, the planners, the doers, the successful people with their heads in the clouds and their feet on the ground. Let their spirit ignite a fire within you to leave this world better than when you found it.

—Wilfred Peterson

ACKNOWLEDGMENTS

This memoir would not be possible without the assistance of my dedicated American and Moroccan families and the encouragement of my many friends. I am indebted to my grandparents, parents, godmother, and aunts for their stellar guidance and sacrifices and thankful for the love of my sister, niece, nephews, and cousins.

I am obliged to Ambassador Kenneth L. Brown, Daniel F. Whitman, and Marilyn Bentley of the Association of Diplomatic Studies and Training (ADST), an independent, nongovernmental organization that advances the knowledge of U.S. diplomacy. ADST is located at the Foreign Service Institute (FSI) at the State Department's George P. Shultz National Foreign Affairs Training Center in Arlington, Virginia. I am honored that my story is included in their historical archives. Throughout the adventure of writing this book and my oral history interviews, Dan Whitman's patience, enthusiasm, and cheerfulness never wavered. I am forever grateful for his willingness to accompany me on this long voyage. His curiosity and tenacity during our interview sessions enabled me to document my memorable Foreign Service experiences.

Heartfelt thanks to Dr. Mamphela Ramphele, Judith Mudd-Krijgelman, Susannah Brooks, Dr. Marcel Gomes Balla, and Dr. Badi Foster and his wife Juanita—historians, genealogists, writers, academics, and mentors whom I am fortunate to call friends. Their insights significantly strengthened the various iterations of my manuscript.

To Marion Hird, Carolyn and Jimmy Lee, Miki Markoff, Lois Gore-Thompson, Shirley Wilson, Nancy Andrews, Cynthia Farrell Johnson, Katherine Lee, and Marilyn Martz, our friendship grows deeper with each passing year. Thank you for your steadfastness and your caring spirits. Much gratitude is extended to Michelle Debrosse, Leigh Anne Terry, Margaret Dean, Claudia Anyaso, Sally Kearney, Eddie Lodie, and Lawrence Cohen for moving my vision forward. Bobbie Wilinski, Pat and Dick Kalla, Peter and Lynn LaMontagne, Vanessa Britto Henderson, Dennis Halpin, Beatrice Beyer Ancheta,

Rick Gray, Loretta DiGennaro, Angie Villanueva, and Billy Wright— you are all truly a blessing in my life.

Rachel Jeanty, Mary Chin, Sarah and Rob Wagner, Becky and Tom Yun, Betty Coley, Nancy and Chuck Reid, Stephen Graham, Janice Clements, and Anthony Butler contributed in numerous ways to my personal and professional growth, as did others mentioned in my memoir. It is impossible to name each person who has touched my life, but you know who you are and what you did. I am grateful to all of you for showering me with so much kindness over the years.

Sincere appreciation to Mary and June Rose, Momma Habiba Zefri, Mohamed Jamal Akahloun, Souad Akahloun and Abderrahman Loukili, Elsie Parker, Frankie Andrews, and the late Emma Roderick for selflessly sharing their family history. Their wealth of wisdom inspires me to be a greater human being.

Finally, God bless my children, Leila and Omar, who provided invaluable advice. My book greatly profited from their suggestions. Finer fans cannot be found anywhere. Their love, support, smiles, and boundless humor constantly uplift me.

INTRODUCTION

Because I understand the significance of valuing one's own roots, I embarked on this lengthy project of recording my oral history and then converting it into a memoir. The intention of my book is to document the achievements of those who came before me as well as my personal experiences so as to inspire present and future generations the world over. Retirement from my forty-three-year career in the U.S. Foreign Service afforded me a golden opportunity to put pen to paper in hopes of honoring my ancestors and awakening the prospect of others to achieve their dreams.

My professional and personal goals were accomplished largely because of a supportive mother and father and a nurturing Cape Verdean community. The perseverance, stability, drive, and willingness of my parents to create better lives for their children paved the way for my good fortune. Much respect and gratitude are owed them.

Some people's lives are transformed gradually. Others experience swift changes. The epiphany of my life's purpose came during a family vacation outside of Massachusetts when I was eight years old. The trip broadened my horizons and stirred my imagination. From that moment, my dream was to travel far and wide and positively influence the lives of people around me. Throughout the years, successive challenges threatened my plans. However, determination, unshakable faith in God, and the kindness of others propelled me forward.

Although I have recorded events to the best of my recollection, time is capable of distorting facts. Memories fade, especially as we age. Frequently there is a tendency to weave separate events together. Researching for nearly seven years and digging into my journal entries, family records, photographs, letters, and old newspaper articles provide a fair degree of accuracy to this memoir. Additionally, elders in the Cape Verdean community filled in gaps in my memory bank as they graciously shared their thoughts and experiences. Genealogical research at the Library of Congress and the National Archives in Washington, D.C., verified some of the folklore and led to intriguing discoveries.

There is more to life than what is seen or can be explained by rational means. An invisible energy or force can—and at times does—direct us. I am convinced of this. Writing my memoir, I clearly sensed the presence of departed family members. When stymied or discouraged, their unrelenting voices were steering, guiding, and preventing me from veering off course.

Working with the U.S. State Department for forty-three years, I learned all humanity is interconnected. It was a privilege meeting people of all races, nationalities, and backgrounds. Foreign Service life was enjoyable, adventuresome, and meaningful. As in all professions, there were occasional bitter periods, but experience taught me that there is no avoiding strife and pain, as they are necessary for growth, the pursuit of new opportunities, and the realization of goals. But thankfully, setbacks are also temporary. I am grateful for the entire tapestry of my experiences. My choice of profession was a perfect match for me and one I genuinely consider to be a gift. As you struggle with seemingly unattainable goals, I hope my story in some small way is a reminder that living our dreams is possible.

PART ONE

CHAPTER ONE

Courageous Cape Verdean Beginnings

MY FORMATIVE YEARS, 1943–1965

I was born on April 6, 1943, and grew up in Onset, Massachusetts. My journey—documented by Daniel F. Whitman of the Association of Diplomatic Studies and Training (ADST) in the form of an oral history interview—reveals how my Cape Verdean ancestry significantly influenced my life's goals and aspirations. Here is my story.

Q: *Very often our names are a reflection of the hopes, dreams, and perceptions held by our parents and grandparents. How did you acquire your first names?*

AKAHLOUN: My maternal grandfather, Lawrence Fernandes, chose my names. He was a Cape Verdean immigrant who gardened for some prominent Bostonians at their summer home in Wareham, Massachusetts. His employer's wife's name, Eleanor, fascinated him. When my mother became pregnant, he said, "You know, Alesha [her pet name], when the baby come, we gonna name her Eleanor. It's a good name for a good lady." After seeing me at the hospital, his eyes sparkled. "Alesha," he chuckled, "I think we call her Penny. She's a round, she's a copper tone, and she's a short. She looks just like a penny!" Even today the description fits. Although my birth certificate welcomed me into the world as Eleanor Faye Lopes, from the outset I was called Penny and consider the nickname to be my authentic self.

Q: *You seem to be very connected to your family history. Tell us more.*

AKAHLOUN: I had always been one to cozy up to the elders and listen intently to their wise words. I enjoyed the intriguing stories of their existence in the Cape Verde Islands and their tales of immigrant life in the U.S. and admired and respected their courage, sacrifice, and resiliency. They instilled in me an appreciation of my heritage. I also learned of my family history from the journals of Aunt Katie (Katherine Fernandes) and from memorable, in-depth conversations with older members of the community.

After retiring in April 2008 from the State Department, I began formally exploring my family genealogy at the National Archives and Records Administration (NARA) and the Library of Congress (LOC) in Washington, D.C. The latter is our country's biggest public library and has the world's largest collection of books. Just about everything ever published is there for your reading pleasure. In the main reading room of the Thomas Jefferson building, researchers are dwarfed by magnificent bronze philosophers and stucco cherubs perched beneath a splendidly decorated dome. The atmosphere is captivating and stimulating.

Few people know that Cape Verdeans are an ethnic and racial minority of Portuguese African origin and that they immigrated to America beginning in the early nineteenth century. My ancestors, as other immigrants from different parts of the world, endured and overcame many hardships as they established themselves in the U.S. The deeper I probed, the more I empathized with their struggles. They fought against overwhelming odds but never gave up. Their voices need to be heard, and I hope to give them life through this memoir.

Q: *What brought the Cape Verdeans to New England?*

AKAHLOUN: As my elders recounted to me, life was miserable in the Cape Verde Islands—they were plagued by chronic drought, famine, and poverty. The islands were dry and barren and had few natural resources, but there was one saving grace. Its geographic location—about 350 miles from Senegal astride mid-Atlantic shipping lanes—made it a convenient spot for ships to refuel. As early as the 1740s, U.S. whaling ships began recruiting crews from the Cape Verde islands of Brava and Fogo. The earliest record of a Cape Verdean arriving in the U.S. is around 1790, but the first significant wave was between the 1880s and the 1920s.

Q: So early Portuguese explorers understood to advance their interests they needed a way station, which is why they settled in Cape Verde.

AKAHLOUN: Precisely. Portugal wanted access to the Far East's gold and spices. Because the Arabs controlled the trans-Saharan trade and the Ottoman Turks dominated the overland Western European and Asian routes, they were forced to look elsewhere. They commissioned traders and sailors to explore new routes around Africa, which would lead to India.

The islands were officially described as "uninhabited." Because of the prevailing winds and ocean currents in the region, some historians suggest the islands may have been visited by the Moors or Phoenicians centuries before the arrival of the Europeans. Explorers, however, sailing under Prince Henry the Navigator of Portugal claimed discovery. Portugal's King ultimately awarded the distinction to Antonio de Noli from Genoa in 1460. Two years later, he began colonizing the islands and founded Ribeira Grande (now Cidade Velha), Santiago. According to the State Department's "Background Notes," this settlement was the first European city in the tropics.

Incidentally, Dr. Marcel Gomes Balla, a painter and a historian who has written several volumes about the islands, mentions in one of his books, *The "Other" Americans,* that Christopher Columbus stopped in the Cape Verde Islands during his voyages. Marcel currently lives in Portugal and is an active board member of the Antonio de Noli Academic Society. In addition, he speaks seven languages. His sister, Ruby Balla Brown, and I were classmates at Wareham High School.

Q: It appears that the island's history resulted in the fusion of diverse cultures.

AKAHLOUN: This is true. Initially, the settlement included an elite group of Portuguese and their Italian, Spanish, and North African trading partners. Slaves mostly from the region of Senegal and the Gambia were then brought over. The French and other people from far-flung places, such as Goa and Macau, also made the islands their home. Moroccan Jews sought refuge here during the Spanish and Portuguese Inquisitions. As a result of this history, Cape Verdeans are multiracial and multicultural and have roots and branches extending to the African continent, the U.S., Europe, Asia, and South America.

For three generations, the islands acted as a depot for the African slave trade between Europe and the Americas. In the U.S., the abolition of slavery occurred in 1865, but the islands finally liberated their slaves around 1876. European settlers did not routinely bring wives or families with them. They mixed with the local women. Growing up as a child, I heard stories about the *brancamento* (whitening) process practiced in Brava, where women tried to marry lighter-complexioned men in an effort to advance social stature. Colonialism gave birth to the hierarchical concept of race and class. The darkest Cape Verdeans were seen as inferior while the lighter ones were perceived as more desirable: more refined—essentially more like the Portuguese. This mentality, unfortunately, followed the Cape Verdeans to the U.S. As in the old country, those with fairer skin were generally considered to be of greater importance and given more privileges than those of a darker skin. "Colorism" and discrimination existed on the island and in the diaspora. The lighter your skin color, the better treatment you received.

Cape Verdeans received a relatively good education and had a reputation of being the most literate of Portugal's African colonies. They became civil servants and assumed midlevel administrative positions throughout the region. For example, in 1971, en route to Nairobi, I traveled to Dakar, Senegal, to visit my cousin, Jose Lopes, a Pan American catering manager. While there, I met U.S. Embassy officials who spoke highly of Cape Verdean employees.

Q: Enlighten us about the trajectory of Cape Verdean immigration patterns to the U.S.

AKAHLOUN: In the 1750s, New England whaling ships regularly visited the Cape Verde Islands. The vessels, mainly from New Bedford, Massachusetts, came first for supplies and then for crews. When the industry went into a decline, the captains experienced recruiting difficulties. Young American seamen were no longer interested in the dangerous seafaring job. During the early 1800s, young Cape Verdeans were so eager to find any means of survival that they jumped at the chance of working on these vessels. They had few skills but were determined to make a new life for themselves. The mass exodus to New England was so great that around 1818 formal U.S.–Cape Verdean diplomatic relations were established. In fact, the first American Consul-General to the Cape Verde Islands, Samuel Hodges Jr., was from Stoughton, Massachusetts, a neighboring town of mine. When the ships made port calls in New Bedford or Providence, Rhode Island, a few sailors stayed behind and began working on the docks. That is how the Cape Verdeans gained a foothold in America. This migration is unique because it represents the first large group of Africans to have made the transatlantic voyage to America voluntarily.

Q: It seems that the whaling industry fashioned a U.S.–Cape Verdean connection. But what triggered the movement to hire Cape Verdeans over other groups?

AKAHLOUN: Cape Verdeans were willing to do the ship's dirty work. They were considerably cheaper than their American counterparts, and they were also very brave. It may well be that they tolerated whale-hunting risks better than most groups because their existence on the islands conditioned them to withstand harsh environmental conditions. Eventually, they became very skilled and gained a reputation as being the best harpooners, steersmen, and all-around crewmen.

These voyages were incredibly difficult and dangerous not only for Cape Verdeans but for the entire crew. The ships hunted whales from the Arctic to Antarctica and were often confronted by blizzards, raging seas, and fierce winds that washed them overboard. Then there was the danger of angry whales smashing their boats and dumping them into the sea. If they were not instantly killed, they drowned or were eaten by sharks. And the pay was low. According to some accounts, after clothing, tobacco and other deductions, Cape Verdeans earned as little as $14—sometimes less—a year. Fights broke out over skimpy rations and unfit drinking water. Seamen living a solitary, lonely life frequently were away from homeports for two or three years at a time. With the advent of the steam ships, these old sailing vessels became obsolete.

Q: When the whaling industry collapsed, what took place?

AKAHLOUN: The Cape Verdeans in America were survivors and responded by developing a transatlantic system known as the "Brava" Packet trade. As early as 1892, they pooled their resources and began purchasing a fleet of dilapidated whalers, which were converted into cargo and passenger ships. The Cape Verdean-owned and operated trade was crucial in preserving the island's language and culture in the U.S. The roughly 3,545 mile voyages between southeastern New England and the Cape Verde Islands took about six weeks and opened up a line of communication between those who departed and those who lived in the motherland.

The biannual trips were also a means of bringing cheap labor into the U.S. The schooners carried migrant laborers who worked in the cranberry bogs and the New Bedford textile mills. Household items, clothing, food, cars, and other supplies were also transported. The arrival of the ships on either side of the Atlantic was cause for a big celebration. The atmosphere was exciting and welcoming. Different from any immigrant group in the U.S., either black or white, the Cape Verdeans controlled their own means of passage into this country. The Brava Packet trade also permitted them to have firm control over their collective identity. The Great Depression, the new immigration laws of 1921 that were prejudicial to non-Europeans, and the outbreak of World War II (German U-boats were patrolling the Atlantic Ocean) largely contributed to the demise of the trade by the end of the 1930s. The Ernestina, which I will talk about later, was the last schooner to bring Cape Verdean immigrants to America.

Q: What happened to the Cape Verdean immigrants in the first decade of the twentieth-century?

AKAHLOUN: Similar to many immigrants, their entry was a struggle. Whatever their skin color, due to the legacy of colonialism, Cape Verdeans considered themselves Portuguese. Yet, once in America, those with light skin were labeled European and the darker ones as African. Because no separate category recognized Cape Verdeans as a distinct ethnic group with a country of origin, immigration authorities checked either a black or white box. The difference between how most

Cape Verdeans wanted to be identified and the way official government records or the wider society perceived them often varied. This forced them for the first time in their lives to come to terms with the notion of a bewildering identity based on color and nationality. Were they white, brown, or black? Portuguese, African, or American?

In my particular case, during early childhood, when asked about my background, I replied Portuguese because my parents identified as such. Inside, I always felt Cape Verdean American, but outside my circle I was considered Negro, colored, black, or African American based on existing politically correct terminology. Who exactly was I? Portuguese? Cape Verdean? African American? These racial categories confused me until I realized it was possible to be all three. I had inherited European facial features, curly African hair, and a café-au-lait complexion. Grandfather named me with an open heart. He made no judgments about race, religion, or politics, which freed me to be my unique self—different, multicultural. In the end, I concluded I was purely a woman of Cape Verdean African American ancestry who respected all humanity and was happy with my own self-identity.

Cape Verdeans come in all hues, facial features, and hair textures. Many of my cousins had a fair complexion and straight hair, which were miles apart from my brown skin and wiry hair. As children, we did not dwell on physical appearances. None of this mattered to us, but it made a big difference to the adults within our community. Skin tone or colorism bias was alive and well. Later in life, I learned this is a common problem within communities of people of color globally. The concept is a method of discrimination, which profits lighter-skinned people. Frequently, they earn more money, complete more years of schooling, live in better neighborhoods, and marry at a higher level than darker individuals of the same race or ethnicity. Sadly, I know of families where siblings representing both extremes of color were torn apart because of this destructive mind-set.

Q: How did the Cape Verdeans work through this crisis?

AKAHLOUN: Their faith, strength, and sense of humor sustained them, but finding a niche in their newly adopted country was complicated. As previously mentioned, Cape Verdeans perceived themselves to be Portuguese, but because of their mixed African and

European ancestry, they were unable to find acceptance as immigrants of European descent. Society looked upon and treated them as an inferior racial group. Although they initially sought recognition as Portuguese Americans, they were excluded from the white Portuguese social and religious associations and suffered similar discrimination in housing and employment. Much of this information was acquired from my grandparents, my parents, and their peer group, and from my own personal experience. I also researched extensively.

According to a book, entitled *Crossing Boundaries: Comparative History of Black People in Diaspora*, under Portuguese colonial rule, Cape Verdeans were granted a different status from other Africans living on the continent in Mozambique, Angola, and Guinea Bissau. They were deemed unique because of their exposure to Catholicism and a history of miscegenation, which created a large mulatto population on the island. Consequently, Cape Verdeans brought with them a distinctive cultural identity.

As such, they were immigrants who proudly came to America from Africa of their own free will rather than in bondage. They elected not to identify with the largely slave-descendant African American population in New Bedford because the Cape Verdeans were quickly learning about the racial liabilities associated with being "non-white" in America. They believed identifying as American blacks would limit their upward mobility and jeopardize their children's chances for advancement. So my grandparents and the others hastily checked the "white" box on all official documents. In essence, they rejected being branded as black Americans and defined themselves as belonging to a separate ethnic group.

They stuck together as a means of survival—built their own community organizations, tended to marry their own kind, and clung to old country ways. In these close-knit circles, they spoke Creole *(Crioulo, Kriolu, or Kriol),* a mixture of Portuguese and African dialects, exchanged island tales, ate ethnic food, including *jagacida* (rice with beans) and *manchupa* (a corn lima bean and ham dish), played *uril* (a board and bean game), listened to *mornas* (Cape Verdean blues), and danced to *mazurkas* (lively folk music). Inside their communities they were sheltered, but once they ventured out, it was a different story— discrimination confronted them at every turn. They were looked upon as second-class citizens. Sorting out the question of who they actually were in the new country was a bewildering, painful process. They were marginalized people, walking a tight color line. During the first two decades of the twentieth century, they started forming a collective identity. According to some sources, a few community leaders began to prefer the designation of Cape Verdean to describe their ethnicity rather than being pigeonholed as Portuguese. Cape Verdeans perpetually shifted identities and projected themselves in the most favorable light possible. Social, political, and economic developments governed how they viewed themselves from one moment to another.

In the 1960s, Cape Verdeans of my generation were exploring and emphasizing their African heritage. They participated in the Civil Rights movement, which sought to improve opportunities for all Americans of color. At the same time, soldiers drafted into the military were shocked and dismayed that they were being lumped together with the blacks. This exposure and other developments caused them to identify more with their blackness. The intergenerational dynamics at play at the time was quite interesting. While Cape Verdean parents were still staunchly maintaining their Portuguese identity and Creole culture, those in my age group were developing a stronger appreciation for their African roots.

Coincidentally, Cape Verdeans on the islands were grappling with issues of national identity as well. In West Africa, Amilcar Lopes Cabral began organizing the African Party for the Independence of Guinea and the Cape Verde Islands (PAIGC). He was an anticolonialist who led a protracted political and armed struggle for the liberation of both countries. Cabral and his sympathizers saw themselves as part of the world's majority being exploited by an oppressive white minority. They wanted to rid the territories of Portuguese rule and to unify Cape Verde with the continent of Africa. In September 1974, Portugal finally liberated Guinea-Bissau, and the Cape Verde Islands won their freedom the following year on July 5, 1975.

Following independence, there was definitely a shift of Cape Verdeans recognizing themselves as Africans as opposed to Europeans. But this position was not embraced by the older community in America, which now accepted they were a combination of European and African ancestry. They were prideful of both and felt no more one than the other. This segment of the population had worked tirelessly to project this image. Now, part of their heritage was squashed, and they felt betrayed.

Today, the sense of Cape Verdean camaraderie in Onset, Massachusetts, has nearly disappeared. Many former residents have moved away or intermarried. The demographics have substantially changed, and there are few old-timers left. Apparently, a new wave of Cape Verdeans largely in the cosmopolitan areas of New England seem to be reviving the culture—passing down the language, recipes, and music from one generation to the other. Nowadays, the young tend to be part of a global Cape Verdean diaspora. There is a substantial Cape Verdean presence on the Internet, and a large number of these social networks are centered on music. At various clubs, weddings, and christenings, some of the *mornas* are being played along with popular tunes. The world was introduced to Cape Verdean music mainly through the songs of the late and well-known singer Cesaria Evora, the "Barefoot Diva." The islands have few exportable resources, but its musical legacy is internationally celebrated. Cape Verdeans still seem to be mindful and appreciative of their multiculturalism.

Q: Let's switch gears slightly and talk about your maternal grandfather. Do you know the date he arrived in the U.S.?

AKAHLOUN: My maternal grandfather, Lawrence Fernandes, came to America in 1903, and the story is riveting. On April 1, the *Vera Cruz II* sailed from the Cape Verde Islands (Fajã d'Água, Brava) and was originally bound for New Bedford, but the twenty-nine-year-old vessel drifted completely off course.

Q: Oh, what happened?

AKAHLOUN: According to historical documents located at the National Archives and the Library of Congress, the *Vera Cruz II* went aground at Portsmouth Island in North Carolina on the eighth of May 1903. (The Outer Banks area is treacherous. It is where the warm Gulf Stream meets the cold arctic currents and produces dangerous sand bars and violent storms.) Around 2:00 p.m. that day, a beach patrol spotted the stranded vessel three miles offshore and alerted the "keeper" of the Portsmouth Life Saving station, Ferdinand G. Terrell. He and his crew rushed into their surf boats and headed out to sea. One hour later, they reached the wreck and removed twenty-two women, three children, and two men. One man who died of dysentery was also taken away and buried onshore. Back at the station, the group was fed and sheltered. Meanwhile, a fight broke out on the ship among the remaining passengers. Keeper Terrell returned and "quelled the riot." That evening he wired the U.S. Immigration and Treasury Departments in Washington for help.

The next morning a fierce storm broke out. Mr. Terrell's June 20 report said, "Wind, NE [nor'easter], raining, sea getting up." As a result, he hired extra skiffs and oarsmen. They battled the raging waters and finally reached the ship, where the passengers stood in knee-high water waiting to be rescued. It took forty-four overloaded boat trips to bring 421 Cape Verdean passengers, including twenty-two crew members, to safety. The Life Saving Station's expenses for the three-day rescue operation totaled $179.15. The ship's entire cargo, allegedly 214 barrels of whale sperm oil, valued at $6,000, was also salvaged. It was the biggest rescue operation in the history of North Carolina.

Q: *Amazing. Did the barrels contain something else?*

AKAHLOUN: More than likely he was also transporting contraband cargo. According to newspaper accounts, Customs official D. W. Patrick and Internal Revenue Representative C. M. Babbitt conducted an investigation. By that time, Captain Julio M. Fernandes—and perhaps his first mate—jumped ship. (Incidentally, my grandfather, Lawrence Fernandes, was not related to the captain. His last name is very common. Just want to clarify this.)

During the investigation, two men were caught selling rum from a barrel to local residents. Nuno Antonio Fernandes (a second mate and part owner of the *Vera Cruz II*) was arrested and placed under Mr. Terrell's custody. His accomplice, Manuel Antones (a cook whose real name turned out to be Manuel Penilia), was locked up later.

Q: *This is captivating. Were the passengers well treated?*

AKAHLOUN: In Portsmouth, yes. The villagers surprisingly placed the survivors' well-being before color, nationality, or language. Bear in mind this was taking place when North Carolina was enforcing oppressive "Jim Crow" laws. The islanders provided shelter, clothes, and food. Four-and-one-half barrels of flour were used to make bread, and 2,540 meals were served. Meanwhile, the USS *Boutwell*, stationed in New Bern, North Carolina, was dispatched to Ocracoke Inlet. It played a significant role. On May 10, Captain J. A. Slam received word and prepared for departure. The crew started the ship's fires, filled tanks with freshwater from the hydrant, and took on board extra rations—five boxes of corned beef, two boxes of baked beans, and six boxes of biscuits.

Two days later, about 417 passengers were transported to New Bern, North Carolina. A local physician, Dr. Primrose, aided by an interpreter, examined them. Despite the journey taking a physical toll, he found everyone in fairly decent health. They were then moved to a windowless flood-damaged coal shed on the dock. To make the quarters more inhabitable, the rotted-out floor was replaced with two thousand feet of rough pine boards.

There is conflicting information, however, as to how well they were treated on the ship. At the time, *The Charlotte Observer* reported some passengers ate one biscuit sprinkled with brown sugar from the beginning of the trip. When water was low, they drank a mixture of one part of freshwater to two parts of seawater. Other sources disputed the claim.

In any case, some of the passengers required medical attention, but there were no hospitals in New Bern, North Carolina. In three hours, Surgeon M. W. Glover of Baltimore's U.S. Marine Hospital and Immigration Inspector B. Stump had the nearly impossible task of setting up a temporary clinic. They rented cots and purchased blankets, sheets, pillows, food, and medicine and then the patients were transported to the makeshift hospital and treated. All this information was contained in Glover's June 3, 1903, report. It also noted that "a Negress was secured as nurse and a white man as watchman and orderly."

The doctor found the passengers "insufficiently clad" and "suffering from cold temperatures at night." Diarrhea was also a problem. He thought the enormous quantity of canned meats and bread, eaten after landing in New Bern, might have caused the condition. Malnourished from their journey, they "gorged themselves" on potted ham, tongue, and canned beef for nearly three days. "The illness afflicted almost all the men and one woman, due in all probability to the fact that the males were the stronger and the greedier." The report continued, "They were a *cleanly* docile class of Negroes . . . with proper diet (soup, mush, milk, bread, and coffee), bed rest, and simple medication the disorder yielded." After this, Commissioner Stump took over.

The inspection of the ship and passengers took three days. And the results were staggering. Stump discovered the ship carried nearly double the amount of authorized passengers. There were 180 extra men, including my grandfather who were not manifested and categorized as "stowaways" (smuggled passengers). Huge quantities of rum were hidden under a fake floor of the ship. Prior to fleeing, the captain stole all the money, around $2,300, which the passengers carried with them. This included five dollars belonging to my grandfather.

The weary travelers ultimately reached New Bedford, Massachusetts, but before departing on May 17, they asked for *benson* (a Creole word for God's blessings) for a safe journey at Reverend Father George's 10:00 a.m. "divine service." This was at St. Paul's Catholic Church in New Bern. By the way, three Cape Verdeans—Manuel Jose Barboza, Francisco Piers, and Eugenio dos Santo—were too sick to travel and were left at the hospital. I can't help wondering what became of them.

The *Boutwell* logs noted that "404 guarded immigrants" were escorted to the train depot at 5:00 p.m. After Commissioner Stump and the accompanying doctors confirmed their "chargers" were on board and in their assigned seats, the train pulled out of the station forty minutes later. After two-and-a-half days, they reached New Bedford.

Q: What an adventure. I wonder if the ship was insured.

AKAHLOUN: The U.S. Treasury Department was also curious. It contacted one company in New Bedford, which disclaimed involvement. The U.S. Consul at Brava also had no information. There are many unanswered questions surrounding the ship, crew, passengers, and practically every other aspect of the ill-fated journey.

Q: And how did the Portuguese government react to the incident?

AKAHLOUN: It followed protocol. On July 13, a diplomatic note was sent to North Carolina's governor, expressing gratitude for the "kind and human steps" taken by the local authorities toward the "Portuguese subjects." The note might have influenced the judge to release one of the men jailed for illegally selling liquor.

The *New Bern Daily Journal* reported that Nuno Antonio Fernandes who was imprisoned at the time wrote to Governor Aycock, pleading his case. I suspect this letter, together with the Portuguese government's message, led to the August 22 release of Fernandes and the reduction of his bail from $500 to $100. We can only surmise this because the *Vera Cruz II* story is riddled with holes and intrigue.

Q: *How does a ship, sailing from Cape Verde for New Bedford, Massachusetts, end up wrecked in the Outer Banks of North Carolina? It's very puzzling.*

AKAHLOUN: The crew said the ship was heading for New Bern to replenish its supply of freshwater. Immigration officials believed the captain attempted landing his smuggled passengers and cargo in a secluded area to avoid detection. Apparently, he was on the U.S. government's watch list. My grandfather volunteered little information about the incident. He only said the trip took longer than usual, because the captain was romancing a female passenger on board and his head was in the clouds.

Q: *So the captain was distracted by his lady friend and lost his way. Was he ever found? And what explanation was given regarding the stowaways?*

AKAHLOUN: Over one hundred years later, the captain's disappearance still remains a mystery. Rumors say after the shipwreck, he fled the country in a sperm oil barrel aboard a New Bedford whaler. No one really knows. As for the stowaways, a March 14 article in the *Boston Journal* said a former passenger who inexplicably appeared in New Bedford claimed the morning after departing Brava the captain discovered the stowaways. Supposedly, he tried to turn the ship around, but strong winds prevented the vessel from returning to the Cape Verde Islands. After a day of trying, the captain gave up and decided to take his chances with the immigration authorities when he landed in the U.S.

Once the passengers were transferred to New Bern, there were jobs available for those wishing to earn money. The *Charlotte Observer* on May 14, 1903, advertised "railroad work in West Virginia for Portuguese immigrants at $1.50 per day: transportation free." Evidently, a few Cape Verdeans were hired as temporary farm hands. On October 23, the *New*

Bern Daily Journal reported that the immigrants had so impressed farmer A. B. Dawson with their "industriousness, honesty, and faithfulness" that in the fall he sailed to New Bedford and returned with 106 helpers, some of whom had previously worked for him. Allegedly, there were twelve or fifteen women in the group. The article said the Cape Verdeans were distributed to nine different farms and businesses in the area.

Q: *That stirs the imagination. Do you suppose some residents in this area are related to Cape Verdeans?*

AKAHLOUN: It is possible. Curiously enough, there were 435 *Vera Cruz II* passengers listed in a book I read, entitled *Between Race and Ethnicity: Cape Verdean American Immigrants, 1860–1965* by Marilyn Halter. National Archives records showed a similar number—436. Yet, the Treasury's USS *Boutwell* logs indicated 404 Cape Verdeans departed for New Bedford. Why the discrepancy? Were some people deported? I do not know. We can account for three individuals too sick to travel and two others in jail for illegally selling rum, all of whom remained in New Bern. Did they and farmer Dawson's group permanently root themselves in North Carolina? On the area's 1910 census reports, three Portuguese-sounding names surfaced: John Guman (maybe Juan Gomes), Manley Loxes (Manoel Lopes), and Mandy Fosky. All three immigrated in 1903. Judging from this, I believe some local residents might have Cape Verdean ancestry.

My grandfather kept to his original plan of building a new life in New England. Steve Fernandes met him and his two companions, Lorenzo and Phillip Pina, twenty-eight and twenty-two, respectively, at the train station. They were taken to their new home—a crowded East Wareham shantytown sixteen miles from New Bedford, Massachusetts. Steve's Wareham Savings Bank account spared my grandfather from deportation, as he arrived in New Bedford penniless since the *Vera Cruz* captain stole the $5 he was carrying.

Q: *With everything going against your grandfather, he survived. This took some gumption.*

AKAHLOUN: He was resilient. His small five-feet-seven frame, and sunny disposition betrayed a sad childhood filled with rejection.

Aunt Katie recounted stories of how he was a product of an extramarital affair. As an illegitimate child, he incurred his stepmother's wrath, but his father was unsympathetic to the disdain he faced. So he became very independent and learned to rely on himself. His sense of humor and a philosophy embodied by the Creole saying of *Kai un dia levanta kel otu dia* (Today we fall down; tomorrow we get up.) sustained him.

Q: *In America, there were more challenges. What type of work did him and the other immigrants find?*

AKAHLOUN: You name it, they did it. They tackled the low-paying, less-attractive jobs, shunned by the older well-established New England community. Most were agricultural workers on cranberry bogs and fruit and vegetable farms. Some toiled in New Bedford mills. Others served as porters and chambermaids in local hotels and boarding houses. A few worked as sailors or dock hands in New Bedford, Massachusetts, or Providence, Rhode Island. Several were construction workers, building roads, bridges, and railways and generally commuted long distances to their work sites.

In summer, they picked strawberries mostly near Falmouth, Massachusetts. Around 1907, a quart sold for ten cents. Later, they gathered blueberries. When steady work eased up, they sold Mayflowers door-to-door. During the fall, they scooped cranberries on the bogs throughout the region. In winter, my grandfather and other Cape Verdeans gathered and sold shellfish (clams, quahogs, oysters, and scallops) or chopped wood for burning in stoves. They worked tirelessly. My mother said her father's first jobs were washing dishes at a restaurant called Squirrel's Nest and carrying boarding house guests in a horse-drawn carriage to and from the train station. This piecemeal employment helped him later to acquire property, build a house, raise a family, and own a sizable farm.

One memory of my grandfather lingers. He worked as a caretaker for Henry Burgess who owned the Crocker Estate that dramatically overlooked Onset Bay. He rode his bike there, and I remember him preparing for the long ride. He tucked his pant legs inside his socks to prevent tangling them in the wheel spokes, secured his black metal lunch box (weather-beaten, dome shaped with a thermos inside) behind his seat, arranged his sweat-stained hat on his head, mounted his battered bicycle, and with a smile and a wave, he pedaled away. He was the personification of perseverance and possessed an incredibly strong work ethic.

Q: *You stated Cape Verdeans were involved in the cranberry industry. How was life for them on the bogs? What treatment did they receive? How did the industry impact their lives?*

AKAHLOUN: Cape Verdean immigrants largely helped build the cranberry industry. The multimillion dollar empire of Ocean Spray, one of the world's top grower-owned cranberry cooperatives, has the Cape Verdean community to thank for contributing to the company's growth and profit margin. Much detail can be found in the *Spinner Publications*, which records and promotes the history and culture of various southeastern New England neighborhoods.

Cranberries, a native fruit to Cape Cod, were found on the borders of shallow ponds. Around 1850, the swamp areas were cleared and turned into bogs. By 1900, there was a demand for cheap labor in the expanding cranberry industry. Cape Verdean immigrants from the island of Fogo and transient pickers filled the void. Their living and employment conditions were deplorable. They were housed in crowded, filthy, company-owned shacks without toilets or waste disposal systems. And they supplied their own food and dishes. Many of them died of pneumonia and tuberculosis. Others perished in accidental fires.

The bog owners employed Cape Verdeans because they were efficient, reliable, honest, and docile. In essence, they were ideal workers as they complained little about their low wages, inadequate food, substandard shelter, or the severe climate. Moreover, they had a reputation of paying their bills on time. The bogs were frequently damp in the morning, but by afternoon, they were sweltering. It was a very unhealthy situation. And the work was poorly paid. Some reports indicate the workers received eight cents for a six-quart pail and only five cents if it contained stones or vines. Because the employment allowed them to save and send money back home, they withstood the misery.

By 1910, the number of cranberry-picking Cape Verdeans, including my grandparents, swelled to about three thousand. Children were very much part of the scene. Babies rested in baskets near their mothers. Older children picked alongside the adults using smaller scoops. Cranberry harvest was so significant to the subsistence of Cape Verdean families that it took priority over education. School-age children received permits from superintendents, allowing them to begin their classes after the six-week September to November cranberry season ended.

Q: I believe child labor regulations did not exist and young children routinely supplemented the family income.

AKAHLOUN: That is correct. Economic conditions presented parents with few alternatives. Throughout the nineteenth century, young children labored in the agricultural and industrial sectors. As early as 1904, the National Child Labor Committee began advocating for children's rights, but it was not until 1938 that the Fair Labor Standards Act adopted more sweeping laws governing child labor. One of the provisions prohibited children from working in the farming industry during school hours, which was a blessing for the Cape Verdean immigrant community.

Q: After the bog dried, what was the process for harvesting cranberries?

AKAHLOUN: Under a hot sun, everyone knelt down and began combing the vines with their wooden-teeth scoops. Each person had a row, and everyone headed toward the bog's center. Overseers were posted every twenty or thirty yards, ensuring everyone followed their "picking line." As soon as the scoop filled up, the workers removed the loose vines and poured the berries into empty bushel boxes. My mom was a fast scooper and easily filled up her boxes.

Mary Rose, a classmate of my mother's who is now ninety-nine years old, shared her childhood memories with me during one of our oral history interviews. She told me about life on the bogs and the respect the elders commanded. "We picked cranberries together, and listened to their entertaining stories. In the early morning, they waited for the vines to dry and puffed on their pipes. Others smoked in front of people, but my mother never did." She made it perfectly clear that her mom would never entertain the idea of doing such a dreadful thing. Mary loved spending time with the old folks. According to her, the work was very taxing, but life was not all drudgery. Sundays, a day of rest, were filled with praying, singing, and dancing.

Most of the cranberry pickers were women. Planting, draining, and flooding the bogs were tasks left to the men. During harvest, they also wheeled small carts—stacked with six or more boxes—carried them to shore, loaded the cranberries into trucks and delivered them to the Ocean Spray plant on Routes 6 and 28 in Wareham. My mother later worked at this sprawling canning and processing plant as a screener. She and the other women sat for hours in one position, examining thousands of tiny berries. They removed the imperfect ones from a conveyer belt by hand. The complex also had a refreshment stand, which sold cranberry frappes, juice, and ice cream.

Today eating cranberry sauce, especially during the Thanksgiving and Christmas holidays, reminds me of the central role Cape Verdeans played in the development of the New England cranberry industry. I also think about how much they endured and sacrificed to give their children and grandchildren a better life. Even though they were paid at the end of the season, Cape Verdeans had a reputation of wisely managing their meager salaries and were able to open savings accounts, pay bills, and send money back to the islands.

Reportedly, 80 percent of residents in a certain southeastern New England community in the early 1920s had titles to their homes. Conceivably, this area was Onset, Massachusetts. The 1920 Wareham census listed my grandfather's house as owned and "free of mortgage." The 1930 census valued his house at $4,000. My grandfather arrived in America as a penniless stowaway in 1903 and worked relentlessly under horrendous conditions to gather enough money to build a house and then promptly pay off the loan. This is a testament to his persistence and serves as a lasting legacy for several generations of his family.

Q: *In 1921, during President Harding's administration, Congress passed a stop-gap immigration measure slowing the flood of immigrants entering the U. S. How did this and the subsequent 1924 immigration law affect the Cape Verdean community?*

AKAHLOUN: As a result of tighter immigration controls, fewer Cape Verdeans entered the country and those already here were afraid to leave unless they had U.S. citizenship. The steady stream of new immigrants became a trickle. As stated previously, this was one factor that ended the Brava Packet trade.

Q: Did the cranberry workers try to organize? Demand better working conditions?

AKAHLOUN: Apparently, they did. By September 1933, the seasonal bog workers became so frustrated over unfair treatment that about 1,500 of them went on strike. This was not typical behavior for the usually complacent Cape Verdeans. They demanded higher wages (seventy-five cents instead of fifteen to twenty cents an hour), guaranteed employment until the end of the season, and the right to organize. The strike spread to forty bogs throughout the Onset, Wareham, and Carver region. Violence broke out during an Onset rally, when a local bog owner shot Alfred Gomes in the hand. Police arrived, wounded several, arrested about sixty-four workers and charged them with assault. Eventually, the strike was broken, and everyone returned to work under police escort. According to one labor union report, it was the first agricultural strike in the history of Massachusetts and later on influenced other strikers in the state. A 1938 flood in Onset destroyed many public records, making it challenging for me to research and reconstruct all the events.

Q: What are your memories of the cranberry bogs?

AKAHLOUN: Happy ones. I had no problems or worries. As a carefree child, I ran through the bog, trampling the vines, much to my mom's dismay. She wore two pairs of overalls and had thick pads to cushion her knees. They were made from cloth remnants—plaids and stripes and stiff backing (maybe vinyl)—and she stitched them to her jeans.

In winter, we went ice skating on the bogs, which were flooded to prevent the vines from dying. Reaching them was a hike in summer, but winters posed yet another challenge. We had to winterize ourselves. We dressed in padded ski suits, wore fur-lined boots with double socks, woolen caps, thick gloves, and long scarves wrapped tightly around our necks. We trudged through deep snow in blisteringly cold weather to reach what seemed to be the edge of the earth. Ah, the joys of youth. For hours we skated and skated around and around the bog, jumping and twirling to our hearts' content. We went home only when it was absolutely necessary—our hands and feet grew numb. These were bone-chilling days filled with wonderful memories.

Q: Changing the focus somewhat, did your grandfather ever return to the islands? I imagine the Vera Cruz II incident and its aftermath somewhat dampened his spirit.

AKAHLOUN: By now you know Grandpa Fernandes was not easily discouraged. After five years, he saved enough money for a ticket to the islands. As indicated by his Petition for Naturalization, he departed New Bedford for Cape Verde in October 1908.

Q: What led him to brave another trip?

AKAHLOUN: He was lonely and decided to risk another transatlantic crossing. While in America, relatives in the old country had chosen a sight-unseen-bride for him. It was one of these traditionally arranged marriages. Once back in the islands, however, he caught sight of my future grandmother, Louisa Mott. Within three months, they were married at the São Lourenço (St. Lawrence) Church on the island of Fogo. Naturally, the marriage infuriated his betrothed fiancé. Family folklore has it that in a fit of rage she cast a spell, *mal d'odju* (evil eye) on my grandparents. This belief in the power of good and bad spirits is so ingrained in Cape Verdean culture that mothers often pin a *conta d'odju* (bead protecting against the evil eye) on their baby's undergarments. Adults often adorn themselves in protective amulets as well. I wear mine as a necklace.

On May 24, 1909, about four months after the marriage, he sailed for Massachusetts. My grandmother stayed behind as my grandfather was not able to pay for her fare to the U.S. His round-trip boat ticket, the wedding, and other island expenses had drained his bank account. At the age of thirty-one, he was still young. His plan was to return to America, work hard, and accumulate enough money to send for his bride.

Q: What was the curse? Did it linger?

AKAHLOUN: According to all accounts, the curse meant my grandmother was never to bear a son. In Cape Verdean culture at the time, male children were revered and the most prized possession. It is believed to be the cause of Grandmother losing her boys. She carried nine children, and all four male offspring died prior to or shortly after delivery. The tragedy was openly discussed. In a 1977 recorded interview, my mom reminisced. "When I was in the fourth grade, my mother gave birth to a male child. The arm of the baby was coming out first, and I recall Dr. Goldfarb whispering in the kitchen about the unusual position of the fetus, which complicated delivery." She went on to say, "My father was grief-stricken and repeated, 'Save my wife, save my wife.' The doctor vowed to do the best he could, but he was not optimistic." She paused and said, "I vividly remember this. It stuck with me a long, long time. I believe the curse was real."

During another interview, my Aunt Katie remarked that something supernatural occurred during the wedding of my grandparents and that their marriage was plagued by the mythology of the loss of male children. My aunt said she believed it because Grandmother Fernandes related the same story many times as an explanation for the death of her boys. Not having sons was one of the worst Cape Verdean curses. However, my grandfather accepted his fate. He loved his devoted daughters, who continued living in the neighborhood and showered him with love and affection throughout his life.

Q: Earlier you spoke about your grandfather leaving his bride in the islands. When did he build up sufficient funds to send for her? Were there any complications?

AKAHLOUN: It took him five years to gather enough money for her trip. Even though he arranged for her brother, Joao Correia Motta, to accompany her, there were some glitches. Evidently, twenty-one Cape Verdeans sailed from the islands to Lisbon, Portugal (date, ship, and port of departure unknown). On July 26, 1913, they were scheduled to board the *Roma* bound for Providence, Rhode Island. The vessel, however, departed without them. The ship's manifest showed the names of the ticketed Cape Verdean passengers were crossed out. Why they missed their connection or what happened subsequently is subject to conjecture. Twelve days later, the convoluted trail of her journey to the U.S. is picked up again. They boarded the *Canada* and landed in Quebec City on August 18, 1913, where more surprises awaited them.

Canadian Immigration authorities quarantined her brother, who become ill on the ship, and then deported him back to the Cape Verde Islands. According to family records, she begged to return to the islands with her ailing brother, but Joao could not disappoint my grandfather.

So he entrusted his sister to a stranger who promised to deliver her safely. She was brokenhearted leaving her brother and terrified at the thought of meeting her husband, virtually a stranger whom she only knew four months and was separated from four years. Full of anxiety, she arrived in New Bedford on August 23, 1913, and reunited with my grandfather.

For the record, tracing this history and locating my grandmother's ship was very tricky. Her name was listed as Luiza Fernando Motta vice Louise Mott Fernandes on the manifest. A further complication in following her trail was the rare Canadian border crossing, as most Cape Verdeans entered the U.S. through New Bedford, Massachusetts.

Q: *Did your maternal grandmother, Grandmother Fernandes, regret coming to America?*

AKAHLOUN: Grandmother became accustomed to life in America, yet her soul belonged to the islands. Like many others, she suffered from what Cape Verdeans call *sodade*—the longing, the nostalgia, the desire for home. She missed her family and needed to stay connected with them and the islands. At the same time, she looked forward to setting up a better future in her new homeland. She was often homesick. Being the only daughter, she was pampered by her mother and left the islands with the expectation of returning. Grandmother longed to see her parents but could not afford a visit. She never forgot them and frequently sent care packages to the island.

Q: *When you think of your early childhood, was your grandfather very much a part of it?*

AKAHLOUN: Yes, indeed. I spent considerable time with him. During World War II, my mother worked at Aerovox, a mill in New Bedford manufacturing electronic capacitors and transformers. In the morning, she left me with my grandparents and fetched me in the afternoon. Those were impressionable years. Like a sponge, I absorbed everything. The house and farm were surrounded by apple, pear, and peach orchards. There was also a big vegetable garden. Grandfather raised chickens and pigs as well. The stench of the rice-blood sausages (a Cape Verdean delicacy) made from slaughtered hogs was overpowering, but they were quite tasty.

During winter, I recall sitting in the kitchen next to the wood-burning stove, listening to his colorful tales, as he puffed away on his curved pipe. In the summer, we sat under a sprawling tree next to the grape arbor. Regardless of the setting, his wit and theatrics made his characters come alive. Best of all, whenever I incurred Grandma's wrath, he rescued me.

On Christmas Day, New Year's Eve and during other special occasions, my grandfather and his two brothers would take their fiddle and guitars and go house-to-house singing Cape Verdean *mornas* and *coladeras*, which were slow-rhythm, mournful, and melancholic folk music. They were warmly received and invited into the homes to share some *canja* (chicken soup with rice).

Grandfather was fond of working and had a thirst for knowledge. As a case in point, by trial and error and with few resources, he constructed the family's two-story seven-room house. He never stopped challenging himself. At sixty-five years old, he became a U.S. citizen. My grandfather was an intelligent, caring, fun-loving person with a variety of talents and interests. Success never spoiled him. His pragmatism, resilience, and generosity largely shaped my views on life and played a significant role in my development into adulthood.

When I joined the Foreign Service in 1965, and before departing for my assignment to the Philippines, I went to my grandparents for their *benson*. (This traditional Cape Verdean spiritual blessing is intended for healing, protection, guidance, and the alike. It is often imparted by elders who place their hands on top of a person's head as they recite a prayer asking God to bless the individual.)

"You no find us when you come back," they said. "Of course, I will," I reassured them, "Two years will pass by quickly." But they were wise and seemingly knew their fate. Two months after arriving in Manila on November 8, 1965, Grandfather died at eighty-eight. On his certificate, Dr. Abram Krakower listed his ailments: bronco pneumonia (immediate cause of death), hypertensive heart disease (eleven years), arterial hypertension (fifteen years), and diabetes mellitus (eleven years). Despite all the illness and the loss of part of a leg that was amputated from the knee down, he continued smiling. One of his favorite expressions was "That's what it is and that's how it's gonna be." His life experiences conditioned him to accept things beyond his control. No self-pity. Grandmother passed away at eighty-three (estimated age) on August 10, 1967, of a ruptured aneurism. That was two months shy of my return from the Philippines.

Q: *Obviously, they were very much part of your childhood, adolescence, and adulthood. Any other recollections?*

AKAHLOUN: Yes. When I was about ten years old, I started taking dancing lessons and became a contortionist—a fancy word for an acrobatic dancer. Prior to recitals and competitions, I always went to my grandmother's house to receive my *benson*. Tiny but not timid, she was a disciplinarian who liked enforcing rules. As a youngster, I learned to appreciate that she always had the last word. Later, I discovered her softer side. She raised five daughters and two of the neighbor's children after they lost their mothers. Grandmother Fernandes was the matriarch of the family who took her role seriously. She was an expert cook. Much to the delight of the neighbors, the top of her stove was lined with huge kettles, filled with delicious home-cooked meals.

Here is an amusing story. Her culinary talents also helped her cultivate a lasting friendship with the parish priest, which spelled trouble for her husband. According to my mother, my grandfather disliked church because it involved too much time. He calculated attending service at St. Mary's Catholic Church entailed a forty-five-minute hike to go and another forty-five minutes to return, plus the time lost listening to a long-winded sermon. Although he believed in a higher power, or, at least, that is what he professed, he felt the exercise squandered huge quantities of precious time that could be spent plowing his field. My grandmother worried about his spirituality. So she convinced the pastor to hold services at her house. When Grandfather's activities prevented him from participating (this happened frequently), the priest trudged out to the field. Behind his horse-drawn plow, Grandfather received Holy Communion. His protests were muted for fear of unleashing his wife's temper. Neither did the priest raise any objections as he loved the exceptional food Grandmother prepared for him. It was a win-win situation.

Q: *Extraordinary. Few of us know that much about our grandparents. Your grandfather had everything to gain by coming to the U.S. Your grandmother, after she thought about it, had everything to lose except her husband. They achieved goals. You received their blessings when it was time to go on stage and perform. Your grandfather had a sense of humor. He was an outstanding citizen. What else about them impressed you?*

AKAHLOUN: Their ability to be content with bare necessities in life and the grace in which they dealt with hardships. I was fortunate to interview Emma Roderick, one of the orphaned girls living with my grandparents who described their humble living conditions during the 1930s. She said a potbelly stove in the kitchen heated the entire house. At night, summer or winter, my grandfather shoveled coal inside. In the morning, he added a layer of wood, so there was sufficient heat to start cooking. Immediately after breakfast, my grandmother began preparing dinner.

To conserve heat during winter, they closed up the living room and an adjacent area that doubled as a bedroom in the summer and a cold storage unit in winter. Before entering this part of the house, they bundled up with winter coats, hats, and gloves. The nearby room contained a big tub filled with fifty pounds of lard, which preserved slabs of pork. Additional canned fruit and vegetables were stored in the small cellar accessible only from outdoors. The place reminded me of a cave. It was cold, dingy and had a musty smell. I avoided going there except when the urge for my grandmother's strawberry jam overwhelmed me.

There was no electricity, radio, or television. After supper, they sat around the kitchen table, talking, laughing, playing cards, or listening to stories. A kerosene oil lamp supplied the only light. If someone needed the lamp, it was removed and the others sat in darkness until it returned. Emma said poverty was a way of life for them, but they were filled with contentment. At the time of our conversation, she was eighty-five years old and has since passed away.

Q: We heard about your grandparents but not too much about your parents? Tell me more about them and the effect they had on your upbringing.

AKAHLOUN: My parents were equally special. They aimed to give my older sister, Rita Ellen (Lovie), and I a meaningful life. They encouraged and supported us but were not afraid of applying discipline when we misbehaved. I was my father's pet. In his eyes, I could do no wrong.

Q: *Oh, I think I can imagine that.*

AKAHLOUN: My father was a gentle soul with purity of character. He was quiet, considerate, unassuming, and comical. He recycled everything. He had trouble parting company with his possessions and good-naturedly reminded us, "You never know when these things [referred to as 'junk' by my mother] will come in handy." His rusted pickup truck, held together in several places with duct tape, overflowed with buried treasures, including abandoned coffee-stained paper cups, years' worth of ragged-edged grocery receipts, and a generous supply of scattered rubber bands. He slipped two or three of them on his wrists. His trusty rubber bands held his broken eye glass frames together or prevented slips of paper from dropping out of his dilapidated wallet, which was bursting at the seams. He was a thrifty one.

His cellar was his favorite place. He would store old suitcases, bicycles, electronics, gardening tools, clothes, and anything else he felt could be of value to him. Today, my children control my hoarding tendencies inherited from my father. They buy me self-help books and sit me down to watch reality shows about people who are compulsive hoarders. The therapy is working—my now clutter-free closets, which were beginning to resemble the "unkempt" cellar of my father's, are proof.

My father was also resourceful and intelligent. He did well in school and skipped two grades. Sadly, at age thirteen, he was forced to end his studies and became a construction worker to help out with family finances. Every project he tackled was done to perfection. By day, he was a construction foreman for Frank Smith in Taunton. At night and during weekends, he worked at his private landscaping business. At one point, he took care of some twenty-three homes for their owners. Somehow he found time to care for his award-winning garden. In September 1994, the *Sunday Standard Times* wrote a lengthy article entitled, "Floral Beauty Surrounds Onset Home." The newspaper clipping pointed out at seventy-eight years old, "Mr. Lopes is a bit annoyed that bending over, planting, and pruning is a bit harder than it used to be." Quitting was never an option. When he got tired and his severe arthritis bothered him, he came inside the house, rested awhile and then returned to his chores.

A green velvet lawn framed the property, which was saturated with colorful plants, flowers, and trees. There were meticulously sculptured shrubs next to flowering pink azaleas, rhododendrons, roses, and purple and white hydrangeas that impressively surrounded the house. Either side of the driveway was lined with large bricks filled with white, red, and pink flowers. Pink was my mother's favorite color and the original color of our house. Along our cedar fence, he planted purple dahlias. Every year before the frost arrived, my father patiently dug them up, stored them in his cellar, and replanted them the following year. It was an enormous investment of time. On the other side of the property line, he planted white and purple snowball bushes. In the backyard, more plant life circled the Blessed Virgin Mary's statute and the barbeque pit. Beyond this was another garden, filled with rows of yellow, orange, red-and-white gladioluses, bright red salvia, and other trees and plants. There was also a small plot reserved for vegetables. He even grew strawberries in a wheelbarrow. It was extraordinary. Our home was quite a sight to see with passersby and cars often slowing down to marvel at his work of art. I failed to inherit my father's green thumb.

Q: Are there other special memories of your father?

AKAHLOUN: He was very honest. Once, a cashier gave him incorrect change. When he discovered the mistake, he drove three miles back to the grocery store and returned the dime. My father was also the lifeline for my budding dancing career. For over four years, he chauffeured me to various events in neighboring towns and cities. After the routines became more challenging, he built a sturdy wooden staircase for me. On top of the platform, I proceeded to twist my body into knots. For each performance, he loaded the heavy contraption in the back of his truck. The prizes the amateur variety shows doled out were not in the megabucks category. One talent show awarded me a $3 music store gift certificate. On the "New Stars of 1956" television program in Providence, Rhode Island, I was the lucky winner and received a sixteen-piece set of stainless steel tableware. The Boston Community Auditions television show that was sponsored by Morton Salt Company did a little better. It gave me a $25 U.S. savings bond for my first place finish. Fortunately, for my father, my acrobatic career was short-lived and ended when adolescence hit.

At times, my father baked scrumptious home-made apple-cinnamon muffins. They were restaurant quality. One day, Jimmy Hayes, a close family friend, raved about the goodies to his friends—Boston Celtics basketball players Bill Russell, K. C. Jones, and Sam Jones. They asked to meet my parents who invited them and their wives, Rose, Beverly, and Gladys, respectively, to our house. This was in the late 1950s early 1960s—the exact dates escape me. After the first visit, they became summer guests at Jimmy's (one of my father's nicknames) and Rita's "bed and breakfast." We danced, exchanged amusing stories, and laughed and laughed. At that moment, I realized people were alike regardless of money, power, fame, or physical characteristics and that something special—whether defined as a spirit, energy or light—powerfully connected them.

Q: *Interesting. What about your father's later years?*

AKAHLOUN: His health deteriorated but not his spirit. During my Foreign Service assignment to Canada in the early 1980s, he had two knee replacement surgeries but rapidly mended. He was retired then but served as a senior usher at St. Margaret's Catholic Church in Buzzards Bay, Massachusetts, worked at his landscaping business, and tended to his flower gardens. He also farmed. A neighbor loaned him a sizable parcel of land, which my father plowed and planted rows of green and yellow squash, peas, shell beans, tomatoes, cucumbers, and other vegetables. Despite the woodchuck raids, the crops thrived. We (my parents, aunt, niece, nephews, and my children) sat in the patio for hours cheerfully shelling peas and beans, discussing current events, and listening to my parent's stories of their youth and my grandparents' tales of the Cape Verde Islands. What memorable times.

In 1998, my father suffered a massive carotid artery stroke. Later, he entered the Forestview Nursing Home in Wareham, where he was bedridden and tube-fed for nearly five years. "It could be worse," he would say. His glass was always half-full rather than half-empty. He was well liked and a tremendous source of inspiration.

For his eighty-fourth birthday, six union members from the Taunton Chapter of the Construction and General Laborers Local 876 visited him and presented him a special Fifty-Year Gold Membership Award for his "kindheartedness, generosity, hard work, and faithful contributions to the union and the community." It was touching. His old friends never forgot him. My father fought a courageous battle, which ended on August 15, 2003, when he died of lung cancer and other complications. My optimism comes from him. Whenever anything terrible happens, I counter by doing something positive and constructive. In the midst of planning the funeral, I made folders for family members, containing letters, photos, and other treasured memories of them and my father. Bringing happiness to others was one method of working through my grief. It was very therapeutic.

Q: This buoyancy was an unwavering perspective in your life. It really carried through consistently, from adolescence to the present.

AKAHLOUN: It is interesting you say this. During the State Department's retirement seminar, we were given a Myer-Briggs Aptitude test to gauge our personality type in order to make our transition into the so-called "bonus years" as painless as possible. When I first joined the Foreign Service, we took the same exam. The questions dealt with perception and judgment issues, such as the way we look at things and the way we go about deciding them. After forty-three years, my personality was essentially the same—extraverted, sensing, feeling, and judging (ESFJ). I am talkative, cooperative, and a team player. I seek harmony, dislike technical subjects, and prefer handling issues that directly and visibly affect people's lives for the better. This still holds true today.

Q: What recollections do you have of your mother?

AKAHLOUN: My mother is best identified as a mover and a shaker. The thought of failing at anything never entered her mind. She was a community activist, a trailblazer, and a perfectionist. Her favorite expression was "a place for everything and everything in its place." She was an elegant, dignified, articulate woman with artistic tendencies. She was well-organized and excelled at multitasking. I acquired time management skills from her. When I was about ten, she started a youth center, which provided educational and recreational outlets for the neighborhood kids. We attended lectures, went on field trips, and performed in plays that she wrote and directed. She took pleasure in organizing these activities and chaperoning our parties.

Q: *Why did your mother do this? Was it done mainly for your advantage or was it for the community or both?*

AKAHLOUN: It was partly for us, but she also wanted to convey the message that an idle mind was a devil's workshop to others as well. I suspect her father's charitable activities shaped her humanitarian views. She was a model of civic involvement, and a staunch supporter of the Cape Verdean Relief Association and the Cape Verdean Scholarship Committee. She was a founding member of both organizations. As one of the presidents of the Wareham Friends of Ernestina, she actively campaigned to bring the schooner to the U.S.

The ship was part of the Brava Packet trade that strengthened links between the Cape Verdean communities in New England and on the island. The vessel, first named the Effie M. Morrissey, was built in Essex, Massachusetts, around 1894 and sailed in the Arctic. In 1982, as a symbol of friendship, it was given to the U.S. by the Cape Verdean people and later became a sailing school and training ship. My mother championed senior citizen causes and formed a group called the Friends of Wareham's Elderly. She was also elected to the Board of Directors of the Wareham Council on Aging.

Q: *Now wait. She picked cranberries, toiled in an assembly plant, created a community center for the children, worked as a volunteer, and was involved with the schooner. What did she do in her spare time?*

AKAHLOUN: Well, there wasn't much downtime. She was constantly on the go. Church affairs also consumed an enormous amount of her time. She formed the Saint Margaret and Saint Mary's Star of the Sea Guild and administered to the sick, the homebound, and nursing home residents. She was also a Eucharistic Minister and lector. For many years, she was on the Confraternity of Christian Board of Directors and chaired the "We Care, We Share" program, which encouraged interdenominational fellowship. For her contributions, the bishop of

Fall River, Massachusetts, presented her the coveted Marian Award, given to outstanding parishioners.

She was also prolific at making rosary beads. Over the course of time, as a member of Our Lady's Rosary Circle of Onset, she turned out about 2,500 of them, which were sent to the less fortunate around the world. Mary Vieira Rose, a close friend of my mother's and the founder of the club, confirmed this in one of several oral history interviews. By the way, I still have several drawers overflowing with these prayer beads.

Mary Rose is a person of deep faith, who has devoted her life to helping others. As a reward, in April 2014, her son and daughter surprised her with a visit to Rome, Italy, where she was lucky enough to meet and shake hands with Pope Francis, the current head of the Roman Catholic Church. She was born in December 1914 and will soon turn one hundred years old! When asked what the secret formula is for living so long, Mary responded, "It's hard to say. Don't hurt anybody and try to do good for someone if you can." Miraculously, she is still healthy in mind, body, and spirit.

My mother also had a passion for politics. She was on the Wareham Democratic Town Committee and belonged to the Plymouth County Democratic League. When veteran Massachusetts Congressman Barney Frank (now retired) first ran for office, she campaigned for him. Rummaging through some old papers, I discovered she was once made an Honorary Deputy Sheriff of Plymouth County. I also have a foggy recollection of a Rhode Island mayor proclaiming a special "Rita Lopes Day."

Q: *Quite impressive. I think you covered seven full-time jobs: her work, the community center, the church, the elderly assisted living, the Cape Verdean activities, politics, and the school board.*

AKAHLOUN: I lost count. She retired in her early fifties from the Aerovox assembly plant so she could devote more time to community activities. After this, she became busier than ever. Her den was flooded with awards, citations, and honors. One marble plaque on the wall said, "When faced with a mountain, I will not quit. I will keep on striving until I climb over, find a pass through, tunnel underneath, or simply stay and turn the mountain into a gold mine, with God's help." No mountain was too high for her.

Q: *What about your mother's later years?*

AKAHLOUN: I learned of my mother's ovarian cancer via a phone call from my sister and immediately requested leave to travel home to Onset. On September 3, 1997, during my fourth year in China, the State Department's Medical Unit authorized the visit. The following day I flew home and stayed with her one month. After her condition stabilized, she continued to be a doting grandmother, watched her beloved "stories" on ABC'S daytime television, and was quite the social butterfly. I returned to China to complete the remaining ten months or so of my assignment. Meanwhile, emotionally and physically, she responded well to her treatment and her philanthropic work resumed. Subsequently, we were reassigned to Caracas, Venezuela. In December 1998, however, I again rushed home as she had taken a turn for the worse. She was lucid right to the end and said, "You know, I just don't want to go because I have so much more to give." God called her home on January 9, 1999, at eighty-three years old.

From this four-foot, ten-inch lady, I learned that everyone can make a positive impact in their communities. My maternal grandparents and my parents are my foundation and my finest instructors. I am a reflection of their hopes, dreams, and aspirations. Through my best efforts, I want to honor them and inspire others just as they did. Their struggles showed me it is not what we have but who we are in life that counts. The phenomenal Maya Angelou, a celebrated author, poet, historian, actor, dancer, singer, playwright, producer, and civil rights activist, also influenced me. She once wisely said, "When you learn, teach. When you get, give." I have taken the advice to heart.

Q: *Yes, I can see this passion. I think the grandparents you described were your maternal grandparents. What about your paternal side?*

AKAHLOUN: My paternal grandparents, Mary and Manuel Lopes, were also from the island of Fogo. Unfortunately, they died before I was born. Although my father indicated he was close to his mother, he spoke sparingly about his childhood. By studying the U.S. Federal 1920 census, I discovered that Grandfather Lopes was a gardener and came to America around 1900. Grandmother Lopes arrived about seven years later. At the time of the census, she was listed as twenty-five years old, four months pregnant, and had five children (ages one to six). Less than five months later, tragedy stuck.

A devastating fire swept through their home in Great Neck, Massachusetts, killing their two youngest children, Ennis (two years, seven months) and Dorothy (one year, four months). After the burial, my grandfather's health began deteriorating. That same year, in 1920, he purchased a new house in Onset. Shortly after this, at approximately forty, he died of Nero syphilis. The following year my grandmother married Manuel Fontes. She also was in poor health and passed away due to myocarditis (death certificate) or pneumonia (church records) on December 4, 1937. Although I never knew them personally, my genealogical research brought us closer together spiritually.

Q: *Let's talk about your childhood memories. As a child, you were very much part of an extended family, which is not the case with most Americans. As a young girl, did you find the community supportive, nourishing, and positive in all respects? Or was it suffocating?*

AKAHLOUN: We lived in a modest four-room house on a thin slice of land in the neighborhood of Bay View Park in Onset, Massachusetts. My father's sister, Auntie Irene, lived next to us. A dirt driveway separated the two homes. There were no inside toilet facilities. We used an outhouse. Eventually, my mother convinced my father to upgrade. Instead of abandoning our cottage, it was somehow rigged up on wheels and moved to another spot a quarter of a mile away. It was a delicate operation. Gradually, more rooms and a bathroom were added on to the house.

I enjoyed a very traditional and structured childhood. In our neighborhood, we addressed everyone respectfully and lovingly as uncle and auntie, even those not directly related to us. There were two Syrian families. We played together and attended the same schools. The entire village (known as the "twenty-four-hour, neighborhood watch committee") raised us. From sunrise to sunset, we played outdoors virtually unsupervised. We rode our bikes up and down the streets or ran behind rubber tire tubes, beating them with sticks to make them go faster. I also recall walking on tall stilts, double my size, and holding competitions to see how far and how fast our wooden legs would carry us. Miraculously, there were only minor scrapes and bruises—no broken bones. The nurturing atmosphere made us feel secure, loved, and treasured, not stymied. But there were pitfalls as well. With an army of watchful eyes, nothing went unnoticed or unreported in our village. Everything got back to our parents.

Q: *Oh, you mean you weren't a saint?*

AKAHLOUN: Not at all. I was an ordinary, mischief-loving kid. Let me tell you about an incident, involving a neighbor. From my ten-year-old perspective, she was a busybody. She had so many children that I ran out of fingers counting them. I wondered how her full schedule allowed sufficient time to terrorize the community, including my friends and me. She was one of our least favorite people. So we decided to even the score.

One evening, I slipped out of the house and met my friends at her corn patch where we began reaping havoc. We ran through the field, gleefully hurling ears of corn at each other. Although, admittedly, some trampling of the cornstalks took place, under cover of dark skies the extent of the damage was not visible. Besides, we were too busy having fun. After our jaunt, I safely returned to bed. Early the next morning, I woke up to booming voices and ear-deafening pounding. Literally, there was so much commotion that I thought the house was burning and firemen were breaking down the door trying to rescue me.

Our neighbor burst into my bedroom, shouting, shaking, and jabbing her crooked index finger at me. I nearly lost an eye. I froze and asked God to dig a hole and bury me. She was fuming, "I find you, eh?" Then she turned to my mother, "Alesha, you know what she done, eh?" Answering her own question, she said, "In the night, she come to my land. She killed my corn. Shame on her." My mother was incredulous and thought, "How could her darling baby doll [as I was affectionately known] do such a shocking thing? What are people going to think?" My mother was a very proper lady and mortified at the disgrace I had brought on the family. The neighbor refused to accept my profuse apologies and stormed out of the house. The exact punishment escapes me, but I never stepped in that field again and avoided eating corn for several years thereafter. Indeed, in our tightly knit community, the village raised us and kept us in line.

Q: Let's discuss language. Was Portuguese spoken in your home?

AKAHLOUN: No, only English and Creole. My mother and father spoke English to me, and my grandparents conversed in Creole. Grandfather Fernandes learned English but not Grandmother. By the age of five or six, my comprehension level of Creole was high, but oral communication was low. My generation tended to speak English so as to assimilate into mainstream America. I think the desire to speak English was motivated by peer pressure and a growing awareness of being visibly different, especially when I entered school. That year I attended Onset School about a mile from my house. This was in 1949.

Q: Was that traumatic, or was it natural to go to the Onset school, where the cultural background of the majority of your classmates was different from your own?

AKAHLOUN: I was happy and excited to be there. The day before my mother starched and ironed my green-plum-red plaid dress that had an outrageously large white collar. Each year she saved money to purchase my sister and me a school wardrobe, which she tastefully selected from distinctive New Bedford stores. She stylishly coordinated our outfits. Taffeta bows on my pigtails and ribbons on my sister's hair complemented our outfits. Education was of great importance to her. If we dressed our very best, we were going to be confident and self-assured and consequently we would do well in school. That was my mother's philosophy.

My first-grade teacher, Mrs. Pye, was seasoned and treated everyone with the same degree of kindness and respect. There were thirty-three students in our class, four of whom were Cape Verdeans. No other minorities. I studied at this school for two years and felt comfortable. Then the Cape Verdeans were transferred to Oak Grove, a segregated school one block away from my house. We were all Cape Verdeans, except for a few Syrians. My mother's protest and those of the other parents in the neighborhood fell on deaf ears.

Here is some interesting background information. According to a report I discovered written by Laura Pires Hester, a social worker and anthropologist who was a former Cape Verdean Wareham High School class valedictorian, the origins of Oak Grove School initially dated back to 1905 when town officials started discussing the necessity of establishing separate public schools. This was the result of a growing number of Cape Verdeans who were planting roots in Cape Cod. Following the cranberry harvest more joined the ranks. The steady influx was alarming and generated resentment among the townspeople.

Prejudice was rampant. In 1917, Belmira Nunes Lopes, born in 1899 in Harwich, Massachusetts, begrudgingly turned the townsfolk's heads because of her academic achievements. She was the first Cape Verdean to attend Wareham High School and the first to graduate at the head of her class as valedictorian. The title of Belmira's valedictory address was "The Ideal Town," where she described an environment free of discrimination. One receptive to all ethnic and racial groups where people mingled naturally and avoided trading racial slurs and insults. Belmira later became the first woman of color to graduate with honors and a special distinction in the Romance Languages from Harvard's Radcliffe College. Despite her brilliant record and endorsements from her professors, she was refused a teaching position in the schools of Massachusetts based on racial bias. She went on to receive a Master's Degree in Education from New York University. Ultimately, she taught at various colleges and universities, including Columbia Teachers College, City University of New York, Brooklyn College, and the Catholic University of Puerto Rico.

Belmira Nunes Lopes was truly an icon. She was ahead of her time in many respects. Her choice in strategy for ethnic identity was pragmatic. She took pride in her Cape Verdean heritage but also expected recognition of her mixed cultural heritage on the part of others—white Americans as well as African Americans. Obstacles did not deter her from realizing her many goals. Although she suffered a life of humiliation and discrimination, she was not embittered. She championed racial harmony and was mentally tough, resourceful, and adaptable. Belmira possessed an amazing amount of stamina and perseverance. She became one of my mother's cherished friends, as they collaborated on several community projects. I was honored to know this gracious lady who led such an extraordinary life.

As a footnote, there are two other Cape Verdeans who followed the example of Belmira Lopes and became Wareham High School class valedictorians—Nancy Andrade Reid and Vanessa Britto Henderson.

I am proud to state that they also went on to pursue successful careers and to make positive contributions to their respective communities.

Now back to Oak Grove School. I spent my third, fourth, and fifth grades there. Except for very few Syrian students, we were all Cape Verdeans at our tiny red-brick neighborhood school. In the fourth grade, I shared a classroom with fifth graders. Combined we were twenty-three students. Oak Grove School was neglected and lacked proper staff and resources. No school nurse was available. For medical attention, we walked about thirty minutes to the East Wareham Elementary School. Later, when my classmates and I were bussed three miles to the town of Wareham for junior high (sixth, seventh, and eighth grades) and then for high school, the inferior curriculum at Oak Grove manifested itself. Because these new schools were more academically and socially challenging, we Cape Verdeans struggled a bit but eventually were able to keep our heads above water.

Q: *Do you think Cape Verdeans have this tendency to adapt themselves to the special and peculiar needs of their condition because of the varied components of their character—their mixed background? The Italians, the English, the French, and others went through the islands on their way to the Cape of Good Hope and points beyond.*

AKAHLOUN: I believe so. The mixture encouraged tolerance of diverse lifestyles, which in turn helped us adjust to our surroundings more readily.

Q: *You had many identities. You were Cape Verdean. You were Portuguese. You were a New Englander. You were an American. Was it challenging to be five or six different personalities and basically be Penny simultaneously?*

AKAHLOUN: The transitions were mostly automatic. I learned from my grandparents and parents who took pride in themselves and accepted others. In turn, I was proud of my heritage and my station in life. Their sense of self-worth and faith in humanity grounded me. Essentially, my "culturally wired" mind was controlled by multiple switches that reacted to changing circumstances. Yet I never lost sight of my true essence. This was helpful when entering the upper grades.

The adjustment to Wareham High School required some effort. As a child, I was spared the humiliating experience of being dealt with as "less than." We were cushioned from the blow of life's reality. In my community, a person's background or economic status was irrelevant. In high school, it was a different ball game. To illustrate the point, in my junior and senior years, 1959 and 1960, respectively, I was elected class secretary. Traditionally, student council officers took part in school-wide assemblies, but I was overlooked. Instead, the former class secretary participated. It happened two years in a row, and school officials never volunteered an explanation. The situation was awkward and insulting. The thought of being treated inferior based solely on race rather than on personal qualifications infuriated me, and I was determined to show them I was their equal.

Q: *What percentage of children in your class were New England WASPs? Cape Verdeans? Others?*

AKAHLOUN: Out of 149 seniors, there were thirty Cape Verdeans, one Jewish student, and the rest were primarily white Anglo-Saxon Protestants. Not exactly a melting pot. We were clearly a minority and often rudely reminded of our ethnicity. To cite an example, our school bus driver resented driving to what the majority derogatorily referred to as "Jungletown" to pick up and drop off Cape Verdean students. One afternoon, without being provoked, he exploded, "You people are animals! You don't know how to act." He abruptly stopped the bus, grabbed a couple of boys, and tossed them out, forcing them to walk home. They were having fun laughing at their own jokes. At no time were they being disrespectful. Their only crime appeared to be the color of their skin.

Q: *Why was your section of Onset called Jungletown?*

AKAHLOUN: A 1913 *New Bedford Sunday Standard* report shed some light on how this pejorative label began. I forgot the name of the article and how it surfaced. At any rate, it said that upon arriving in the area "the non-English speaking Cape Verdean immigrants had limited opportunities, faced job discrimination, and lived under poor conditions." It stated that the "townsfolk looked down on them" and referred to the "forty-shanty settlement as Jungletown."

When I grew up, Wareham, including the village of Onset, had about ten thousand residents. Our part of town was a peaceful middle-class Cape Verdean community with neatly painted houses, manicured lawns, beautiful gardens, and white picket fences. The owners, like my father, often worked two jobs to support their families. Through two generations of selfless sacrifice and hard work, the community transformed itself into a respectable neighborhood, but the negative stereotype persisted.

Q: Were you in high school in the late 1950s, early 1960s, when the race issue exploded in America?

AKAHLOUN: Oh yes. My freshman year in 1957, nine African American students enrolled in the racially segregated Little Rock Central High School in Arkansas. It was a monumental event for our nation. The National Guard blocked their entrance until President Eisenhower intervened. In 1961, my senior year, the first Freedom Riders left Washington, D.C., on interstate buses, testing a U.S. Supreme Court decision. The topic was not raised in class, but I was deeply moved and highly respectful of the courageous protesters. Despite occasional snubs, I was grateful for the opportunity to study at Wareham High School. At least, on the surface, there was more racial harmony than the ruthlessness experienced by other people of color in the American South.

Since childhood I believed in viewing things from a balanced perspective. By high school, my values and beliefs began to take hold. A few mantras shaped my life:

- Don't personalize things.
- People are inherently good.
- Give others the benefit of the doubt.
- Choose your battles.
- Be true to yourself.
- Don't let anyone make you feel inferior.
- Always do your best.
- If at first you don't succeed, try and try again.

This mind-set and a desire to fully experience adolescence led to my involvement in many school activities—including student council, band, choir, drama, newspaper, modern dance, sports, gymnastics, and the prom committee. The high school yearbook listed me as the "peppiest" and "most talented" in the class. I think people get out of life exactly what they put into it. If we expect good things to happen and work hard pursuing our goals, eventually we will be rewarded for our efforts.

My last year at Chamberlayne Junior College in Boston was another seminal moment in race relations for me. In 1963, Martin Luther King Jr. was imprisoned for leading a nonviolent protest march on Birmingham's city hall. This is when he wrote his famous "Letter from Birmingham Jail." And in August of that year, a quarter of a million people marched on Washington, D.C., where Dr. King delivered his historic "I Have a Dream" speech, calling for freedom and economic and racial equality. Hearing his inspiring words helped build my resolve to excel in my studies, pursue my dream of blazing trails, and to travel throughout the world.

Q: You were saying when dealing with prejudice and discrimination you chose your battles and you sought to prove you were as good as the others by taking key challenges.

AKAHLOUN: Truthfully, I strove to be better than the rest. We had to be twice as clever to survive. While I forgave people, I did not necessarily forget the slights or piercing comments. The Cape Verdeans motivated one another and were determined to discredit the notion of being insignificant human beings. During hurtful or angry times, I forged ahead more determined than ever. I knew deep down inside no one was going to dictate who I was or make me feel inadequate. Fortunately, I drew strength from my family and my classmates of color, and never believed I was beneath any one.

Two other students—Eddie Lodie and Sally Rhodes—were exceptional. Eddie, the class valedictorian, and I shared the same homeroom. We got along well because I did all the talking, and he did all the listening. I tried to turn him into an extrovert but never altogether succeeded. In our yearbook, I encouraged him to write at least something. He obliged and wrote, *Something, Ed Lodi*. I admired him for many reasons, including his views on racial tolerance. Not surprisingly, he went on to teach English at North Carolina's Shaw University, where he participated in Civil Rights marches. Since then, he has published several books, including his memoir. Sally, the band's gifted trumpet player, had short flaming-red hair that suited her effervescent personality. During our football half-time shows, I cart wheeled around the players in a *W* (for Wareham) formation on the field. When I became winded, I spotted Sally and somehow found extra energy to finish the routine. She always went out of her way to be friendly and encouraging.

Q: The benefits of having a strong culture and the merits of not having such permeable contact with others helped you to overcome. You say you experienced discrimination but sought to rise above it and forgive. Was it that simple? Where you not shocked or dismayed?

AKAHLOUN: Yes. At times, I was very upset by these mindless acts of bigotry. My zodiac sign is Aries, which is associated with the element of fire. When necessary, I am quick to defend myself and others who are unjustly treated. Better not incur my wrath as sparks will fly.

Q: Well it sounds as though you got the point very quickly of realizing there was a challenge here. The way to surmount it was to pick your battles, to forgive, and to surpass expectations. Now that is an enormous psychological voyage taken in a pretty short time.

AKAHLOUN: But consider my upbringing. I was raised in a devout Catholic family. My mother walked around the house with a rosary, dangling from her neck. When my father retired, he said multiple rosaries a day. I can still picture him in the cellar praying and riding his stationary exercise bike. I was conditioned.

Q: I think your outlook resulted from a balance between what you were taught and what you came to believe yourself. At what age did you realize your calling in life?

AKAHLOUN: My path was always clear. I realize it sounds odd, but as far back as I can remember, I wanted to enrich the lives of others— help steer people in a favorable direction and empower them. We all possess different strengths. The fortunate ones recognize their calling early. Others make the discovery later in life. Some never realize their potential. But it is extremely important to pass on our gifts and give back to the community.

As an eight-year-old, I realized my purpose in life. One day during school break, my father squeezed our suitcases into his beat-up four door Chevrolet; we headed for a life-altering vacation in Vermont, New Hampshire, and Maine. One event had potential to ruin the perfect outing. While climbing the steps to a state capitol building, we passed a family. The mother was holding her young son's hand. Unprovoked, the child began laughing at my father and then deliberately spit on his face. My father's reaction was more of disbelief than anger. He shook his head and said, "I don't believe a kid that size is allowed to do such a bad thing." Admirably, he put the degrading incident behind him, and we continued to enjoy our vacation. It was a powerful example of how to exercise self-control in the face of humiliating situations. To see my father disrespected in such a disgraceful fashion stung me and awakened an indelible awareness within me. The vacation in its entirety also exposed me to a universe beyond my tiny Onset town. It broadened my horizon.

I vividly recall returning home, going to the backyard, and walking on my father's step ladder lying on the ground. I forgot the exact date, but it was summertime. The sun was bright and hot. My cousin, Carol Andrews, joined me. "You want to play?" "Sorry," I replied, "I'm not feeling well, but tomorrow let's climb our tree house in the woods." At that moment, I needed solitude to reflect on our trip and why my universe in seven days had turned upside down. Pandora's Box had been opened—a world outside of southeastern Massachusetts existed, and I wanted to explore every inch of it. I visualized each step of the ladder as a different corner of the globe. The vacation instilled a strong desire to learn about diverse cultures and to ensure equal treatment of people. For some inexplicable reason, from a very early age, I felt a powerful force guiding me, shaping my thoughts and directing my footsteps to unknown places.

Q: *You were lucky. A glimpse of one's direction in life at such a young age is unusual. Now, returning to your high school days. You became the class secretary and held certain positions of honor, even though prejudice prevented you from performing some duties normally associated with them. Tell me what you were learning as a high school student in Wareham and more about your teachers and friends.*

AKAHLOUN: We studied traditional subjects. Our stern English literature teacher, Mrs. Rose, comes to mind. Every time she lowered her head and peered over the rim of her spectacles, we felt threatened and expected her ruler to land on our knuckles. In retrospect, her high standards and love of diagramming those horrible sentences helped her students acquire excellent writing skills and a sophisticated vocabulary.

Q: Was English one of your favorite subjects?

AKAHLOUN: I had several favorite subjects—English, civics, geography, sociology, art, and history. My main interest was in people and what affected their lives. I never had an aptitude for algebra, geometry, or scientific courses. Yet studying different cultures, and topics associated with sociology and anthropology intrigued me. It was fun peering into the past, learning where and how people lived, how they dressed and their inner thinking. Civics also attracted me. It educated me as to how the U.S. government functioned and taught me about citizen rights and duties. Music, art, and drama also appealed to me.

Back then, the girls studied home economics and learned to sew and bake pies and cakes. The course was preparing us to become mothers and homemakers, similar to the majority of women at the time. The boys who elected "shop" tinkered with automobiles and hoped to become mechanics. These two courses mirrored the times. In my junior year, my friend Anita Baptiste and I were chosen to attend a precollege summer program at the Museum of Fine Arts in Boston. Some of the art classes and workshops included painting, drawing, sculpturing, graphic design, and jewelry making. I loved it.

Q: Apparently, American government and social history ignited your passion. Was your sense of being an American representing the U.S. in other countries reinforced?

AKAHLOUN: I believe so. During school, I sometimes sat at my desk observing the different mannerisms and attitudes of my classmates. It was then I resolved to treat others, particularly the disenfranchised, with dignity and compassion no matter their background. My community also contributed to this strong conviction.

Q: *Most of us would like to feel this way but don't succeed. You used these observations as a model for your own behavior. Was there a particular teacher who inspired you?*

AKAHLOUN: Oh yes. Mr. Mazeiko, our Polish teacher at Oak Grove School. He was extraordinarily dedicated and gifted. He had the credentials to teach at Boston's finest private schools but chose to invest his time in our underresourced community. There were many problems confronting him. To begin with, he commuted from Brockton—about a seventy-mile round-trip. Town officials neglected Oak Grove. Our school supplies were inadequate and scarce. Low enrollment resulted in combined classes. Some of these issues were raised earlier. None of them fazed Mr. Mazeiko who simply soldiered on. He never gave up and always endeavored to give us the quality education we deserved.

For instance, one day he wrote a tricky math problem on the board. Instead of asking the resident math genius to solve it, he called on me. I was terrified and slowly walked to the front of the room, stared blankly at the board, and after a few futile attempts sat down again. However, he patiently worked with me until I found the correct answer.

It was a humbling experience, but I learned that encouragement and perseverance builds self-esteem. Thanks to Mr. Mazeiko, I left Oak Grove with a sense of self-confidence, which benefited me during my high school years.

Wareham High had a powerful sports program, led by Mr. Spillane, a burly coach whose philosophy was "when the going gets tough, the tough get going." He certainly knew how to fire up the boys' basketball and football teams. Wareham won several regional competitions, including the coveted Tri-County Football championship. Many of the talented players were Cape Verdeans, including my cousin, Lenny Lopes, known as "Mr. Wareham." Tragically, he died at the age of twenty-six in a fiery automobile accident days before his wedding. We were very close. His smile always lit up the classroom.

I enjoyed participating in sports and wrote about athletic events in the school newspaper. I was on the girls' basketball and gymnastic teams. After school, I played football with the neighborhood boys. I don't know whether it was touch or tackle football. In either case, when my anatomy started changing at age thirteen, the boys began calling less aggressive plays and whispering, "Be careful, she's Rita and Scotty's precious little girl. Don't hurt her." The last thing they wanted was to incur my parents' wrath.

This reminds me of another story. Some of the neighborhood boys I thought were somewhat condescending. At age ten, I remember, my classmates Jose Valles and Lebaron Baptiste always selected me last for their softball teams. I was the only girl on the field. In my eyes, this was unfair and discriminatory. So I started practicing long hours with the Wilson glove my father gave me, and finally my small hand and the oversized glove were in sync. I was scooping up balls from the ground, rather than dirt and rocks, and hitting my target. Then, I organized a baseball team of girls my age to take on the boys. My recruits were less than enthusiastic. As an incentive, I rewarded them. I saved my allowance and bought some candy, ten-pieces-for-one-cent, from the neighborhood store, *Chiquinho's*. It sweetened up the practice sessions.

After some training, I felt we were ready for the challenge. During the game, however, things unraveled. I kept encouraging the girls. "You can do it. Step into that swing. Keep your eye on the ball." In the end, we lost, but I was not angry or disappointed. The girls made an effort, and we proved the point that we could at least compete on the same playing field. We were good sports about being beaten, and I channeled my energy elsewhere. "Penny," I said to myself, "You lost this fight, but there are others you can win." Sometimes, the measure of success is how we come back from defeat.

Q: *This seems to be a central theme throughout your childhood to the present: the glass half-full, accepting defeat, making the most of it, and rebounding. After an active four years of sports, academics, social life, band, and newspaper, you were on stage receiving your diploma. What were your emotions?*

AKAHLOUN: I was pleased but realized it was only the beginning of my journey. A year or two before graduating, a friend introduced me to Ruby Dawson, who was studying at Sarah Lawrence in Boston, preparing for a State Department Foreign Service career. Meeting her, rekindled my interest in traveling.

ELEANOR LOPES AKAHLOUN

Q: How did you spend your summers before you graduated from high school in 1961?

AKAHLOUN: I worked to help out with family expenses as a child and later saved money to defray college expenses. Actually, my first job was delivering newspapers at the age of ten. For two summers, I woke up every morning at four-thirty. My father drove me around. A few years later, there was another interesting experience, working alongside my aunts at a local bed and breakfast as a chambermaid. I cleaned bathrooms, made beds, washed windows, and mopped floors. The owner begrudgingly served us lunch. One day she caught sight of my plate and blurted out, "Oh my god, this girl is only thirteen, and she's eating half of the restaurant's profits." (I always had a hearty appetite. I still do.) My aunts defended me by saying I was young but cleaned like an adult. At first, I was amused. Then I felt offended.

Later our relationship warmed up because she organized summer programs at the Onset pavilion and invited me to participate in her shows. These acrobatic performances proved invaluable as I learned how to be at ease with audiences. I also picked strawberries and blueberries during the summer. At fifteen, I started cleaning house for the Horowitz family. Their summer cottage was only two miles away from my home. I rode my new shiny English bike with the brakes on the handlebars there. Sometimes at night, I babysat for their four children. I felt a sense of pride being entrusted with so much responsibility. The entire household treated me well. Mrs. Horowitz is ninety-one now, and we still speak on the phone.

At the time, Cape Verdeans, especially teenagers, had few employment opportunities. We could not become bank tellers, sales associates, law clerks, or hold administrative jobs within the local government. People of color were excluded from these positions. Despite these limitations, I was well on my way to becoming a workaholic.

Q: Evidently. So you graduated, wanted to be in the Foreign Service, but did not go there immediately. What happened during the succeeding years?

AKAHLOUN: Since the age of eight, I knew my "calling in life" was to have a career working abroad. After high school, I toyed with the thought of going to art school but ended up at Chamberlayne Junior College, a small liberal arts school, located on Commonwealth Avenue in Boston, Massachusetts. Not all the colleges accepted my less than stellar SAT math scores. Moreover, I was influenced by Ruby's academic journey. After receiving her two-year secretarial degree, she successfully joined the State Department. My immediate plan was to study at Chamberlayne then transfer and pursue a bachelor's degree. Either way, my sights were set on the Foreign Service.

For individuals unfamiliar with the State Department's purpose, the organization is our main agency dealing with U.S. foreign affairs, and its primary goals are to serve U.S. global interests, to protect American citizens living and traveling abroad while advancing peace, economic prosperity, and human rights in foreign countries. Members of the Department's diplomatic corps make up the Foreign Service. They frequently travel far and wide, generally rotating assignments every two to three years. The Civil Service side of the State Department is populated by domestic civil servants who remain mostly in Washington, D.C. A substantial number of Foreign Service Nationals (frequently referred to as Locally Engaged Staff, LES) are employed at our diplomatic missions abroad and are citizens of our host countries.

Life in the Foreign Service can be stressful, as employees are sent to any embassy, consulate, or other diplomatic missions anywhere in the world, at any time, to serve the needs of the U.S. These assignments can include difficult and dangerous posts, which are categorized as "hardship" assignments or tours of duty (often known simply as tours). Mandatory "home leave" is a vacation given to personnel for relaxation purposes and to reacquaint them with stateside living. This break is usually taken during the middle or the end of each overseas tour. The Foreign Service, unlike any other profession, allows its public servants to uniquely advance U.S. interests abroad while contributing to the global community, and to experience cultures, customs, and people of different nations. The work is stimulating and rewarding, but it can be challenging.

Q: *Being flexible, having good coping skills, and possessing a strong sense of humor seem to help out. Meanwhile, you moved from Cape Cod to*

Boston, about fifty miles away. You went from a small town to a major city. Did you adjust easily?

AKAHLOUN: Yes, because I lived with Mary Gomes, her husband, and two daughters in Dorchester, a Boston neighborhood. Ma Gomes belonged to Onset's extended family. If I missed supper, she left me a plate of food, warming up in the oven. Nancy and Karen were like my sisters. For two years, I was completely at home. They served as a critical support network for me. The transition was also smooth because I was moving a step closer to entering the Foreign Service.

Q: What were your activities and area of study at the college?

AKAHLOUN: My activities were similar to those in high school—class secretary, newspaper, drama, and music. In addition, I was a cheerleader and made the dean's list. The studies included stenography (shorthand), typing, office procedures, business, English, bookkeeping and accounting, business law, and other forgotten subjects. In those days, the secretarial field was fashionable among young professional women. In fact, stenography served me well during my final assignment at the Foreign Service's Board of Examiners (BEX) some fifty years later. Taking shorthand notes was faster than longhand and enabled me to work more efficiently. I guess all acquired knowledge is meaningful and can become useful when least expected.

Q: Skills you would never imagine could be put to use as an examiner for the Foreign Service came in handy some years later. Where did you move after graduation?

AKAHLOUN: I am glad you asked this question, as it leads me to a rather revealing story. A classmate told me there was a vacancy at Bethany Union, a church-subsidized home for unmarried women on Newberry Street a few blocks from Copley Square. So I applied. Mrs. Dumar, a refined silver-haired lady, interviewed me. I informed her I had graduated, was looking for lodging, knew her home had a fine reputation, and wanted to become a resident. She politely replied, "Thank you, dear, but there are no vacancies." I knew differently. "How unfortunate," I calmly replied. "Thank you for meeting with me." Mrs. Dumar underestimated me. I was not willing to accept no for an answer.

I immediately phoned my friend, "Are you certain about the vacancy?" "Of course," she said, "I live there." "Well," I added, "apparently, Mrs. Dumar is confused. She said none existed." "Don't worry," she reassured me, "I will handle this." My Irish girlfriend then spoke with Mrs. Dumar, explaining she had a friend who wanted to live at Bethany Union. My name and race were never mentioned. The deal was then sealed. This is how I came to live in my tiny room on the third floor of Bethany Union. The rent was ridiculously low—$25 a month—which made me even happier. I never raised the issue. Neither did Mrs. Dumar. But we both knew she previously rejected me because of my race.

I have another unrelated gem of a story. This one highlights some of my frugality that enabled me to survive living alone in the big city of Boston. My father and I appreciated the necessities in life, but we also believed in economizing. My parents paid for my education and continued to subsidize me. Whenever possible, I wanted to lighten their burden. One day, I told my father, "Daddy, this week, I'm going to tighten my belt and see how much money I spend." Things looked promising. My father paid the rent, Bethany Union furnished meals, and I walked to work. Besides, I was dieting. At week's end, my father asked, "Baby doll, how did you make out?" I responded, "My expenses totaled twenty-five cents. I splurged on gum." He and I were two peas in a pod—very thrifty and cautious about the way we handled our finances.

Soon I found gainful employment. I did some waitressing, telephone solicitation, and worked part time for an attorney. After a number of job interviews, I landed a position in the office of Attorney General Edward W. Brooke who later became a U.S. Senator. Back then he was the nation's first African American to hold this position. He impressed me as being affable, caring, intelligent, and dedicated. But obtaining the job was not straightforward. I took the test, administered by his personal secretary, and promptly failed the exam. I was devastated. However, a favorite adage of my parents kept ringing in my ear. "If at first you don't succeed, try and try again." So instead of giving up, I explored other avenues. I spoke to my mother, who was involved in politics but held no public office, and asked for her intervention.

Rita A. Lopes was one persuasive individual with exceptional oral and written skills. She immediately wrote Attorney General Brooke and suggested he meet with me. Astonishingly, he agreed. Entering his office, I was nervous, yet I found my voice. When he asked if I was able to do the work, I unhesitatingly answered, "Yes. I have the skills, the temperament and the desire to perform the work." After a few rounds of questioning, he hired me. I assured him he would not regret his decision. This was a pivotal moment in my life. Afterward, I thought about the disappointing test results and critiqued myself. I jotted down some notes for future reference. "Not sufficiently prepared. Panicked. Lacked confidence. Potential there. Try harder." I also decided that in the future, as Ed Brooke did, I was going to give others the benefit of a doubt. Everyone deserved a second chance.

Q: Do you think that he recognized there was an important constituency in southeastern Massachusetts? Or was it actually the impression you made during the interview?

AKAHLOUN: I think there were several factors at play. Obviously, he was focused on politics. At the same time, the interview went well. He was a respectable person, and I got the impression he genuinely wanted to help me. I realized it was imperative I measure up to his expectations.

Q: I am sure you surpassed them. You said he was attorney general before being senator?

AKAHLOUN: That's right. In 1966, he became the first African American senator since the U.S. Reconstruction era and the first one to be reelected by popular vote. Quite a feat.

Q: Wow! That really is a slice of history. Please, let us focus on that. The daily ambiance of the office—Edward W. Brooke, attorney general (future senator), the pace, the activities, and the kinds of outreach. Do you think he had the Senate on his mind at the time?

AKAHLOUN: His persona was bigger than just a chief lawyer and law enforcer of the Commonwealth of Massachusetts. He was brilliant and destined for the national scene. The office was bustling—plenty of work. I will never forget how one senior attorney, Mr. Kelleher, described the workload. "It's akin to sweeping the tide back with a broom." It was an apt description. The attorney general's office handled Medicaid and unemployment fraud, fair labor practices, civil rights, appeals, energy matters, consumer protection issues, financial investigations, corruption, and other matters. Two major investigations consumed the office—organized crime and the Boston Strangler. Between June 1962 and January 1963, thirteen single women were murdered; three of them in the Back Bay area—my neighborhood. I was always looking over my shoulder. It was a dangerous time to be a woman walking on the streets alone.

Q: How long were you there? What was your function? Were you the only person assigned to that particular role?

AKAHLOUN: I worked there two years—from 1963 to 1965. I was part of the executive branch, but my duties were more operational in nature. My boss, Betty, and I provided administrative rather than policy-making support. We handled the logistics of his engagements. Attorney General Brooke visited every morning to discuss the day's upcoming activities. In addition, I coordinated Mrs. Brooke's schedule. He was very popular, so they attended numerous social and political functions. There was also a human resources component to the job and other tasks, which are now buried somewhere in my mind.

Q: You seemed to be into two-year segments.

AKAHLOUN: Well, I was biding my time until reaching twenty-one, which was the minimum age to join the Foreign Service. I did whatever was necessary to follow through with my goals. I capitalized on all the opportunities presented and left no space for self-despair. Meanwhile, I worked full time and studied at night at Boston University. I also took the Foreign Service stenographer's test at the Federal Building.

Q: You sat for this exam in 1965 after two years in the attorney general's office.

AKAHLOUN: Yes, and that was another disaster. I flunked the examination the first time and was crushed. Once again, I was in the unenviable position of having to try and try again. I refused to let failure paralyze me. So I studied harder than ever and the second time met with success.

At my request, the State Department delayed processing my security clearance for one year. I was attached to my parents, particularly my father, and wanted to allow sufficient time for us to adjust to being separated. Living abroad for prolonged periods of time often is a traumatizing lifestyle. Would I be content? Was I being realistic or simply romanticizing? To answer these questions, I bought an inexpensive thirty-day Eurail Pass and traveled with my girlfriend by train throughout Europe. The experience was fantastic and shored up my enthusiasm for joining the Foreign Service. Now, I had to sell the plan to my parents. I continued working for the attorney general, went home on weekends, and spoke incessantly about my glorious European vacation.

Q: Did they understand why you were in Europe?

AKAHLOUN: Not at first. Slowly, I shared my thoughts and hoped for the best. After all, both sets of grandparents emigrated to the U.S. Moreover, at an early age, my mother left home to live and work in Boston. Once they embraced the idea, assurances were given that I would stay in touch and not abandon them. And I never, never, ever did.

After six months, the State Department cleared me, but I felt I wasn't ready—it was too premature to come on board. I needed more time to prepare myself and my parents for my departure. The building blocks for my new career were not yet securely in place. The foundation was still wobbly. Thankfully, the Department agreed, and I was able to make the necessary psychological adjustments and finish out my second year with the attorney general.

Q: After one month in Europe and an additional year of working at Attorney General Brooke's office, the day arrives when you pack your bags. What happens next?

AKAHLOUN: I went to Washington for Foreign Service training. There were only fifteen women in my orientation class. Prior to that, I received a letter from a placement officer offering me a grade nine

Foreign Service secretarial position at the $5,010 base salary level and a choice of training for six months or three weeks. I opted for the latter as I was anxious to go overseas. The government also covered my packing and travel expenses. I reported for work September 24, 1965, and was housed at the Meridian Hill Home for Women in D.C. The surrounding park and gardens are now a U.S. National Historic Landmark. It was gorgeous, and I was thrilled to embark on my journey—one that began in my imagination at the age of eight.

ELEANOR LOPES AKAHLOUN

Form 1806.

WRECK REPORT.

Portsmouth Life-Saving Station, _Seventh_ District.

Date of Disaster:

May 8", 1903

1. Name of vessel.	1. *Vera Cruz 7"*
2. Rig and tonnage.	2. *Barkentine 605 23/100*
3. Hailing port and nationality.	3. *Buenas Ayres*
4. Age.	4. *29 years*
5. Official number.	5. *90638*
6. Name of master.	6. *Julis M Fernendes*
7. Names of owners.	7.
8. Where from.	8. *Cape Verd Islands*
9. Where bound.	9. *New Bedford Mass*
10. Number of crew, including captain.	10. *22*
11. Number of passengers.	11. *399*
12. Nature of cargo.	12. *Lunm Oil 214 barrels*
13. Estimated value of vessel.	13. *$ 6.000*
14. Estimated value of cargo.	14. *$6.000*
15. Exact spot where wrecked.	15. *Dry Shoal Saint*
16. Direction and distance from station.	16. *S. S. E three miles*
17. Supposed cause of wreck (specifying particularly).	17. *Drug anchor and went in broke*
18. Nature of disaster, whether stranded, sunk, collided, etc.	18. *Stranded*
19. Distance of vessel from shore at time of accident.	19. *300 yds from Dry Shoal Saint*
20. Time of day or night.	20. *2 Pm*
21. State of wind and weather.	21. *N. E. fresh smoky*
22. State of tide and sea.	22. *Ebb sea moderate*
23. Time of discovery of wreck.	23. *2 Pm*
24. By whom discovered.	24. *Keeper and W. Roberts*
25. Time of arrival of station-crew at wreck.	25. *3 Pm*
26. Time of return of station-crew from wreck.	26. *4.40 Pm*
27. Were any of the station-crew absent from wreck? If	27. *J W Fulcher first trip*
30. Number of persons brought ashore in life-boat.	30.
31. Was surf-boat used?*	31. *Monomay and Jersey*
32. Number of trips with surf-boat.	32. *41*
33. Number of persons brought ashore with surf-boat.	33. *420*
34. Was small boat used?	34.

Extract from the 1903 Portsmouth's Life Saving Station's report of the *Vera Cruz VII* shipwreck in Ocracoke, North Carolina.

Grandfather Lawrence Fernandes in the early 1920s
(estimated), New Bedford, Massachusetts.

The 1934 high school graduation photograph of my godmother, Annica Correia Pina. She and my mother were first cousins and best buddies.

My parents' 1939 wedding was an elegant affair.

Grandfather's 1942 Certificate of Naturalization lists his age as 62, but Social Security and other records show his birth date as April 9, 1880, making him 65 at the time he became a U.S. citizen.

Here I am in complete body splendor, 1943.

With Grandmother and Cousin Larry Correia in Onset, in 1946. It was a bad hair day for me. The photographer's visit caught my mother off guard.

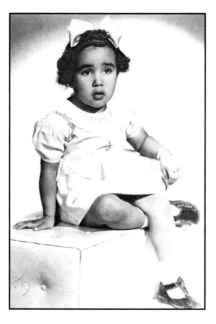

No surprises this time. I am all dressed up (with a pretty hair bow) at a fancy studio in New Bedford, Massachusetts, 1946.

Turning myself into a pretzel in 1955 at one of my dance recitals.

An Easter Sunday outing with my mother and
sister, Osterville, Massachusetts, 1959.

My mother and my father at Edward W. Brooke's second swearing-in
ceremony as Massachusetts Attorney General in Boston, 1964.

My mom, grandfather, and godmother at my parents' 25th wedding anniversary, Buzzards Bay, Massachusetts, 1964.

With my sister and father at the celebration.

PART TWO

CHAPTER TWO

THE PEARL OF THE ORIENT

THE PHILIPPINES, 1965–1967

The Department of State agreed to my last minute request for a posting to Manila, where my friend Ruby Dawson was assigned. Luckily, my first overseas assignment with the U.S. Foreign Service turned out to be a match made in heaven.

Q: Tell me about the day you left the U.S.

AKAHLOUN: I flew from Dulles Airport on October 15, 1965. The long journey was broken up into two legs—San Francisco/Hawaii (rest stop) and then Japan/Philippines. Dressing for success, I donned white gloves and wore a gray dress with a white and black trim circular collar and a thin black border at the hemline. The accessories included a white hair bow, white globe-shaped earrings, and black pumps. I carried an oversized black leather bag filled with everything under the sun to handle any unanticipated crisis. I felt the mandate of officially representing the U.S. government and its citizens abroad required me to be impeccably dressed. Stepping out of the plane, I was ecstatic. At last, my childhood dream had materialized.

Q: Do you have memories of arriving in Manila, or were you too sleepy? This is a major experience. What did you see? What did you feel?

AKAHLOUN: I was a bright-eyed, twenty-two-year-old heading overseas for my first big assignment with the State Department—didn't get a wink of sleep on the flight. I arrived early afternoon and saw some sobering sights. I was surrounded by "third-world" poverty I had only seen on television. Thatched-roof bamboo huts on stilts were everywhere. The oppressive heat, the intense blue sky, the scorching sun, bird of paradise flowers, and palm trees stretching for miles and miles were eye-openers. Flamboyantly decorated jeepneys clogged the streets. These were U.S. military jeeps left over from World War II that were fitted with metal roofs, painted vibrant colors, and adorned with chrome decorations. You rode them at some risk. Inside, the riders hung on for dear life. The masses of people, level of noise, amount of pollution, and general chaos was startling. I also expected Filipinos to look more Latin or Hispanic because of their names. This was not uniformly the case. Many had darker complexions like mine. Despite the whirlwind, there was a powerful connection between myself and my new home. It was crystal clear I was in the right place at the right time.

Q: *You might say this first hypothesis of yours was challenged. You expected to see people who resembled Spaniards or Hispanic but what you found was the opposite. That very first impression was already something different.*

AKAHLOUN: I was caught off balance by my new environment but not for long. I kept an open mind. People are people. We all smile the same. Color was never an issue with me because I dwelled on the commonalities of the human spirit rather than outer appearances. The adjustment was made swiftly, and I got on with the business of being a conscientious, U.S. government worker, serving my country. Thankfully, I did not encounter blatant discrimination or receive the feeling I was being treated condescendingly by other diplomats at the American Embassy or by the Filipinos.

Q: *Did you understand in advance what the work entailed?*

AKAHLOUN: I learned the details upon arrival. As a secretary, I worked for the labor attaché and two political officers who handled external military affairs. This required different office procedures and managing clients with opposing interests. The office overlooked

Manila Bay, but the heavy workload allowed little time to admire the striking view. The three busy men had conflicting managerial styles and lacked a sense of priority. They possessed one thing in common— explosive tempers and each one wanted to monopolize my time. They had difficulty comprehending I was a shared resource, dividing my time equally.

Q: *What you just said proves you are a diplomat. They had trouble getting along with each other?*

AKAHLOUN: Somewhat. Each of them promoted good host country diplomatic relations in their respective fields, but they were not team players and lacked respect for each other's portfolio. The labor attaché analyzed, studied, and reported on the labor market issues; he worked closely with union representatives. The political officers did the same thing but in the national security arena. They networked with high-ranking Foreign Ministry officials, Filipino military leaders, and U.S. commanders at Subic Bay and Clark Air Force base.

Q: *Was there a chain of command?*

AKAHLOUN: Yes. All of them reported to Mr. Usher, the political counselor who was a dear-heart and the epitome of what a diplomat should be—technically qualified with polished interpersonal skills. There I was a bewildered fresh recruit caught up in this madness. A little girl from a tiny town who believed U.S. Embassy employees acted with decorum, at least, that was the message preached at our Foreign Service orientation class. Diplomats do not argue—they use skills of diplomacy and negotiation to iron out differences.

While the men's responsibilities oftentimes put them unintentionally at odds with each other, they were highly qualified and decent people. The solution was to "manage up." I had gained some experience with this at Attorney General Brooke's office without realizing it. When we discuss my Canadian assignment, I will provide more details.

Meanwhile, any one practicing this managing up strategy needs to consider the pressure from the supervisor's angle and take into account higher office demands, which often require the work to be finished yesterday. Know the mission plan and keep abreast of current events. Penetrate the mind of the boss. Analyze his/her strengths, weaknesses, and managerial styles. Identify blind spots. Assess your personality and make comfortable adjustments to accommodate different managerial styles. Be trustworthy and dependable and keep the director informed. Go to your superior with solutions. In this way, you can anticipate a person's needs without his/her awareness of your input. Over time, these tactics opened many doors for me.

My background provided a framework for appreciating people regardless of race and economic status. As the product of a multicultural upbringing, I learned to deal with different ways of behavior and thinking. I had to be nimble in responding to the Cape Verdean, the Anglo American, and the African American cultures. They were not identical, but one had to be equally conversant in all three. I think this gave me an advantage going into the Foreign Service because I had already learned how to be flexible when exposed to diverse cultures. To reiterate, I was fortunate to have excellent role models—parents, grandparents, teachers, religious leaders, and extended family within the community. In my neighborhood, we always "saved face" for people. We tried to spare them embarrassment. Anyhow, through divine intervention and recalling the high school coach's pep talks on toughness, the situation gradually improved.

As for accommodations, upon arrival, I learned there was a three-month waiting list for government-furnished quarters at Seafront, the housing complex where most Americans lived. Staying with Ruby was a convenient way to start a new life thousands of miles away from home, but I did not want to impose on her kindness. Besides, living in this isolated setting defeated the purpose. Why come halfway around the world and end up in an American bubble? After a month, I moved into 5C Palm Court, a duplex apartment building directly outside Seafront's back gate. The Reyes family had just constructed the units and rented them to Filipino families, U.S. servicemen, and me. Next, I joined the U.S. Employees' Association and paid a $75 deposit and a $1.50 monthly fee for access to Seafront's commissary, dining room, snack bar, swimming pool, and the library. Life was akin to having one foot in the east and one in the west. It was an ideal situation.

The Reyeses adopted me, and their daughter, Guia, introduced me to her friends. Soon my social life blossomed. We organized exciting parties and did the *tinikling,* which is a folk dance inspired and named after the heron—a bird that dodged bamboo traps set by rice farmers. Two people sit and slide and hit bamboo poles (about nine feet long) against each other and against two thick blocks of wood on the ground while dancers step over and between the poles. It is similar to jumping rope, except your feet move at lightning speed or your ankles get smashed. We wore traditional Filipino clothing—a *balintawak* (long dress with wide-arched sleeves) for women and a *barong tagalog* (formal shirt) for the men. Believe me these parties were quite a production.

I wholeheartedly embraced the Filipino culture—even tried their local specialty, *balut,* a duck's egg (or chicken) in embryo form. The outside looks like an ordinary egg but inside is another story. The fertilized egg is incubated for about two weeks, boiled, and then eaten in the shell. When broken, you actually see a duckling with eyes, beak, small pink limbs, bones, and gray feathers. One stiflingly hot evening, my friends and I decided to take a stroll in Luneta Park. Several emaciated elderly women were squatting on the ground, yelling, "Ba-luuuuuuuuut!" One of them reached into her straw basket and handed me one. I felt sorry for her and bought it. She gave me a pinch of salt to sprinkle on the warm egg. My companions cheered as I slowly ate the crunchy egg. That memorable evening, I became an honorary Filipina and the talk of the embassy community.

Q: Did you learn Tagalog? What exactly was your job?

AKAHLOUN: I discontinued my classes because of a heavy workload but was able to acquire some basic words and phrases. Because my Filipino friends spoke English fluently, there was scarce opportunity to practice the language.

I was a secretary—typed, filed, took dictation and transcribed shorthand notes, answered phones, greeted visitors, and performed general office management tasks. This was all before computers. We used electric typewriters. One minor mistake and we had to throw away everything and start all over again. Each page consisted of two or three carbons. Invariably, there was a typo at the bottom of the document. The multiple revisions were time-consuming. We revised umpteen times. No such thing as correction fluid in those days. I used a red Eberhard Faber pencil eraser with an inch-long brush at the end to make corrections and then artistically dabbed the smudges with a piece of white chalk. I am my mother's daughter—a perfectionist. This made the process even more laborious.

I picked up the messages from the old Communications and Records Unit (CRU). It was the nerve center of the embassy where incoming and outgoing traffic (classified and non-classified) was processed and dispatched to the Department and elsewhere. All official records were kept there.

The secretaries kept individual files, according to the State Department's standard regulations, as well. Our duties extended beyond record keeping, but not all supervisors fully understood this. We analyzed the boss—his/her personality, management style, preference of resolving conflicts, and communication style (oral or written notes). We studied the mission goals and objectives and questioned how the office fit into the overall plan. We followed current events. Basically, we were troubleshooters. If something was overlooked for a meeting, we diplomatically suggested, "Do you think this document will be useful?" We anticipated the needs of the person in authority and managed up. The point I am making is that secretaries were undervalued. At least, that was my observation.

It is a recurring theme of mine. "People are people" and regardless of setting, color or culture, they have common traits—the same aspirations, the same sensitivities, and the same ego. The problem arises when we lose sight of this. If we dwell on the dark side, then the goodness of others—their light—is concealed. I think everyone has the power to tear down stereotypes if we choose to do so, but it requires an abundance of patience, courage, and energy.

We sent many labor and political reports to Washington. The region was politically and economically active. Ferdinand Marcos was being elected. In addition, the Vietnam War was heating up. Congressional delegations poured into the country. At the end of 1965, up to 50 percent of the countryside in South Vietnam was under some degree of Viet Cong control. That same year, *Time* magazine reported the Filipino population was growing by "a million a year and annually some 360,000 youngsters were entering the labor market" only to find insufficient jobs. The crime rate soared and so did the labor attaché's reporting.

Q: The Philippines is a large country. Did you have a chance to venture out, or were you mainly in Manila?

AKAHLOUN: I went on several adventuresome trips but nothing compares with the first one. It was an unbearably hot and humid Sunday morning, and I was attending mass. Beads of perspiration poured down my face, but I was thinking about our planned trip to Pagsanjan Falls to shoot the rapids. It would be cooler there. Two hours later, we arrived, parked our jeep, and climbed into our respective dugout canoes. There were three of them, each carrying one passenger and two *banceros* (boatmen). It vaguely occurred to me that we were not wearing lifesaving vests.

It was a heavenly day—blue sky, soft white clouds, riverbank filled with lush tropical vegetation and radiant sunshine. As the *banceros* paddled down the river, my canoe suddenly crashed into one of the rocks and capsized. I thought, "Lord, I arrived one month ago. Surely, you did not bring me halfway around the world to end my life here. You know, I have been very faithful. Please help me." I listened to an inner voice that said hold on to the canoe. As the falls neared, the water became more turbulent. I began praying. The canoe continued to roll over and over. Each time, I held my breath, shook the water off, and tightened my grip. Once again there was a whisper, "This is not your day. Hold on. Don't give up." So I fought harder and clung on for dear life. Just in the nick of time, someone swam toward me and pulled the canoe over to a cluster of rocks miraculously saving my life. After that, I never shot the rapids again—one near-death experience was more than enough.

Q: Okay, you narrowly escaped and totally understood you were spared. What continued to happen in the Philippines during your two years?

AKAHLOUN: It was an exhilarating assignment. Reportedly, 110 different indigenous groups of people live in the Philippines. My goal was to interact with as many of them as possible. As a vibrant twenty-two-year-old, I was full of curiosity. Another priority was exploring Manila's nightlife. The Filipinos are known as the musicians of the Far East. Most weekends we scouted out new clubs and stayed out until four in the morning. Because I never tired of dancing, everyone thought my drinks were spiked, but it was simply a natural high, as I do not drink alcoholic beverages.

None of my social activities interfered with my professional duties as my career was my number one priority. It was ingrained in me that whatever the task, "you give it your best shot." I was conscientious, responsible, and managed to find a healthy work–life balance. As time progressed, I was able to multitask, work hard, maintain a lively social life, and travel extensively. And that is a fact.

The Philippines was a bustling culturally diverse country with over seven thousand islands. Although the majority of Filipinos lived in poverty, some city dwellers led sophisticated and privileged lives. There was a huge cultural mixture. One memorable trip was to Baguio City, located in the mountains in the northern part of Luzon. It has a cool climate and is known as the Summer Capital of the Philippines. It was a day's journey from Manila. The narrow twisting road we drove on had no guardrails, and the steep drop-offs were scary. Nevertheless, the view was magnificent. From Baguio I went to Banaue and saw the two-thousand-year-old rice terraces carved largely by hand into the mountainside. This amazing engineering feat spreads out for miles and miles and has been declared a World Heritage Site by the UN Educational, Scientific, and Cultural Organization (UNESCO).

My friends and I also traveled to Mindanao, the second largest island and the southernmost major point in the Philippines. It has a significantly large Muslim presence. To reach there, we took a crowded ferry in questionable condition packed with people, produce, and chickens. I have no recollection of how long we were on the boat, but it was unnerving. Very rustic. Upon arriving, we rented motorized bikes to sightsee the island. I thought it was a great idea until I hit a bump and went flying over the handlebar. Luckily, I did not sustain any broken bones, but the gravel road badly scraped my right arm and leg.

Back then, we didn't have the luxury of carrying bottles of hand sanitizers or tubes of Neosporin. And neither was there a reputable medical facility on the island. We cleaned and bandaged the wounds as best possible, but my leg became inflamed. The next boat to Manila was arriving in two days. Life in the glamorous Foreign Service does have its pitfalls. The morning after I returned, I hobbled to the embassy's medical unit and then to my office. By now, the men in the office and I had bonded. The work required me to jump from one job to another.

The deadlines were relentless and the interruptions endless. Somehow, I retained my composure and sense of humor, which my bosses appreciated. They began entrusting me with increased responsibility and projects. I started drafting cables and other documents.

Q: Well, you almost lost your life in the rapids. You scrape half of your body. You go in the next day and draft cables.

AKAHLOUN: Sure did. That was the way it happened. My vacation ended, and it was time to eliminate the backlog. I was at the bottom of a highly stratified totem pole. Without a college degree, pedigree, or "big city" upbringing, I had to work doubly hard to gain the respect of my supervisors and colleagues. It was crucial to get past the stereotyping and preconceived opinion that people of color were inferior.

Q: Manila was a staging ground for some of the military operations in Vietnam. What were some of the major political activities taking place during your assignment?

AKAHLOUN: Some people believed our diplomatic relations with the Philippines were being tested by communist agitators. There were insurgents in the country identified as leftists. I think our worsening relations with the country were caused by multiple factors. One component was our presence in Vietnam. There was great controversy regarding our military intervention in that country. Several public demonstrations took place outside the embassy gates. The sight of angry mobs protesting and throwing rocks was terrifying. The mission's security procedures were strong, so I felt somewhat reassured.

Q: When you say our relations were declining, do you think the general skepticism for the U.S. went throughout the public or certain sectors only? And was it shared by the government?

AKAHLOUN: Excellent questions. We endorsed President Marcos because he was anticommunist, pro-American, and his campaign had an anticorruption theme. We also had strategic interests and military bases in the region. We needed a foothold in the Philippines to extend our sphere of influence and counter Soviet and communist activity in the region. Domestically, Filipinos in general were angry about their government's inability to govern effectively. There was a growing crime rate, widespread murders, extensive corruption, and rampant smuggling. Public resentment existed for President Macapagal and in certain segments of the population for the U.S. as well. We thought Marcos would be our savior. After becoming president, however, his corrupt practices and extravagant lifestyle disillusioned many. Neither did we envision Imelda Marcos becoming famous for her shoe collection. Allegedly, when Marcos and Imelda fled the country in 1986, she left behind 1,220 pairs of shoes.

Q: *A considerable amount of corruption was taking place. Okay, geographically we are in Manila. There were white water rafting, nightclubs, tinikling parties, balut sampling, and Baguio rice terraces. A trip to Mindanao and scraped knees. Friendships. What else comes to mind?*

AKAHLOUN: I must mention another trip. The location of the Philippines allowed me to explore neighboring countries. At the time, I was single and able to take calculated risks. In early 1966, I naively decided to visit a friend in Indonesia. Upon landing, there were military tanks and antiaircraft missiles lining the runway. Two Indonesian political figures—Sukarno and Suharto—were engaged in a power struggle. There were coup attempts, and it was a dangerous period of social and political unrest. October 1965 to March 1966 witnessed the eclipse of Sukarno and the rise of Suharto as the supreme leader. I underestimated the gravity of the situation but boarded the plane and returned safely to the Philippines. What a nightmare.

Q: *Considering your track record, I think you didn't need any more daring adventures.*

AKAHLOUN: One would think so. In March 1967, my friend, Judy Fest, and I were seized with the desire of taking a southeast Asian Circle tour to Hong Kong, Thailand, Malaysia, and Singapore. Did I mention Vietnam? Judy, incidentally, worked at the U.S. Embassy as a secretary in the Economic Section. Vietnam dominated the headlines, and we wanted to investigate firsthand. On my father's birthday, March 4, 1966, we landed in Saigon. We were two fish completely out of water.

Two servicemen rescued us. In disbelief, they asked why we were there. We actually weren't sure. Just knew I wanted to visit the country. In the background, we heard mortars and rockets being fired. We sought refuge at a safe-haven hotel. Our self-appointed escorts turned out to be gentlemen—very respectful and protective. We went to dinner, but our nerves were frazzled. Bombs and grenades exploded all around us. The waiter placed salt-and-pepper shakers on the table, and we jumped. Even this simple sound scared us. It was the most frightening thirty-six hours of my life.

Sunday morning before departing I asked our good Samaritans, "Do you know where the nearest Catholic Church is located?" They were mortified at the suggestion we wanted to venture out into the streets again. Miraculously, the church was a few blocks away, but getting there was horrifying. It was 5:00 a.m. when we set out. The streets were deserted and pitch-black. Falling bombs in the periodically illuminated the sky. Suddenly, we heard quick footsteps behind us. "Judy," I whispered, "do you hear that?" "Yeah," she replied. Terrified, we started running faster and faster. The noise came closer and closer. I thought the end was near. We ducked into an archway and crouched down. A silhouette passed us. It was a farmer carrying baskets of vegetables. The darkness had concealed him. In our imagination, he was the enemy. It was too early, too dark, and too dangerous for two young impressionable Foreign Service gals to be out in the war-torn streets of Saigon. We attended mass and left Saigon double-quick.

Q: *You definitely tested the limits of normal life there. The rapids, warfare, falling off a bike. I think you lived in a state of grace. Meanwhile, doing your work and putting up the front of just nose to the grindstone.*

AKAHLOUN: I took pride in my work. It was an obligation to me and my superiors. I had much to prove to myself and my parents who had deep faith and confidence in my ability. While overseas, I was eager to learn and experience as much as possible.

One unforgettable experience was the Easter procession during Holy Week in Bongabong, Oriental Mindoro. I was there with friends as an observer rather than in an official capacity to watch the flagellants and other activities. The scene was far from anything I had ever witnessed. The copper-tone Mangyans, indigenous people of the island, walked around barefooted. They wore loincloths, and some of the women covered their breasts with bark scraps. It was strange seeing them with ice cream cones. Young boys and girls danced around us, gawking at our big-rimmed sunglasses and fancy clothes. Precious old ladies covered their heads with veils and buried their faces in prayer books while we—the Filipino and American city folks—snapped away with our sophisticated cameras.

The four participating flagellants atoned for their sins by flogging themselves with wooden flails. The shirtless penitents were cleansing their souls—the greater the pain, the more meaningful the sacrifice. They were without shoes and wrapped palm leaves around their waists, which partly concealed their tattered trousers. To hide their identities, they covered their faces with black hoods and leaves. For me, fasting forty days during Lenten season is an endeavor. However, it clearly pales in comparison.

The process was elaborate and appeared excruciatingly painful. First, the flagellants whipped themselves until their back muscles swelled. The preparation was supposed to numb the pain. Then, another person made some thirteen rows of neatly lined cuts with a knife on their backs. Under the boiling sun, they marched around for three hours, beating themselves from side to side. Blood oozed out. What an unbelievable sight. *Moriones* led the Good Friday procession. They dressed in red capes and masks, carried sticks, and whirled around, mocking the flagellants who trudged along slowly and silently to the sea where they washed their wounds. The salt acted as a cleanser and accelerated the healing process. Can you imagine the agony? It was a sobering moment.

Q: *Well, this was very exotic. A little bit shocking and somewhat out of the ordinary. Is this partly why you wanted to be in the Foreign Service? To have these unusual encounters?*

AKAHLOUN: Partially. Seeing life enfold in real time fascinated me. I suffer from wanderlust—an old-fashioned expression that explains why people make the effort to become familiar with the unknown. Then there was a desire to make the world a more humane place.

Q: What is your sense of your own experience in the Philippines? Do you feel you made a difference through your embassy work or your extracurricular activities?

AKAHLOUN: I made an effort by submerging myself into the culture. I lived outside the U.S. government compound, began studying Tagalog, rode jeepneys, joined a local theater group, and traveled to surrounding barrios and neighboring islands. In my efficiency report, my boss wrote "Penny is a one woman Peace Corps." He was overly generous with his comment, but I tried to portray Americans in a favorable light. There was a growing resentment toward us because of our involvement with the Vietnam War. We were scrutinized and generally considered privileged and inaccessible. Some people live abroad without leaving home. This expatriate lifestyle did not suit me, and that is why I rode local transportation, but it was also fun.

There were no bus stops, but the jeepneys with their flashy colors and designs were easily spotted. My weight was considerably more than the average Filipina, and this presented a bit of a problem. I occupied two seats and sometimes received side-glances from slimmer passengers. Space was at a premium. Anyone suffering from claustrophobia would find it difficult to cope. The drivers were speed demons. You had to really hang on because they "stopped on a dime." No cords to pull. You simply yelled, *"Para, para"* (stop, stop), and the jeepney came to a screeching halt. They would brake and accelerate without showing tenderness for the riders. But these excursions were culturally insightful and helped me better represent the U.S.

Q: I must say your endurance is impressive. We made it through a lot of material, high school, parents, Senator Brooke, and a first assignment, which is sometimes the most notable. Before moving on to the next segment of the interview, I suggest we end on a high note. What are some observations about your first Foreign Service tour?

AKAHLOUN: The Philippines exceeded my expectations. The assignment was exotic, fun, and adventuresome. Yet the level of poverty and political conflict I witnessed distressed me.

When it was time to leave, it was especially heartbreaking to say good-bye to Guia Reyes, the landlady's daughter. It was a bittersweet departure. Endings in the Foreign Service, however, are a way of life. No matter how sad they are, it is vital to think they signify a new beginning and new possibilities. Guia and her sister eventually moved to Canada. Some thirteen years later, we met during my assignment to Ottawa. Despite the passage of time, we spoke to each other as though it was only yesterday. This is a test of true friendship.

Q: Can you speak about "fishing around" for your next assignment. Do you recall the circumstances?

AKAHLOUN: Oh yes. During the May 1967 Foreign Service post inspection, I was asked about limitations that should be taken into consideration in transferring me. My response was, "I am open to any post, providing there is a Catholic Church available." And my preferences? Beirut, Israel, Tunisia, Algiers, Morocco, or Greece. At twenty-four, I was in many ways still an adolescent and very naïve.

After pouring through the open assignments list, I narrowed my choice down to one—Rabat, Morocco. The grade level and location was perfect, and I could visit Uncle Ti Tom (Bartholomew Jose Correia) who earlier retired in the Cape Verde Islands. Both Foreign Service and personal needs would be satisfied, so I began lobbying and received the assignment. Soon, I was hunting for a Catholic Church in a Muslim country.

Q: Before venturing on to Morocco, delve a little deeper into the political scene in the Philippines. We spoke about Manila being a staging area for U.S. military operations in Vietnam and the resentment of some of the public. In addition, Marcos was being elected. Let us hear more about that.

AKAHLOUN: The campaign was downright explosive. There were many rallies, deaths, and curfews—official and self-imposed ones. It was a tense period, and the embassy personnel moved around the city cautiously. Marcos was the establishment candidate. The one backed by the U.S. We were counting on him to reverse the country's downward spiral. Unfortunately, it did not turn out this way. He took his Oath of Office on December 30, 1965. Vice President Humphrey came to town for the swearing in and later President Johnson visited.

Q: *These trips reinforced Marcos and demonstrated to the Filipinos that we took their geostrategic role seriously. Were you involved in the logistics of any of these visits?*

AKAHLOUN: Yes, the entire mission was mobilized for both events. My first taste of a VIP (very important person) visit was when Humphrey came to town. It was hectic and overwhelming, as one of the men I worked for was heavily involved. One of his responsibilities was to craft the Vice President's speech. The multiple drafts kept me quite occupied. In addition, there were several control rooms—one for the White House, one for the press and another for the embassy—sometimes not all in the same place. Frequently, one location was unable to communicate with the other. I was one of the rovers and delivered classified messages to the various sites. Humphrey briefly visited the chancery. He struck me as being earnest, friendly, and unpretentious.

Q: *Now, let us skip to the U.S. President Johnson's visit, which was in 1966. Anything different about that?*

AKAHLOUN: On October 24 and 25, 1966, President Johnson and other heads of state gathered for a Seven-Nation Manila Summit Conference to discuss the escalating Vietnam War. Each one of them received full military honors, including a twenty-one-gun salute. It was quite an extravaganza. President Johnson was a larger-than-life personality who spoke with a Texas drawl. The ambassador hosted a huge reception, where we shook hands with the president who graciously acknowledged the embassy's efforts. He was charismatic and had a folksy style. I think it is unfortunate he became more known for escalating the Vietnam War, instead of his efforts pushing through sweeping civil rights legislation. His wife, Lady Bird, was well dressed, poised, and polite. It was a thrilling occasion.

Q: *Tell us about your departure from Manila. You took a flight path that enabled you to see half the world in one month. What an adventure.*

AKAHLOUN: When I was younger, many of my dance routines were performed to the music of "Around the World in 80 Days." The melody magically transported me to distant lands. I had already crossed the

Pacific to reach Manila. So after my assignment ended, I decided to travel the other way to circumnavigate the globe. My itinerary took me to India, Nepal, Iran, Turkey, Greece, Israel, Jordan, Austria, and France. The first stop was Calcutta, India. A hot, noisy, and overpopulated city with staggering poverty, bodies on the street, sacred cows roaming the sidewalks, and aggressive flies. The human suffering was beyond belief. India is a land rich in ancient culture and customs. The country's exotic cuisine and spices are world-class, and we are only scratching the surface.

Anyway, the plane landed and taxied to the gate. I cleared customs and went to pick up my baggage, which never showed up. Officials speculated it was still on the plane en route to Geneva. This was definitely not part of the script. The suitcase contained everything, including my winter clothes. My carry-on bag had a few items but no extra clothing. The airlines sent me shopping with $50 and an apologetic guide. The Good Samaritan shop had a limited selection of western-style clothes and nothing for winter. Three days later when I began to despair, my luggage was delivered. Thank God. The following morning I went to Nepal.

Q: *Perfect timing. Now, about the people and the Hindu caste system. India is one of the most stratified societies in the world. Was this obvious?*

AKAHLOUN: India's caste system is complicated and is steeped in two thousand years of culture. People at the top and bottom of the pyramid were generally recognizable, as opposed to those in the middle. As I learned from my research prior to leaving Manila, there are four main castes: Brahmins, Kshatriyas, Vaishyas, and Shudras. The Harijans or Dalits, formerly known as the "untouchables," are the "outcasts." People are born, get married, and ultimately die within their own caste. In Calcutta, I saw those without a caste lying at the edge of the road—unable to move, too weak to speak, eyes glazed over, and minutes away from death. A dreadful sight.

Q: *Do you think the caste system was partly a rationalization for dealing psychologically with disadvantaged people?*

AKAHLOUN: Possibly. Historians have differing viewpoints about its origin. I think we can all agree that the system is unfair to those at the bottom who are considered inferior and have no privileges. The "untouchables" are alienated from society. Today I understand there is less social stratification. I hope so. A person's status should be defined by his or her character and achievements, not by the color of their skin, or to whom they are born.

Q: *During the visit did you entertain the thought of a future posting in India?*

AKAHLOUN: India was fascinating, but I never considered an assignment there. From Calcutta, I flew to Kathmandu to see the snow-capped Himalayan Mountains and Mount Everest, the tallest mountain in the world—over twenty-nine thousand feet. It was sensational. I visited Banaras (now Varanasi) situated on the banks of the Ganges River. The city is believed to be at least three thousand years old and is one of the seven sacred spots for Hindus. Every devout believer hopes to visit the city once in a lifetime and take a dip in the Ganges. The scene defied imagination. People were bathing, swimming, washing their clothes—and animals—in the water. Commuter boats were ferrying passengers. At the river's edge were the famous ghats (a series of vast concrete steps) where literally life and death activities occur. Vendors sold food, drinks, and flowers. Holy men practiced yoga, body massagers were busy at work, as well as barbers, armed with straight razors. Smoke poured out of funeral piles where bodies were ceremoniously cremated. People paused to grieve and then went on to celebrate life. Despite all the activity, it was very peaceful—a place where mind, body, and spirit seamlessly blended.

Next, I stopped in Agra to see the Taj Mahal. It was dazzling. Absolutely magnificent. Afterward, it was on to Jaipur, the Pink City, to view their splendid temples and to take an exciting elephant ride. I I also went to New Delhi, where hordes of people, bicycles, cars, cows, donkeys, and yellow-turbaned vendors squatting by their smelly camels, seemed to mingle nicely together. I was traveling alone but made certain a reputable agency organized the trip. After Saigon, my parents were traumatized. This time, I kept them well informed. Along the way, I sent postcards and checked in at our embassies for security briefings. I kept silent about visiting Saigon to spare them from worrying. In retrospect, they should have been advised.

*Q: You were always mindful of your parents' presence. But at this point,
your credibility was impaired. You had to regain it.*

AKAHLOUN: Right. Damage control measures were in full force. The
aftermath of the 1967 Six-Day War between Israel and its Arab neighbors
prevented me from going to Lebanon and Libya. There were anti-Israeli
demonstrations and riots in many Arab countries, so I decided to visit
Tehran instead. We had diplomatic relations with the country then. On
October 26, 1967—two days after I arrived—Mohammad Reza Shah
Pahlavi crowned himself Emperor of Iran, and his wife, Farah Pahlavi,
assumed the title of empress. Banners, photos of the Shah, and strings
of lights elaborately decorated every inch of the capital.

Outwardly, the city looked prosperous and westernized, but there
was an undercurrent of tension. For the most part, people were cordial
but not particularly receptive to outsiders. English was spoken mostly
at the hotels. There was not much interaction with westerners.

Some women wore a dark chador, a full-length semicircle cape
loosely thrown over their heads and bodies. It was open down the front.
Their faces were not entirely covered. My long-sleeved loose-fitting dress
attracted unwanted attention. At one time, I remember admiring a ring
in a store window when a man suddenly snuck up from behind, pinched
my bottom, and vanished. After the surprise attack, I was a bit on edge,
aware of the vulnerabilities of traveling alone as a woman. Hereafter, I
became much more aware and cautious of my surroundings.

As a side remark, the Shah introduced significant women's rights
measures. For instance, the minimum age for girls to marry was raised
from around thirteen to eighteen. Other reforms included more liberal
divorce laws and educational rights. After the 1979 Islamic revolution,
women lost most of their freedom, and the new regime required Iranian
women to wear the *hijab* (veil) in public.

*Q: From Tehran, you went to Turkey and Greece. Could we focus on that
for a minute? Two countries with strained relations that are next to
each other. Many people prefer one to the other. Did you?*

AKAHLOUN: Given its geographical positioning, Turkey is unique.
East meets west here. It has been a cradle of many civilizations for

centuries and centuries. The country has been influenced by cultures from China to Vienna and Russia to North Africa. Turkey preserved its melting pot identity by practicing goodwill and religious tolerance. It is a very inclusive society. Also, I might add The Blue Mosque, with its cascading domes and six slender minarets, was quite imposing. Its interior was lined with more than twenty-thousand handmade ceramic tiles. An awesome sight.

My entry into Greece was entirely unexpected. At a U.S. Embassy dinner party in Istanbul, I met an American couple who were planning an overland trip to Athens. They invited me to tag along. I have since forgotten the names of the places we visited, but the golden images of the mountains and Aegean seaports and friendly people linger. I do remember briefly stopping in Alos, a rocky village, after we spotted a rugged-looking elderly woman who was charming. She stood outside her straw dwelling, dressed head-to-toe in black (long skirt, sweater, and headscarf). She tilted her sun-beaten face and slightly smiled at us. Then she placed her hands on her hip as if to say, "I am poor, proud, and somebody."

Greece was also rich in history, tradition, and beauty. There was much to see in Athens. The Acropolis was moving. Walking around on its grounds gave me a feeling of awe and a tremendous sense of the greatness of the ancient Greeks. I also loved the food—fresh fish and tasty vegetables picked from the vines. In retrospect, perhaps Greece had a slight edge over Turkey.

Q: Next, you went to Israel and Jordan. What stands out in your mind?

AKAHLOUN: Jerusalem, the holy site for Judaism, Christianity, and Islam—three major religions—was spiritually uplifting. To see Jewish temples, the spot where Jesus died and was resurrected, plus the place where Mohammed ascended to heaven all in the same location was an emotional experience. Other unforgettable attractions included the Wailing Wall, the Via Dolorosa, the Dome of the Rock, the Tomb of King David, the Cenaculum (Last Supper Room), and the Garden of Gethsemane. Dipping my feet into the Sea of Galilee, where Jesus delivered sermons and performed miracles, is embedded in my mind.

Near the end of the trip, events and dates all meshed together. I had been traveling for nearly one month and stayed in twenty-one hotels. My memories were becoming foggy. Only after reaching Washington was there time to savor the victory of completing my grand odyssey.

CHAPTER THREE

Around The World And Home In One Piece

WASHINGTON, D.C., AND HOME LEAVE, LATE 1967

It felt wonderful being on U.S. soil again. I looked forward to reuniting with my family and friends. In my absence, however, the domestic scene profoundly changed. And so had I.

Q: This is now the end of 1967. You returned to the U.S. for an extended period of time before your onward assignment to Morocco. You are twenty-four years old and have circled the globe. After expanding your horizons, did Washington, D.C., look the same?

AKAHLOUN: It was less intimidating. Overseas I became more familiar with the roles of various U.S. foreign affairs agencies and how they operated. I learned the inner workings of the bureaucracy and felt more confident. I had grown as a person—more self-assured, worldlier, and more comfortable in the woman I was becoming.

Q: During 1967, there were tremendous differences of opinion in the U.S. on the Vietnam War. Lots of hard feelings on everybody's part—those opposed and those in favor of the war. This really developed while you were in the Philippines. Once you arrived, did you detect some tension in the air?

AKAHLOUN: Yes. There was some restlessness, and I experienced "reentry shock." That's when we feel anxious and nervous returning from an international location and must readjust to our culture and the old way of life. It is very similar to the culture shock which takes place when we go abroad and sense confusion, uncertainty, or uneasiness caused by exposure to a foreign environment. Life was different now, and I felt somewhat out of place in my own country.

There was an "informational" divide. A tremendous gap. There was no Internet or a cable network such as CNN. We were not digitally or instantaneously connected to developments taking place internationally. No cable television news reporting in real time. I arrived in Washington, D.C., late November in a vacuum and was surprised to learn a few weeks' earlier over one hundred thousand antiwar protestors rallied at the Lincoln Monument, where Dr. Benjamin Spock and other celebrities condemned Lyndon Johnson for escalating the war. Life in America seemed to be unraveling.

Q: Let us talk about your home leave. For the reader, this is a vacation that Foreign Service officers receive generally after or midway through an overseas posting. You checked in with your family in New England.

AKAHLOUN: Yes, I returned home and received royal treatment. My mother and father rolled out the red carpet, hung up welcome home signs, and put up Christmas ornaments and lights everywhere. A beautifully decorated tree and presents filled the living room. I was extremely happy as I had missed my close-knit family deeply. My dear niece and nephews joined us. It was a marvelous celebration.

My mother staunchly believed in self-improvement, especially for her children. Soon she started probing. "While overseas, what did you learn? Have you taken advantage of your gifts?" She was referring to my artistic talent. Traveling for travel's sake was not enough for her. To appease her, I promised to sign up for art lessons during my Moroccan assignment.

Q: Politically did you detect any difference in your Massachusetts community? What about social changes? Was it pretty much the way you left it?

AKAHLOUN: Essentially, the isolated community was the same. My world had significantly expanded, but that was not the case with others. My friends were pleased to see me, yet sometimes I sensed they felt awkward in my presence. I politely answered their questions and then redirected the conversations, focusing on them and their families. These were friends I grew up with, and I wanted them to feel comfortable. There was no need to bore them with my activities or have them think I was snobbish.

Q: You departed the U.S. after your home leave, obviously, not knowing exactly what would await you in your next assignment of Rabat, Morocco. It was closer to Cape Verde and you were going to take up art. That's all you knew. Little did you suspect it would be a life-changing assignment.

AKAHLOUN: I had no clue. Being near the Cape Verde Islands was a factor in choosing Rabat, and the personnel division in Washington thoughtfully accommodated the request. After a few weeks at home, I was off to Morocco. I didn't speak Arabic, and there was no time for French training in Washington, D.C., so my plan was to study the language at the embassy in Rabat. I was excited about the adventures awaiting me in my new adopted country.

CHAPTER FOUR

LAND OF HOSPITALITY, MINT TEA, AND LOVE

MOROCCO, 1968–1970

Life sometimes unfolds in an unpredictable fashion. I had specific personal and professional goals upon arriving in Morocco. After landing in Rabat, however, these plans suddenly derailed—but for the better.

Q: Let us get your first impressions of Rabat.

AKAHLOUN: Wednesday, the third of January 1968, I arrived. The North Africa panorama was very different from anything I had ever seen and completely fascinating. In contrast to Boston's gray sky and bitter cold weather, Rabat was sunny and mild. The clear, blue sky, colorful gardens, red earth, and palm trees invigorated me. It was Mother Nature at her best. Moroccans walked around in *djellabas* (long outer garments with hoods). Some of the men wore yellow *babouches* (slippers with no heels) and a turban or a *tarboosh* (red fez) on their heads. The pace of life was leisurely, and the people were enchanting.

In Manila, I tended to greet everyone with a smile, handshake, and a hug. According to the State Department's briefing on Moroccan etiquette, women gave out handshakes in limited situations. Otherwise, the gesture sent a message of promiscuity and disrespect. I tried to curb my extroverted enthusiasm and my natural inclination to warmly greet people. I began training myself. "If I keep my hands folded behind my back, it will be harder to thrust them at a stranger." I looked Moroccan, which was a double-edged sword as I was readily accepted by the people, but also was expected to adhere to the subtleties of the culture. There was a greater sense of conservatism than I had experienced in the Philippines or in the U.S.

Q: *Did you give any thought about being unable to initiate handshakes, or did you accept this?*

AKAHLOUN: "When in Rome, do as the Romans do." We adapt to the customs of the places we visit. In the Foreign Service, we try to avoid embarrassing ourselves or the U.S. government. We are guests in a particular country and are held accountable for our actions. I accepted the way of life. On the other hand, the society was tolerant enough so that wearing western clothes and behaving somewhat differently presented no major problems. For me it was not burdensome easing into the culture. Yet I must confess to missing my nightclub excursions—at least initially.

Q: *So women were limited to certain types of behavior. Tell me more about some of the differences you encountered in this captivating country.*

AKAHLOUN: Morocco is a beautiful country filled with a huge variety of natural landscapes from the sands of the Sahara to the majestic peaks of the High Atlas Mountains. It is surrounded by the Atlantic Ocean and the Mediterranean Sea and offers an amazing diversity of cultures. I found that most people were thoughtful, educated, and incredibly kind. It is one of my favorite places in the world.

When men met on the street, at home, or in restaurants, they tended to greet each other with a handshake and touched the right hand to their hearts as a sign of respect. The Moroccans, a family-oriented society, inquired about a spouse, children, and parents repeatedly, as though reciting a litany. If the person was a friend, the greeting was accompanied by kisses, usually twice, once per cheek. Couples, even married ones, rarely touched in public. These were some of my first impressions.

The people were hospitable and graciously served guests traditional mint tea, which they drank throughout the day. For Moroccans, it symbolized warmth, generosity, and friendship. They steeped the green tea leaves and generous amounts of spearmint or mint leaves and added rock sugar. The tea was ceremoniously poured from a distance into small glasses. It was very sweet, soothing, and refreshing. Even vendors in the *souk* (market) served us tea. A wonderful tradition.

The Moroccan *tagines* (stews) made of meat, chicken, or fish and plenty of fresh vegetables were delicious. I particularly liked the lamb dish with olives and a light, nutty Argan oil exclusive to Morocco. I loved the aroma and the colors of the different spices—saffron, turmeric, paprika, cumin, and cinnamon. The sights, sounds, and smells of the country were stimulating.

Another notable difference was the way Moroccans worshipped compared to Christians. Under Islam, they prayed five times a day—generally at dawn, noon, afternoon, sunset, and evening. The call to prayer boomed from the mosques and echoed throughout the city. Friday, not Sunday, is the Holy Day. Their piety was inspiring.

Linguistically, the country is rather complex. The official languages are Modern Standard Arabic, Moroccan Arabic, and Berber. French, however, serves as a second language for many Moroccans and is primarily used in government, business, and by the upper class. In the north of Morocco, Spanish is commonly spoken due to the area's colonization by Spain.

Q: What about the political situation?

AKAHLOUN: At the time, it was stable, but there was a history of turmoil. Briefly, King Hassan II succeeded his father in 1961. A few years into his reign, a plot against his life was discovered and one of the organizers, Mehdi Ben Barka, subsequently vanished. This was in 1965. King Hassan later suspended Parliament and assumed supreme control. His loyal friend, General Mohamed Oufkir, supervised the brutal repression of politicians, unionists, and the religious establishment. He was notorious and feared throughout Morocco.

Q: We will go into this in greater detail later. But first, tell me how you integrated into the embassy. Your tasks and types of encounters with Moroccan counterparts.

AKAHLOUN: The Moroccan employees at the U.S. Embassy were polite and courteous. Siad, who worked at the snack bar, was especially friendly and a great storyteller. He entertained us with his humorous tales about life in the *bled* (the country side). Siad made the best tuna fish salad sandwiches ever. Turns out he was skillful at something else—espionage. For a long time, the embassy was unaware it had a Russian spy in its midst. I am glad I listened to him rather than contributing to his conversations. This was a sign of Cold War politics at play. After this incident, I became less trusting of people, at least, initially.

I worked as a secretary to John Collins, the administrative counselor, who was as tall as he was round and very openhearted. He spoke with an engaging southern drawl and had a disarming smile. Mr. Collins was full of wisdom that manifested itself in his thick crop of white hair. From the outset, he saw my potential as a budding embassy staffer and assumed a mentoring role. He groomed me for higher responsibility.

Our section was involved with embassy procurement issues, U.S. government contracts with local vendors for employee housing, and other administrative tasks. We also supervised the French language training program. I was lucky to be assigned to Morocco as it was considered a choice assignment. The U.S. Mission was much smaller than Manila, and we had close diplomatic relations with the Moroccan government. Actually, in 1786, Thomas Jefferson, John Adams, and Muhammad III signed a Moroccan–American Treaty of Friendship, which is the longest unbroken alliance in U.S. history.

Part of Morocco's charm is its blend of Islamic, Arabic, Berber, European, and African influences. Colonial powers Spain and France also left their imprint. Surprisingly, a sizeable Jewish population existed. This cultural mix was similar to my Cape Verdean background. Despite the different social expectations and roles for women, I felt at home here.

Q: I imagine you explored the country. That is what you did in the Philippines, in Southeast Asia, in the Middle East and everywhere else. Where did you travel outside of Rabat?

AKAHLOUN: I visited Casablanca, Tangier, Fes, Meknes, and other exciting places. Marrakech and its magical Djemaa El Fna Square in the *medina* (old city) impressed me the most. Few other UNESCO World Heritage sites compare to the dynamic Pink City. Its sights, sounds, and smells are intoxicating. The odor from the horse-drawn carriages and donkey-pulling carts takes your breath away. Walking into the square is like stumbling on a Hollywood movie set. It has the feel of an open-air circus. Acrobats, musicians, snake charmers, trained monkeys, and storytellers perform under sweltering heat. Watermen carry cold water in camel skin sacs and pour it into shiny brass cups for spectators. The flute-playing Moroccan snake charmers are legendary. How they mesmerize the cobras is a mystery. Supposedly, the reptiles are in some induced trance, but the one placed around my neck was frighteningly energetic. I was petrified.

Deep inside the colorful bazaar, or souk, was another enchanting world. We walked through a maze of narrow alleyways and nearly got trampled by donkey carts. It was easy to get lost. We entered a variety of workshops—cloth dying, copper beating, leather working, and others. Shop owners lured us inside. *"Aji, aji (*come, come). Sit down and warm yourselves with mint tea." Who could resist?

On my $6,730 annual salary, I could not afford a car. Instead, I drove down to Marrakech with embassy colleagues. The excitement of the city, the chaos, the smell of the spices, the colors, and the warmth of the people captured my heart. One day we spent time with the spice vendors. The next day, we visited the brass and copper sections of the market and on and on it went. In some respects, it was an intimate affair. We never tired of the souk and neither did the vendors tire of us. Marrakech was founded over a thousand years ago as a caravan trading post in the middle of a desert oasis. For centuries and centuries, it was exposed to various types of people and cultures. It is impossible to overstay your welcome in Marrakech. It is a fantastic city.

Q: *During 1968, 1969, and 1970, I believe, there were no tremendous ups and downs at the embassy. You had a protective boss who mentored you. You organized sightseeing trips. You understood that a woman traveling alone was not the best thing, so you accompanied other Americans to these spots. What else would you like to add?*

AKAHLOUN: Some Moroccans working at the embassy invited me to their homes. These gatherings were not part of my official duties. I wanted to move beyond the stereotypes and experience the Moroccan way of life. The country's customs, food, traditional dress (long robes and turbans), written language (left to right), music, palaces, and religion were some of the elements that attracted me. Morocco is one of the more moderate Arab nations and traditionally has been friendly toward the western world.

An invitation to a Moroccan home for dinner was quite special. We washed our hands and removed our shoes before entering the salon, lined with multipurpose sofas. The communal meal was served on a low round table, and the food was mostly eaten by hand from a large platter. Thick slices of bread were passed out for dipping into the serving dish. Thinking back, the choice pieces of meat were given to me. It was polite to have at least two or three helpings to avoid offending the hostess who ate sparingly so that the guests ate sufficiently.

After the feast, no one retreated to another room as we often do in the U.S. We stretched out on the sofa and drank a glass of soothing mint tea. The Moroccan families I encountered—even those with limited means—went out of their way to serve elaborate meals and to properly entertain their guests.

Another point is worth mentioning. Moroccans place high value in honor and pride. A respectable reputation is considered everything. This is why *hshuma*, the concept of shame, is so central to the culture. It dictates a huge portion of daily life (who they talk to, where they go, and what they do). They avoid asking overnight house guests how long they plan to visit because it is *hshuma*—disrespectful.

Q: Now, you told your mother you were going to pursue your art interests. Did you follow her instructions?

AKAHLOUN: I did, which is one reason I speak so glowingly of the Moroccans. My search for an art teacher began shortly after I moved into my downtown apartment at 41 Avenue Allah Ben Abdallah, one floor above the embassy's U.S. Information Service (USIS) center. One instructor—a Russian lady—came highly recommended. I deliberated, "Hmm . . . cold war . . . fraternizing with the enemy . . . engaging her services will require sending reports to the security officer." I thought, "Penny, better think twice about this."

On January 19, 1968, the agricultural attaché's secretary, who was a lovely woman with a prominent southern accent, invited me to dinner. My eyes were drawn to a captivating picture hanging on her dining room wall. It was a gorgeous watercolor painting of a souk. It was enchanting—rich Moroccan colors and lots of texture and depth. After dinner, I asked Iris, "Where did you buy that?" She replied, "Oh, this little boy in my office gave it to me." I mentioned the Russian art teacher and my reluctance to embark on that journey. She replied, "If you want, I can introduce you to him. His name is Ahmed."

All weekend, the beauty of the painting haunted me, but I was in a male-dominated society and women had to respect their boundaries. After all, I did not want to humiliate myself or the artist with an impromptu visit. I entered into a dialog with myself, "Should I introduce myself or not?" So half of me said, "You must be insane. In this culture, females do not approach strange men and shake hands. Much less propose taking art lessons." The other side countered. "What harm is there? He works for the American Embassy. Besides, you are a world traveler and can handle the situation. No need to make eye contact. Focus on his forehead." Finally, I gathered my courage and took action. Early Monday morning, January 22, 1968, I walked into his office.

Ahmed was employed by the embassy as a Foreign Service National in the agricultural attaché's office. He was sitting behind a large desk. "Hi, my name is Penny Lopes," I said. In contradiction of all my training in cultural sensitivity, impulsively I extended my hand for a handshake, which startled him. He then mumbled something in French. I thought, "Oh no, what have you done? No handshakes and looking men in the eye!" I collected my composure and continued, "I saw your painting at Iris's house. I want to take art lessons and wondered if you could recommend a teacher?" I honestly had no ulterior motives. My plans were to study painting, to learn French, and to visit the Cape Verde Islands.

When he stood up to invite me to sit down, his desk shrunk. He was twice my size—six feet, three inches tall. Recovering, he said with a thick accent, "Oh, what type of art are you interested in?" I was on guard waiting for him to make a false move. Instead, he was polite, friendly, and had a sense of humor. Even though we struggled to communicate, there was some chemistry. I thought to myself, "This is very perplexing. The guy is atypical of how an Arab is supposed to act." Another alarm went off when he offered to give me art lessons and to shop for art supplies that afternoon during his lunch hour. Events were moving rapidly. It was unsettling. "Stay alert, Penny. See where this eventually leads."

ELEANOR LOPES AKAHLOUN

Q: Probably, you were thinking it was too good to be true.

AKAHLOUN: That is exactly right. He promised to call in the afternoon, and he did. Speaking half-English and half-French, he explained art was a subjective discipline. Everyone had a particular style, so he felt I needed to make my own choices and suggested we go to the *medina* (market) together to purchase my supplies. "Oh boy," I thought, "This guy is a real con artist. He is trying hard to squeeze in a date." Nonetheless, that evening we went shopping together for art supplies, as I was anxious to begin the lessons. I wrestled with the idea of inviting him to my apartment for dinner. "Would he misconstrue my kindness? What would I serve him?" My cupboards were almost bare.

Q: You have known him less than twenty-four hours.

AKAHLOUN: Yes. This is true. It was unusual for me because I was generally cautious.

Q: Although, some of your travels are utterly adventurous. I don't know exactly how cautious. Well, let the reader decide.

AKAHLOUN: Let us say, I took calculated risks, but in Morocco more precautions were necessary. I went with my gut feeling. He was kind, gentle, and sensitive. Moreover, he seemed sincere. The invitation was extended. Pork and beans was on the menu, as it was the only thing I had in my pantry.

Q: Oh my gosh, for a Muslim? Consumption of pork is prohibited.

AKAHLOUN: I made a complete fool of myself. The meal preparation was quick—no culinary skills necessary to open a can of beans and boil hot dogs. But internally I was bubbling over with excitement and confusion. He was seated at the opposite end of the living room. I was standing near the kitchen door, glaring at him, and said, "You know, I want art lessons, nothing more and nothing less. Do you understand?" He flung his head back in shock and calmly replied, "But of course." Satisfied, I marched back into the kitchen just in time to salvage my hot dogs. The water in the pot had nearly evaporated. Poor guy. He ate everything on his plate and never complained.

The next evening, January 23, 1968, I apologized for my cultural faux pas. He took no offense, and art lessons then commenced. (I was recording the dates and events in my journal.) Communication was largely through our English-French dictionary. We spent more time searching for words and laughing than painting. It was increasingly challenging to concentrate as he was quite handsome and charming.

Q: The plot thickens.

AKAHLOUN: Initially, each of us sat at the opposite end of the room. Once the lessons began, we kept moving closer to the center. To slow down the momentum, we invented this imaginary person, Madame Goofy, through whom we communicated. We wrote letters to each other but addressed them to her. I don't know how we derived at the name, but she was a counselor with whom we shared our inner feelings. We frequently asked her for advice. Although my right brain, the creative part, usually dominated, this time I needed help from the other side—the more controlled and analytical left brain.

Madame Goofy was logical. She allowed for deeper reflection. We were attracted to each other, but how strongly? Did we want to jeopardize our employment and commit to an uncertain future? If we were to marry, Ahmed would lose his job, and I would be forced to resign from the Foreign Service. I gave him a Harvard University–designed compatibility test, and he scored an eighty-nine. It was a struggle not to like the guy. Feeling somewhat conflicted and because no progress was being made on the art front, I proposed we temporarily switch to French lessons. He agreed.

Q: You took the lead. This wasn't the normal cultural pattern.

AKAHLOUN: It was unusual. The switch made matters worse. We had to practice rolling the Rs. The key was to carefully watch his mouth and notice how his tongue vibrated. Oh brother! We were closer than ever.

ELEANOR LOPES AKAHLOUN

Q: This is going downward fast. From Art, to French, to music . . .

AKAHLOUN: After nineteen days, the bells began ringing. We were reading the newspaper and listening to our favorite songs when our lips tenderly touched. The next day, Ahmed poetically wrote to our counselor. This is what he said: "Madame Goofy, one evening I will remember all my life. I was in a very romantic mood. I felt I was burning, and this sort of flame that I cannot determine the origin, was hurting me in the deepest of myself, to a point that I lost the control of my emotions. My lips touched hers—thousand bells rang in my head, almost paralyzing me, I was in the clouds. When I landed, I discovered her smile, mixed with purity and color and love—I felt love. I will love her dearly, within the limits of the respect. She became a part of me. I am happy. I would like to drop you some questions because I need their reply so badly. Should I see my baby doll as often as I do now? Should I refrain myself and hold everything in. In other words, should or may I love her more and more dearly. As I am also young, I would like you to be my adviser, and you will have more letters describing the emotions that 'perturbate' my clean heart."

Because we were an improbable couple, we had to cross-examine ourselves and sort out our inner hopes, beliefs, and feelings. To begin with, Ahmed was six feet, three inches, and very lean. I was barely five feet and pleasantly plump. To gain weight, he drank my homemade eggnogs. To slim down, I ate more fruits and vegetables. He had an olive complexion. My skin was brown. We practiced different religions—Islam and Catholicism. It was a huge no-no for a Muslim man to date or marry a Christian woman in an Arab country. As a result, Ahmed would have to deal with a heavy dose of societal disdain and cultural complications. At the time, the concept of American female diplomats dating Foreign Service Nationals of Arab descent raised eyebrows. We grappled with many issues that threatened to separate us. We were deeply in love, but both of us knew that this alone was not enough to sustain a happy marriage. We had to be sensitive to the issue of compatibility as well.

There were some positives. Ahmed voluntarily accompanied me to Sunday mass at the cathedral. He was a very open person with an inquisitive mind. Moreover, he realized I respected all religions and did not advocate for proselytizing. Another factor helped. He was born in Marchand, an affluent international quarter of Tangier, the port city in the north of Morocco. At the time, his father was a prosperous merchant who educated Ahmed in the best French schools, where he acquired a leaning toward the west. Still, we were not completely out of the wilderness.

Q: *When did he take you home to meet the family? Being introduced to them is of some importance. Were they as open? Was this an issue or was Ahmed an independent spirit?*

AKAHLOUN: Less than four months of knowing Ahmed, he invited me to his home, which was a joyful event. The date was Saturday, May 11, 1968. My main goal was to eat with my right hand instead of the left one, which is prohibited in Islam. Their one-bedroom apartment was immaculate. They had the typical multipurpose living room couches, circling the room. Before we ate, Momma Aini, one of his mothers, came around with a pitcher of water and poured it into a basin for us to wash our hands. They served a delicious couscous meal with plenty of lamb and fresh vegetables, salad, bread, and fruit. We capped the evening off with traditional sweet mint tea.

They were open-minded, and I think Ahmed's liberal thinking largely influenced them. The Akahloun family consisted of Jamal, the youngest brother; Aziz, a second brother now deceased; and Souad, a younger sister. Ahmed's father was polygamous and had two wives. So his two mothers, Momma Aini and Momma Habiba, were finally meeting me—the mystery woman monopolizing their son's time. After his father's death, Ahmed, who was sixteen at the time and the eldest son, became the household's breadwinner. He then left school and started working as a teletype operator at the post office in Tangier. Four years later, he was employed by the American Embassy and everyone moved to Rabat. Both of his mothers doted on him.

Q: *Islam allows a man to marry more than two wives, but how did the mothers adjust to this?*

AKAHLOUN: They seemed to accept the situation. Ahmed's father, who was also active in the French Resistance movement, ran a wholesale grain

ELEANOR LOPES AKAHLOUN

business that extended from Tangier to Marrakech. Because of his wealth and influence, he could easily support two wives. The religion sanctions up to four wives, if all parties consent to the "expansion." Because Momma Aini, his first wife, was unable to bear a child, she consented to her husband marrying Momma Habiba, a fourteen-year-old second cousin of his. One year later, Momma Habiba gave birth to Ahmed. From the outset, the two women bonded and jointly raised the children. Both mothers were equally loved. I was surprised to see how much harmony existed between the two of them and how smoothly the household functioned.

Q: *Ahmed was so open to another culture that he accompanied you to church. The fact you were another religion was apparently not an issue with his siblings or his two mothers. In what other ways did you bridge the cultural gap? He learned English, you learned French. He gained weight, and you shed some pounds.*

AKAHLOUN: Well, to be honest the mothers initially harbored some doubts. At first, they were not so accepting of Ahmed dating a non-Muslim, but he was able to change their opinions. They began to appreciate the fact that he looked healthier and happier. Also, as head of the household, his judgment was respected. Both mothers were kind and loving, but Momma Habiba and I were kindred spirits. We communicated with hand gestures, smiles, hugs, laughs, and muddled Spanish, French, Arabic, and English. We read each other's minds. To this day, we are still very close.

Q: *What an amazing lesson in cross-cultural communication. Where is Momma Habiba now?*

AKAHLOUN: She still lives in Rabat and is in her eighties. Whenever we meet, she touches her heart, smiles, and says I am inside. Some say I am her favorite daughter-in-law. She truly is an exceptional woman.

Q: *The outsider, the one that is different, is not only accepted, but the favorite. That's remarkable. Obviously, they were tolerant, but would you say they were devout Muslims?*

AKAHLOUN: They were practicing Sunni Muslims. Ahmed was not a devout Muslim, but he realized that such a potentially divisive issue needed to be thrashed out early. Was I willing to convert to Islam? What religion would our children follow? The twenty-first of March we started deliberating the future implications of our differing religions. Our sessions were agonizing but never confrontational. One month later, Ahmed decided it was important to raise the children as Catholics because my faith was stronger than his. As adults, they would decide for themselves. This was very courageous of him.

Ahmed frequently gave me flowers. Each morning, he wrote love notes and placed them on my desk. For instance, one message said, "You are my heart, soul, body, and everything I own. I love you more than the stars in the sky and sand in the beaches and flowers in the field." At the end, it said, "This is not poetry."

I am not dramatizing, but our situation was like climbing a mountain with a bag of rocks strapped to our backs. No one could lead the way or rescue us because there were no scripts to follow on how to make an interracial, cross-cultural, interfaith relationship work. At least, we were unaware of any such help. There is a proverb in Arabic, which states, "A friend is one to whom one may pour out all the contents of one's heart, chaff, and grain together, knowing that the gentlest of hands will take and sift it, keep what is worth keeping and with a breath of kindness blow the rest away." Establishing a concrete friendship with each other helped us build a solid relationship.

Q: *You met Ahmed about two weeks after your January arrival, talked about marriage and religion in March, and you were introduced to his family in May. Events were swiftly unfolding. What happened next?*

AKAHLOUN: I informed my mother about our relationship. She was skeptical and not an immediate fan of my falling in love with a Moroccan who was a non-Catholic and barely able to speak English. She requested an eight-by-ten color photo of Ahmed and asked for a recorded tape (reel-to-reel back then) so she could listen to his voice and get to know him better. Then he wrote a touching letter, asking my parents for my hand in marriage. Once convinced, she was ecstatic. On June 1, 1968, she replied, "I have never received a letter that penetrated my heart like this one. As I read it over and over, tears of joy blinded my eyes . . . We extend our open arms from the depth and breadth of this continent and accept you as our own dear son . . ." Turns out she was a poet as well.

After receiving her blessings, we became engaged. She planned to announce the engagement in the newspaper and arrange a party. My assignment was to inform her of "everything and anything you feel I should know so that I can answer all the questions at the gathering." The only thing she felt badly about was the missed opportunity to see the Cape Verde Islands. The visit was postponed but never erased from my mind.

Q: Reel-to-reel tapes? That's very methodical. Your parents accepted Ahmed. They transcended the religious differences, which never became a problem between the two of you. You were concerned about his parents and your parents.

AKAHLOUN: My mother was highly organized and applied a great level of detail to every aspect of her life. After she passed away, I found lists, containing outfits including matching jewelry, scarves, hats, gloves, and shoes she planned to wear during the week to church, social engagements, and to the community center. We paid attention to our families and made sure they were not bypassed. Without their approval, our relationship would not blossom. We were engaged on the twentieth of September 1968. It was a romantic affair. Ahmed proposed marriage in my apartment in Rabat on bended knees as I serenely sat on my ornate fan-backed princess chair. I was over the moon but also realized our work was just beginning. Embassy requirements, especially the fraternization policy, needed to be tackled.

Q: Embassies can be rumor mills. How did it react to your engagement? Were embassy people involved in any way?

AKAHLOUN: Our friends, Eleanor and Conrad Bellamy, were very supportive and encouraging. Conrad was an embassy communicator, and his wife was a teacher at the international school. They arranged a formal reception to celebrate the news. There was the usual idle gossip over a Foreign Service National dating an American. This was frowned upon by some as "lowering" standards by mixing with the locals. The reaction did not upset me at the time, as much of it was anticipated. We remained true to ourselves and our love. We were very happy.

Being together, however, had severe and immediate implications for us career-wise. Three days after our engagement, I submitted a letter to Ambassador Henry J. Tasca, seeking permission to marry Ahmed and requesting my employment with the Foreign Service be continued. According to Department of State policy then, if a woman married anyone—a Foreign Service officer, a foreigner, or another American—she was expected to resign. Men were exempt from this regulation. Five attachments were included in my request: a statement acknowledging upon marriage to an "alien," I no longer was available for worldwide assignment, a resignation letter, Ahmed's photo and biographical information, the names and addresses of twenty-three of his blood relatives, and a declaration that he agreed to become a U.S. citizen. The results of his medical examination were also forwarded. I was thinking thank God for those eggnogs and his healthy weight gain. In one year, he went from 143 to 179 pounds.

I cite these details to give you an inkling of the State Department's mind-set and the bureaucracy involved. The waiting and uncertainty was horrendous. Was I going to lose my job and have to give up my career because of wanting to marry the man of my dreams? A short time later, the Department sent notification I was being directly transferred to another country. My heart sank within me. Panicked, I went to the Deputy Chief of Mission (DCM) and told him it was impossible for me to be reassigned. He was sympathetic and successfully intervened.

Q: Did the transfer have anything to do with your personal situation?

AKAHLOUN: There might have been a connection. I cannot truthfully say whether the transfer was by design or by sheer coincidence. The timing, however, is suspicious. Meanwhile, we traveled to Malaga, Spain, Marrakech, and other points in Morocco. Ahmed also earned his University of Michigan's English Proficiency Certificate—a precursor to the Test of English as a Foreign Language (TOEFL).

Q: When you tendered your resignation, what was your expectation? Did you know it would be rejected, or did you have to force the issue?

AKAHLOUN: While the ambassador, the DCM, and the administrative counselor were helpful, the decision rested in Washington. Our hands were virtually tied; we waited as human resources, diplomatic security,

ELEANOR LOPES AKAHLOUN

ethics, and other State Department offices deliberated. There was no indication as to the outcome. We were sitting on pins and needles.

Meanwhile, I was counting on a strong embassy endorsement and developing events in Washington to rescue us. The Women's Action Organization (WAO) and the American Foreign Service Association (AFSA) both were seeking a complete transformation of the State Department's policy on women officers and marriage. Embassy officials knew I wanted to continue working, but a letter of resignation had to be submitted as a formality. Fortunately, on January 28, 1969, my prayers were answered. Permission was granted to marry Ahmed without my having to resign, and I finished my tour. What a tremendous relief, but he was required to give up his job. A few years later, I was informally told that our marriage was a test case, which contributed to changing the Department's policy. There is no proof of this, but it certainly felt as though we were blazing new trails. It was a victory for Ahmed and me and for all female members of the service who wanted to marry and not jeopardize their careers in the process.

Later, in 1972, the State Department issued a directive stating that female Foreign Service officers could no longer be required to resign from the service if they married, nor could any comments about them be included in an officer's efficiency report. Steps were also taken to improve inequities in housing allowances and in the recruitment process for them. In 1978, the State Department went further and established the Family Liaison Office (FLO) that assists families from all foreign affairs agencies at home and abroad. Times have certainly improved for women in the Foreign Service. Although many inequities remain, the Department has opened its doors to three women Secretaries of State—Madeleine Albright, Condoleezza Rice (the first woman of color to hold the position), and Hillary Rodham Clinton.

Q: This was an historical breakthrough. Tell me about the wedding and about your life in Morocco as a married woman.

AKAHLOUN: We were married on May 31, 1969, nearly seventeen months after I arrived in Morocco. I was twenty-six and about halfway through my assignment. There were two weddings—a Catholic ceremony at St. Margaret's Church in Buzzards Bay, Massachusetts, and a traditional Muslim marriage in Tangier, Morocco. We had six bridesmaids and six groomsmen at our stateside wedding. There were not one, not two, not three or four, but five priests officiating! My parents had gathered these "men of cloth" from near and far.

The second event was held in Tangier on June 9, 1969. Momma's father, Abdesselam Ben Mohammed, an Imam, officiated. He gave us a beautiful handwritten wedding certificate in Arabic. I had to play the part of a demure, stoic, respectful Moroccan bride. During the ceremony, the hardest thing was to sit still, hold my hands on my knees, keep my eyes lowered, and refrain from smiling. Gratefully, I was allowed some wiggle room. I wore a richly decorated caftan and was adorned with heavy jewelry and five eighteen-karat gold bangles that Ahmed gave me as a dowry. It was a joyous occasion that also satisfied Muslim law. We were now officially recognized as man and wife in Morocco. Nothing in either ceremony required us to compromise our beliefs. I was not asked to renounce my religion and neither was Ahmed. He only attended prenuptial classes required of all non-Catholics.

Living together in our Rabat apartment was an adjustment. The separation from his family increased the frequency and severity of Ahmed's inherited migraine headaches. Stopping by to see them as much as possible helped. My visits, however, were limited to once a month, as I wanted to maintain a healthy degree of distance and give Ahmed quality time with his loved ones. Essentially, I did not want to wear out my welcome. I wanted our warm relationship to continue. Once Ahmed explained the rationale behind my absences, everyone understood and accepted my decision. Fortunately, there was no bitterness. Toward the end of the assignment, I visited every week.

Q: Now, let me ask you a trick question. What happened to the art lessons?

AKAHLOUN: To this day, I have not picked up a paint brush. But it is still on my mammoth to-do list.

Q: But there was great artistry in your new life. You said Ahmed was obliged to resign his Foreign Service National position and needed to find a new job. What transpired?

AKAHLOUN: On June 25, 1969, he began working for Aerojet-General Corporation, a U.S. private organization building a communications satellite station outside Rabat. His former boss was instrumental in finding the position for him. The company needed an English, French, and Arabic translator/interpreter. Ahmed fit the bill, and the timing could not have been better. He translated official documents, interpreted at high-level Moroccan meetings, operated the telex, typed, and did some accounting work. King Hassan II inaugurated Morocco's first earth station with great fanfare on January 7, 1970. Now it was simple to dial the U.S., and we paid considerably less money—twelve dollars for the first three minutes and three dollars for each additional minute. The job agreed with Ahmed, so the transition was relatively smooth.

Q: *You were in Morocco from 1968 until 1970. For the moment, let us move from your personal experience and dwell on political events and U.S.–Moroccan diplomatic relations.*

AKAHLOUN: Neil Armstrong's August 1969 walk on the moon created a stir. The entire embassy staff watched the event on a big screen setup in the lobby. Sharing this experience at the outset of our new life together was special. Everyone marveled at the historic event. Moroccans generally liked Americans, and our diplomatic relations were close. King Hassan II was a western-oriented, moderate Arab leader. On the surface, the political scene was calm, but the king ruled with an iron fist. Mehdi Ben Barka, a critic of the monarchy referred to earlier, was blamed for a 1963 plot to assassinate Hassan. He went into a self-imposed exile in Paris and two years later mysteriously disappeared. As a result, bloody antigovernment riots took place in Morocco. Hassan then dissolved Parliament, declared a state of emergency, and assumed absolute power. Many opposition leaders were executed under the direction of General Mohamed Oufkir, who was the most powerful figure in Morocco after King Hassan. Some of the positions he held included minister of interior, defense minister, and chief of the armed forces.

Q: *Let's focus on your departure from Morocco. Were you given a list of follow-on assignments?*

AKAHLOUN: Back then, State Department employees with Foreign Service National spouses were required to complete a full tour in the U.S. before reassignment. U.S. citizenship was also mandatory. So we returned to Washington.

Q: Ahmed's family must have had mixed feelings. You had to leave Momma Habiba and Momma Aini and his brothers and sister. What went through your mind at that time?

AKAHLOUN: It was heart wrenching to see Ahmed being uprooted, leaving behind family and friends, familiar places, and his culture. He was the firstborn son and head of the household since age sixteen. His siblings, especially his sister, Souad, depended on him. His "separation anxiety" was worse than mine, and I empathized. He would have to acquire a new way of life and suffer through bouts of homesickness. I was prepared to comfort him during the dark days. He was more than a husband; he was my best friend. We were buddies.

Before departing Morocco, there were many fun trips to the souk for caftans, rugs, and handicraft items. Ample spices were purchased for the Moroccan dishes I had yet to master. The shopping sprees, in part, closed the circle. I was saying good-bye to the vendors and the people and country I cherished. It was agonizing for both Ahmed and me. My father also reached out to him in an effort to ease some of the pain. I kept one of his touching letters, which reads, "You haven't a Father there, but you have one here . . . so don't worry. I don't think that even your own mothers will love you more or do more than we will for you. I want you to put your mind on the good side of life. Have faith in God, and he will never let you down . . . I know it is hard to leave your family and come to live (in the U.S.) . . . but you can always go back for a vacation."

During the ride to the airport, our hearts were heavy and tears rolled down our faces. Momma and Momma Aini were crying out, "My son, my son, we will never see you again." I promised we would not forget them. And I meant it. This time my Pan American jet clipper was not circling the globe, but flying directly to Washington, D.C., where Ahmed and I would build a life together in an unpredictable future.

CHAPTER FIVE

THE NATION'S CAPITAL GREETS THE NEWLYWEDS

WASHINGTON, D.C.

The State Department, Office of East African Affairs (AF/E), 1970–1973

Our return to the U.S. was a period of personal and political upheaval on many fronts. The obstacles encountered required us to create new rules for our survival and well-being, and we adopted a philosophy of "and-this-too-shall-pass." The on-going trials and tribulations made our marriage stronger.

Q: Where did you reside in Washington?

AKAHLOUN: We lived at 1915 Kalorama Road, N.W. We chose this multicultural area because we felt an international setting better accommodated interracial couples. I was also close to work, and there were frequent buses going to the State Department. The apartment building was situated in the heart of two very diverse neighborhoods. The Connecticut Avenue side had an old-fashioned upper-crust feeling. The Chinese Embassy was located in a nearby hotel, and the French ambassador's residence was just down the street. Walking one or two blocks in the opposite direction toward Columbia Road, the eclectic Adams Morgan section, the scene shifted from conservative to liberal.

This vibrant section of the city had exciting residents, boutiques, restaurants, bars, laundries, pharmacies, and grocery stores. The Black Panther headquarters was in close proximity. We transformed our apartment into a Kasbah and an art studio. It was terrific.

Once we settled into our new home, I contacted my former employer—then attorney general, and now, Senator Brooke. My intention was just to phone and say hello, but he invited us to his office. We met and presented him with a gift from Morocco and received this thoughtful letter:

"Dear Penny:

I just want to express my gratitude for the handsome Moroccan leather folder.

You can be assured it is getting a lot of service on my desk and is certainly far more attractive than the old folder it replaced. It was most thoughtful of you to think of me and I am deeply appreciative.

It was wonderful to see you again and to have the opportunity to meet your husband. I do hope that whenever you are on the 'hill,' you will stop by to say hello.

With every best wish to you and Ahmed, I am

Sincerely, Edward W. Brooke"

His gracious gesture meant a great deal to us.

Q: How did Ahmed adapt to his new home in the U.S.?

AKAHLOUN: I always sensed when he was homesick. When he missed Morocco, out came his traditional music, the *derbouka* (drum), and the *tar* (tambourine). He turned up the volume of the stereo set and began singing, dancing, and conducting his one-man orchestra. Throughout all our tours and decades spent in the Foreign Service, nostalgia and homesickness for Morocco plagued him.

He struggled to find full-time employment in the local economy. His efforts encountered strong resistance. While his skin color was not a major issue, his name, Ahmed Akahloun, and birthplace, North Africa, disadvantaged him. On the whole, he was less than welcomed by society. This bias, coupled with his lack of higher education, limited job opportunities. Yet he persevered. He studied computer programming and held a series of part-time jobs—pharmacy clerk, waiter at the U.S.

ELEANOR LOPES AKAHLOUN

Capitol, Spanish and French translator at Catholic University, and instructor at the French Institute. He also sold paintings on the side.

By November 1971, he hit the jackpot and became a Foreign Service Institute (FSI) Arabic Language and Culture Instructor. Some of his students were high-ranking diplomats and military officers going overseas. In fact, Ahmed recorded the Institute's first set of Moroccan Arabic tapes. He was the only person teaching both the colloquial and written forms of Moroccan Arabic. That exemplified Ahmed's multitalented nature and resiliency.

Q: Sounds like he was doing everything possible as a newcomer to acclimate himself to his new environment. How were you adjusting to your stateside assignment at the State Department?

AKAHLOUN: Yes, Ahmed was proactive. I worked in the Bureau of African Affairs but bounced around for a month before entering the Office of East African Affairs (AF/E). I stayed there from 1970 to 1973, performing mostly secretarial duties. The four countries I covered were Zambia, Malawi, Tanzania, and Uganda. The job was enjoyable.

There was plenty of activity in Washington, D.C. During the assignment, I supported four different officers. The Zambian and Malawi Desk Officer Ken Brown eclipsed the others. As you know, after a long tenure, he recently stepped down from being the president of the Association for Diplomatic Studies and Training (ADST). Prior to this, he served as the U.S. Ambassador to the Congo, the Ivory Coast, and Ghana. Ken was unpretentious, energetic, hardworking, and passionate about his work. He possessed an easygoing personality and a keen sense of humor. Moreover, he genuinely cared about the AF/E staff.

Our office handled twelve countries—Ethiopia, Somalia, Djibouti, Kenya, the Seychelles, Tanzania, Uganda, Zambia, Malawi, Mauritius, Madagascar, and one other African country that I have forgotten. Five secretaries (now called office managers) backstopped eight officers. Country Director Wendell Coote, the previous Deputy Chief of Mission (DCM) in Nairobi, headed our office and was the right person for the position. He was a superb administrator with nice interpersonal skills.

The Bureau of African Affairs was big and relatively young. It was established in 1958. In the Office of East African Affairs, we were dealing with countries that were independent since the 1960s. In East Africa, there was a cascade. In southern Africa, Rhodesia (presently Zimbabwe) was in the midst of a struggle for freedom from its British colonizers. There were uprisings in Kenya with the Mau Mau rebellion and political oppression in Uganda under Idi Amin.

Q: A radical political shift in Africa was taking place at the time. The sixties were a period of tumultuous change for the continent.

AKAHLOUN: Yes, but one of optimism and opportunities. Several African countries gained independence from colonial powers and during the Nixon presidency, most of them experienced relatively stable governments. There was one notable exception—Uganda. General Idi Amin overthrew President Milton Obote's government on January 25, 1971. The coup was motivated primarily by ethnic, political, and financial issues. The military coup and subsequent chaotic events kept the African Bureau, particularly AF/E on edge.

Initially, Israel, the United Kingdom and the U.S. supported the coup d'état, because President Obote's regime gained a reputation as being ruthless and corrupt and discriminated against certain elements of the population. The average Ugandan hailed the change and welcomed General Amin. Meanwhile, he became increasingly paranoid. By the end of 1972, Ugandan-U.S. relations soured. As a side note, I must say Forest Whitaker in the *Last King of Scotland* brilliantly characterized Idi Amin as a charismatic, irrational dictator, bent on committing incredible atrocities to secure his stronghold over the country.

Idi Amin's biography is intriguing. He was born near Koboko, located in the Western Nile Province of Uganda near the borders of the Democratic Republic of the Congo and Sudan. He grew up tending goats and working in the fields. Purportedly, he only had a fourth-grade education and could barely read and write. As a teenager, he joined the British colonial army as an assistant cook and rose through the ranks to become a general. He was also involved in operations against the Mau Mau in Kenya. He was married several times and acknowledged at least forty-three children.

During Amin's eight-year reign of terror, it is conservatively estimated that the death toll topped three hundred thousand. However, the figure compiled by human rights organizations and Amnesty International puts the number killed over five hundred thousand. His troops also slaughtered hundreds of thousands in neighboring countries. President Nyerere of Tanzania did not recognize Idi Amin's government. He gave political asylum to Obote who attempted to recapture Uganda in 1972. In retaliation, Amin bombed Tanzanian towns and purged the Ugandan army of Acholi and Lango ethnic groups who supported the abortive coup. It was a nasty situation.

As events unfolded in Uganda and information filtered back to the Department, particularly the Office of East African Affairs. It was believed Idi Amin was likely suffering from hypomania, medically defined as "a form of manic depression characterized by irrational behavior and emotion outbursts." He took drastic measures to stamp out any opposition to his rule. Amin organized killer squads and was suspected of practicing cannibalism and traditional Kakwa blood rituals on slain enemies.

After overthrowing President Milton Obote in 1971, Idi Amin slaughtered so many people that he became known as the Butcher of Uganda. He was also called Big Daddy and had other names, such as His Excellency President for Life and Field Marshal Al Hadji. Our office was receiving hundreds of queries from concerned relatives, congressmen, religious leaders, and foreign embassies. Amin was systematically destroying the moral, social, economic, and political fiber of his country.

In August 1972, he expelled about fifty thousand Asians and confiscated their assets. They had ninety days to leave the country and were only allowed to take two suitcases. Some of them were robbed by soldiers en route to the airport. Perhaps it was a mistake kicking them out. The Asians were the economic backbone of the country—the merchants, teachers, economists, shopkeepers, and more. Economic collapse was inevitable, but he continued the carnage.

Q: What was his rationale for throwing out fifty thousand people who were basically the middle class?

AKAHLOUN: Idi Amin espoused an "Africa-for-Africans" mentality. The thinking was that foreigners had gained too much control of the country. He thought the wealth should transfer to the Africans and started distributing businesses to the military and others. He also bribed people with expensive cars and other luxuries. Things were out of control. An excellent example of this is the disappearance of Nicholas Stroh and Robert Siedle.

Stroh, a freelance reporter and heir to the Stroh Brewery in Detroit, was thirty-three years old. His friend, Robert Siedle, was a sociologist teaching at Makerere University in Kampala, the capital of Uganda. They heard rumors about mass executions of Lango and Acholi soldiers, whom Amin believed to be pro-Obote, at the Simba Barracks in Mbarara outside Kampala. On July 7, 1971, the two men set out for the bush to investigate. This tragically led to their disappearance and eventual death.

The incident created big waves internationally. Their families wrote to congressmen, newspaper editors, and everyone else imaginable. For the first time, the outside world was exposed to the indiscriminate slaughter and the unspeakable torture and rape taking place in Uganda. The men in our office were becoming increasingly busy, so I took on more responsibility by screening calls and personally responding to some of the routine queries.

Q: Did you actually talk to the Stroh and Siedle families?

AKAHLOUN: I certainly did. We tried to support them as much as possible. Ugandan law required the time frame of seven years before a "presumed certificate of death" could be issued. Absent proof and without bodies, the families were left in limbo as to the fate of their loved ones. A death certificate was necessary to claim insurance benefits, and the estate could not be settled without one. Idi Amin denied that Stroh and Siedle were dead. He argued that the men left the country on holiday. Our pleas to the Ugandan government were in vain. Sometime later, an informant came forward and revealed that Stroh and Siedle were dumped into crocodile-infested waters.

Q: This is utterly deplorable. Meanwhile, Ambassador Jean M. Wilkowski, the first female ambassador to Africa, was being appointed. What was your impression of her?

AKAHLOUN: I highly respected her. With twenty-odd years of U.S. government experience, she was a seasoned diplomat and a suitable match for the assignment. The Office of East African Affairs (AF/E) was preparing two U.S. Chiefs of Mission–Ambassador Jean M. Wilkowski and Ambassador Thomas Patrick Melady—for their appointments to Zambia and Uganda, respectively. Melady remained in country less than one year because of the political turmoil.

As the first female U.S. Ambassador to an African country, Wilkowski's appointment to Zambia was groundbreaking. We were busy turning out briefing papers on the country's history, people, politics, and economy. Other activities included producing profiles on key Zambian government officials, arranging appointments, scheduling meetings with scholars, and setting up consultations with White House and high-level State Department officials. Preparations for her Senate confirmation hearings on Capitol Hill were also in progress. Her swearing-in ceremony was held on the eighth floor in the State Department's impressive diplomatic reception rooms, decorated with colonial antiques and historical artifacts. The view overlooking the Washington Mall, the Lincoln Memorial, and the Potomac River was awe-inspiring. I found Ambassador Wilkowski to be capable, witty, and unassuming.

President Kenneth Kaunda was a Pan Africanist, and Zambia was a key country where African freedom fighters opposed to European domination in their countries sought asylum. He was also against our involvement in Vietnam. U.S.–Zambian relations were lukewarm. In her book, *Abroad for her Country: Tales of a Pioneer Woman*, she shares how she waited nearly a month to present her credentials and officially be recognized by the government to take up her post as ambassador. In contrast, the Chinese Ambassador was able to do so within a few days of his arrival. Although the Zambian government treated her politely, diplomatic relations did not thaw completely until the end of the Vietnam War in 1975.

Ambassador Wilkowski listened to Kaunda who felt the U.S. needed to be more engaged and supportive of majority rule in southern Africa. She bombarded us with messages, urging a more straightforward U.S. policy of opposition to apartheid in South Africa and support of decolonization across the continent. Her efforts fell on deaf ears and did not endear her to Secretary of State Henry Kissinger. Relations between the two at best were tepid. Just prior to her departure, she was able to affect some degree of U.S. policy change. Kissinger visited Lusaka and held a historic press conference in April 1976. He criticized South Africa and strongly condemned the country for its institutionalized racism. The U.S. was also opposed to the colonial Rhodesian government under Ian Smith and supported black majority rule in what is now Zimbabwe. Ambassador Wilkowski's insistent pleas finally bore fruit. But it is curious that her career seemed to stall somewhat after Zambia. She retired at sixty, which was then the mandatory Foreign Service retirement age. Congress later reinstated the earlier sixty-five age limit.

Q: So Ambassador Wilkowski was sending messages about Kaunda's positions on various topics. Were the ambassadors from the neighboring countries sending similar reports?

AKAHLOUN: Ambassador W. Beverly Carter Jr. in Tanzania also documented what was going on in the region, but Wilkowski took the lead. The Assistant Secretary of State for African Affairs David Newsom, and Country Director for the Office of East African Affairs Wendell Coote supported the ambassadors, but it was difficult to capture the attention of others in Washington. It took some time to understand that Africa was not colonial Europe. Africa was Africa. It was finding its voice as a continent of independent countries. The U.S. needed to deal with the state of affairs on a different level, but shifting gears required time and seemingly was impossible.

Q: Domestic politics probably clicked in at that point. The Office of East African Affairs (AF/E) was pretty uniform in its approach, thinking and believing that change was in the air and we should be part of it, instead of opposing it. What about U.S. interests in these countries?

AKAHLOUN: Well, Zambia was important for several reasons. It was a key frontline state bordering white-ruled Rhodesia (Zimbabwe) and South Africa and was an excellent listening post. President Kenneth Kaunda supported majority rule in the region and played a pivotal role in the armed liberation struggles of the region. As a classic example, Oliver Tambo, a central figure in the African National Congress (ANC) and Nelson Mandela's former law partner, sought refuge in Zambia. By the mid-1970s, the country was the safe haven for exiles and refugees of the liberation movements in South Africa, Mozambique, Angola, and other countries. Zambia gave these individuals military training and became their rest and recuperation point. Kaunda was against the U.S. presence in Vietnam and felt we knew and understood little about his part of the world. Kaunda and Julius Nyerere of Tanzania were considered heroes by many of Africa's liberation movements.

President Nyerere embraced an economic philosophy contrary to the American capitalistic system. He was experimenting with socialism and village collectives. Nyerere adopted an African *ujamaa* (Swahili for "family hood") policy for his country. He also advocated for Pan African unity, which he thought would solve the continent's economic, social, and political problems. Remember, he also gave refuge to Obote who then launched a failed attack on Idi Amin. Nyerere was also open to dialogue with the Communist Party in China. This strained the relationship between the U.S. and Tanzania, and Nyerere's movements were scrutinized.

The Chinese, in 1970, began constructing the Tanzanian-Zambian Railroad (now Tazara Railway), which connected landlocked Zambia to the Indian Ocean via the port of Dar es Salaam. When it was completed around 1975, Zambia had a new and reliable outlet for its copper exports, reducing its dependence on trade through Rhodesia and South Africa. The Chinese were gaining a foothold in the region by building the Tan-Zam Railroad. It is interesting to see how the Chinese were making political and economic inroads in Africa as early as the seventies. At the time, it did not seem like much, but it was a beginning. Now China has enormous influence.

Q: And you were there in the Office of East African Affairs during this time?

AKAHLOUN: Yes. It was pretty exciting. The office also received reports from Lusaka, Dar es Salaam and Kampala regarding antiapartheid activity taking place in the African National Congress (ANC) and Pan Africanist Congress (PAC) guerilla camps located in many Southern and East African countries. Although my office dealt directly with East African countries, events in South Africa interested me and I kept abreast of developments there. Some of the antiapartheid leaders, who remained in the country of their own volition, suffered severe consequences. Stephen Bantu Biko, a Black Consciousness Movement founder, died in police custody in September 1977. The same year

Dr. Mamphela Ramphele, an influential political activist and medical doctor, as well as a dear friend of mine, was detained without trial and shortly afterward received a banning order.

Q: It is incredible that Mandela survived twenty-seven years of imprisonment, eighteen of which were spent on Robben Island, a desolate, unwelcoming prison off the coast of Cape Town.

AKAHLOUN: A few years ago, my children and I took a turbulent boat ride to the island and visited Mandela's tiny cell, where he slept on a thin mat on a stone floor and used a bucket for a toilet. We also saw the limestone quarry, where he was forced to do hard labor. Rarely was he allowed to communicate with his family. How horrifying. Incidentally, on a fortuitous occasion I had the honor of meeting Mandela and his wife, Graça Machel, and shaking hands with them. It was a brief, but momentous encounter. He was very charismatic and completely down to earth. His passing in December 2013 was a great loss for humanity.

Q: During your three-year assignment in the Office of African Affairs, surprising events were happening in Morocco, your previous post, and in China, a future post. Do you have any recollection of events on the tenth anniversary of King Hassan II assuming power?

AKAHLOUN: We were in Washington, D.C., when Skirat, a town outside of Rabat, made its international media debut. It was on July 10, 1971—an unbearably hot muggy day. Tension was growing over Morocco's widespread corruption. According to some sources, King Hassan II was lavishly celebrating his forty-second birthday at his royal palace with eight hundred prominent Moroccans and diplomats when about 1,200 armed cadets stormed the palace. They attacked and killed over one hundred guests, including the Belgian Ambassador, the Moroccan ministers of justice and tourism, and Hassan's eighty-year-old physician. Some two hundred others were wounded.

The army was planning to set up military rule, but King Hassan II literally outsmarted them. He hid in a bathroom during the prolonged gun fight. When the fire died down, he walked out and confronted the soldiers and began reciting verses from the Koran. Supposedly, some of the cadets knelt and kissed his Majesty's hand, which allowed loyal troops to crush the revolt. Reportedly, some 1,400 to 2,000 rebels were later executed.

Q: *Amazing. King Hassan II understood that he risked being killed, but he believed that he could pull sway through the prestige of his ancestry and through prayer.*

AKAHLOUN: Hassan II is considered by pious Muslims to be a direct descendant of the Prophet Muhammad. He also surrounded himself with top-notch security guards, allegedly, trained in Israel. As the story develops, the soldiers knelt down, faced Mecca, and laid down their weapons. Ahmed had special insight into the incident as he was being fed fresh accounts from relatives back in Morocco, especially his brother Jamal who was closely following political events.

Q: *Evidently, the king reigned on the strength of his lineage, strong leadership, and charisma. After Skirat, did Morocco return to its previous state?*

AKAHLOUN: I am afraid not. Another bold attempt on King Hassan II's life occurred on August 16, 1972. Same story—an attempt to overthrow the monarchy. As the king was returning from a visit to Paris, four or five F-5 Moroccan air force fighters pulled alongside his aircraft and opened fire just as he was landing at Rabat. One of the Boeing's engines was knocked out, and the plane should have gone down. But the quick-thinking king pretended to be a flight engineer, grabbed the radio, and said, "Stop firing. The tyrant is dead!" He told the attackers not to harm the rest of the passengers and to allow the crippled plane to land safely. Once the plane was on the ground, Hassan II emerged unharmed.

It was another narrow escape. This time the trail led to his trusted friend, General Mohammed Oufkir who was promptly arrested and killed. Official reports maintain he committed suicide, but according to Malika Oufkir, his eldest daughter who wrote *Stolen Lives: Twenty Years in a Desert Jail,* his body was found with several wounds that purportedly were impossible to be self-inflicted. Hassan then banished Oufkir's widow and six children to the desert where they were held under house arrest. The military's agenda was to remove the ruling Alouite dynasty, which stretched back hundreds of years. There was discontentment over the king's repressive government, the uneven distribution of wealth, the high unemployment, and the widespread corruption at the top. Pressure for reform also came from Islamic activists.

Q: *What was your sense of the many attacks on his life? The people must have been divided between those who wanted stability and continuity and those who wanted change. Do you think most Moroccans wanted the king to remain? What was Ahmed's interpretation?*

AKAHLOUN: Ahmed believed that King Hassan could and should have done more to improve the average Moroccan's life. On the other hand, he respected the king and believed reform during this stage would best be accomplished within a monarchy and in a peaceful and structured way. I think his mixed feelings were typical of other intellectuals. It seemed to me those who favored Hassan II did so primarily out of loyalty and religious beliefs. Of course, wealthy Moroccans wanted to preserve their fortunes. Most people wanted a transformation but feared a tumultuous one. My feelings were similar to Ahmed's.

Q: *King Hassan did modernize the country. If I am not mistaken, he admitted women into the university. What other things were done to respond to the demands of society?*

AKAHLOUN: He built the Earth Station for Satellite Communication and created *ateliers* (workshops) for artisans to preserve their cultural heritage. At the end of his reign, he took measured steps toward democracy. For instance, he finally freed the imprisoned Oukfir family in 1991, enacted constitutional amendments in 1996, established a two-chamber parliament with expanded powers, and launched an independent commission to examine human rights abuses. I think an argument can be made that the country was somewhat better off during his final years than it was when he first came to power. Yet, I certainly do not condone the atrocities he committed.

Q: *This is fascinating insight as to what was going on in Morocco in the 1970s. Anything else about the King of Morocco?*

AKAHLOUN: Just a few thoughts. His diplomatic relations with the U.S. and the west were closer than his father's. He promoted Arab-Israeli peace negotiations and mediated many Middle East disputes. King Hassan played a backseat role in getting Egyptian President Anwar El Sadat and Israeli Prime Minister Menachem Begin to sign the Camp David Accords in 1978. After the coup attempts, it was rumored the king moved from palace to palace, sleeping no more than three or four nights at each one. The truth may never be known.

Many Moroccans believe he possessed *baraka* (good fortune). This is a concept in Islamic mysticism symbolizing the connection between the divine and the worldly. Special blessings and grace deliberately flow from Allah (God) to chosen worshippers. Whether we accept or reject this notion, it is strange that during his thirty-eight-year reign, King Hassan II survived half-a-dozen coup and assassination attempts and enjoyed one of the longest head-of-state tenures ever. He ended up dying peacefully at the age of seventy.

Q: *Many world leaders, including President Clinton, attended his funeral. Shifting gears to Sino-African relations, while you were working in the Office of East African Affairs, President Nixon was making overtures to China. We are discussing this partly because you went to China and these events later affected you.*

AKAHLOUN: Yes, that is true. In October 1971, the United Nations seated Communist China and expelled the Nationalist government, which fled to Taiwan.

Q: *How did this happen? There was a lot of politics going on here. How did China achieve this?*

AKAHLOUN: Rest assured there were behind-the-scene negotiations with members of the Permanent Security Council. The U.S. had more influence in the UN General Assembly in the 1970s than now. I assume Nixon heavily influenced the outcome.

Q: History will judge if it was more Kissinger or Nixon. They were working together, yet they were rivals. Each one wanted credit.

AKAHLOUN: But it was President Richard Nixon who visited China in February 1972 and met with Chairman Mao Zedong. The trip was monumental, as Nixon going to see Mao gave implicit recognition of the communist People's Republic of China (PRC). The visit broke nearly twenty-five years of Cold War tension between the two countries and paved the way for establishing formal diplomatic relations in 1979. Nixon also came home with two panda bears, which were given to him as a gift.

During this same period, the Watergate scandal broke. Who can forget the "plumbers" and that fatal June 1972 day? It was shortly after Nixon's visit to China that five men broke into Watergate, attempting to burglarize and bug the Democratic National Committee headquarters. The job was bungled, and they were apprehended by police. It was the beginning of the end for Nixon. That was election year—just before the summer political conventions. The irony being Nixon was not going to have any problem being reelected. He had everything to gain, but he blew it. Nixon visited Africa during his vice presidency in 1957. After the trip, he recommended diplomatic relations be established directly with African nationals rather than with the colonial powers. Foolishly, Watergate overshadowed everything he accomplished. It was his downfall and became his legacy.

Q: We cannot decide in this room today how to judge Nixon. But he did initiate direct relations between the U.S. and independent African countries. Of course, later he opened relations with China. Your assignment in the Office of East African Affairs (AF/E) from 1971 to 1973 gave you unique insights into U.S.-Africa relations. Anything further to address?

AKAHLOUN: A few things come to my mind. To begin with, I abandoned the idea of painting and explored other interests—sewing and designing my clothes, did some macramé work, dabbled with decoupage, and made scrapbooks. This way, I engaged in creative activities but avoided competing with Ahmed. It was important to let him own the space of being the artist in the family. At Christmastime I decorated our State Department office entrance with African batiks. The idea spread and soon other doors of the African Bureau took on a similar appearance. Today, the practice continues year-round, and Plexiglas (a hard transparent acrylic plastic) has been cleverly introduced to protect the beautiful batiks.

The Department of State announced it was relaxing the dress code for women in 1972. The new policy somewhat loosened up the establishment's conservative culture. Female employees were no longer limited to wearing dresses or skirts. Henceforth, they could report to the office in tasteful and suitable slacks and pantsuits. This was a welcome change, and I quickly busied myself making a new wardrobe.

I think the period from 1969 to 1979 was pivotal to the feminist movement. A popular television program, the *Mary Tyler Moore Show,* focused on women who wanted to pursue careers outside of marriage, and *All in the Family* made an issue of Archie Bunker's chauvinism. In 1970, Colonel Anna Mae Hays, Chief of the Army Nurse Corps, was the first female in the history of the U.S. Army to become a brigadier general. These are only a few of the breakthroughs that took place.

Another major event occurred—the John F. Kennedy Center for the Performing Arts opened its doors. I was excited about the occasion even though tickets for the performances were beyond our financial reach. Washingtonians celebrated as the prestigious center elevated the city to new cultural heights. Additionally, Uncle Jamal came to America for the first time, and he received a welcome fit for a king. True to our word, we stayed in touch with our Moroccan family.

Q: Tell me about your social life at the time.

AKAHLOUN: Ahmed and I were cautious as to where and with whom we socialized. As previously explained, mixed marriages, such as ours, were not universally accepted or appreciated. We associated with people of diverse backgrounds. Folks like my good friend Lois Gore-Thompson, a former secretary in Rabat for the Foreign Agricultural Service (FAS), Beatrice Beyer, a U.S. Agency for International Development (AID) Officer, and others. Our parties were lively, and we served our guests homemade Moroccan dishes. Artists, diplomats, taxi cab drivers, waiters, and college professors all rubbed shoulders with each other at our Kasbah. We wisely extended invitations to our neighbors. This was to prevent complaints stemming from the ear-piercing music that Ahmed and his enthusiastic musicians provided.

Q: I presume you began hunting for your onward assignment well in advance.

AKAHLOUN: Actually, I began preparing twelve months ahead of time. Uruguay, a tiny, Spanish-speaking country in the Southern Hemisphere seemed to be ideal for us partly because Ahmed spoke the language. The country also had a thriving art community, and the position advertised was at my grade level. So off I went to chat with my career counselor.

Q: You actually picked Uruguay and managed to get that assignment? Who could ever say no to you, Penny?

AKAHLOUN: Plenty of people say no. But I keep asking the same question in different ways to many people until someone says yes. In May 1973, Ahmed received U.S. citizenship. He had entered the country three years earlier. Not sure when the formalities began, but I know the State Department expedited matters. Initially, we were destined for Addis Ababa, Ethiopia. For some reason, the assignment fell through. We had the option of extending in Washington for one year, followed by an assignment to Addis or selecting a new country. Things usually happen for the best, so we were not worried. We looked elsewhere. Uruguay seemed to be a good fit. We read everything we could about the country. One of the books, *Alive,* was an extraordinary account of human survival.

Q: Oh yes. One of the most celebrated stories of its kind. Very inspiring. A Uruguayan rugby team flies to Chile for a game in 1972, the plane crashes into a mountain in the High Andes and only a few passengers survive.

AKAHLOUN: It is a thoroughly fascinating story. The Uruguayans were graduates of the Christian Brother's College of Stella Maris in

Montevideo and had a strong religious base. The survivors were on a mountain top over 11,800 feet altitude for seventy-two days. Twenty-nine died. Sixteen were rescued. To stay alive, they ate the flesh of those who perished. One by one they kept succumbing to their injuries or the freezing temperatures. At one point, an avalanche killed eight of them. Courageously, they continued to pray and console each other. In desperation, two men trekked ten days through treacherous mountains in subzero temperatures to seek help while in constant danger of slipping off icy slopes or dying of hypothermia, frost bite, dehydration or starvation. Yet against these seemingly insurmountable odds, they reached safety. The story underscores the power of prayers, hope, and the human will to live.

Simultaneously, inside Uruguay, something much less uplifting was taking place—a Tupamaro urban guerrilla movement, which wanted to bring about social change by toppling the government. The group robbed banks, businessmen, and staged political kidnappings, including diplomats.

Q: I guess you were concerned for your safety because they were kidnapping diplomats.

AKAHLOUN: Absolutely. I was hoping the threat of the Tupamaros would cease to exist by the time we arrived. In July 1970, the group kidnapped Dan Mitrione, the head of the Public Safety Office (OPS) at the U.S. Embassy. At the time, he was the main American advisor to the Uruguayan police. Mitrione was held for ten days and then was killed after demands for his rescue were not met. As the violence escalated, the military declared a national emergency that stretched over a number of years and arrested or killed scores of people. So-called death squads were responsible for many abductions and disappearances.

Despite the tense atmosphere, we were looking forward to our first Latin American assignment. We were determined to look on the bright side and capitalize on Uruguay's strengths. In Washington, Ahmed and I surrounded ourselves as much as possible with encouraging people. We tried to avoid the skeptics, as well as toxic thoughts, sounds or sights. We endured the highs and lows—home sickness, job uncertainties, cultural shock, multiracial, cross-cultural, and religious hurdles. At this point, we were even more intent on proving to the world that unorthodox relationships, such as ours, could survive. I took comfort in repeating a favorite prayer that fortified me in mind, body, and soul: "Lord, help me to remember that nothing is going to happen to me today that you and I together can't handle." Before beginning our new adventures south of the border, we spent a relaxing and delightful vacation in Massachusetts.

ELEANOR LOPES AKAHLOUN

CHAPTER SIX

FOOTLOOSE AND FANCY
FREE IN LATIN AMERICA

URUGUAY, 1973–1975

Although the political unrest in Uruguay was unnerving, we embarked on the southerly journey with anticipation. We believed the country's art and intellectual communities would benefit Ahmed. I prayed for our safety and hoped the region would be kind to us. It was a leap of faith.

Q: Traveling from Washington, D.C., to Uruguay, nearly at the tip of the Southern Hemisphere, is a lengthy voyage. And the seasons are reversed.

AKAHLOUN: Our trip was not exactly a piece of cake. Because of mechanical problems and lengthy layovers, it took about one day and a half to reach Uruguay. There was also significant air turbulence. We flew from Boston to New York and then Sao Paulo, Brazil, proceeded to Buenos Aires, Argentina, and finally arrived in Montevideo. When we landed in the afternoon on the sixth of August, we were worn out but glad to exchange the chill of winter for the warmth of summer.

Montevideo, the capital of Uruguay, was quaint and noticeably devoid of color. For the most part, the buildings were drab and deteriorating, and many *cachilas* (Uruguayan old cars) roamed the streets. Ahmed commented, "You know, honey, I think this whole country should be packed up and moved into the Smithsonian Museum." The population was only three million people. Curiously, it was the best place in the world to find vintage cars. International collectors purchased these gems from the 1920s, 1930s, and 1940s at bargain prices. There was a reason why Uruguayans were so ingenious about recycling and repairing things. It was partly driven by necessity.

During the first half of the century, the country's beef and wheat exports were booming. Luxury cars from Europe and the U.S. were imported in large numbers. Then, because of a crumbling economy, an overextended welfare system, government corruption, and social upheaval, the high standard of living declined. Cars and other goods became prohibitively expensive, so Uruguayans became more conservative and imaginative. As an illustration, soon after arriving, we saw a man driving a jalopy down the street. He had one hand on the steering wheel and the other one outside his window, holding up a bag with a tube attached to something under the hood. He probably had a leak of some sort.

Here is more local color. Because we could not afford a car, we relied on public transportation. One morning while waiting for a bus, a number of people breathlessly climbed up the hill and joined me. It was puzzling. When the rickety bus—kept alive by resourceful Uruguayan mechanics—arrived, the answer was clear. Apparently, excessive weight was preventing the bus from negotiating the hill. So all passengers were obliged to get out and walk. Once they reached the "summit," they unflinchingly reentered the bus. For the rest of the journey, it was smooth sailing.

Within five days, we moved into a spacious two-bedroom apartment in a comfortable part of town, close to the embassy. Our large sunny terrace furnished a nice view of the Rio de la Plata. Best of all, it had a maid's room, which Ahmed promptly converted into an art studio.

Q: I must ask about the nature of your work. What were the issues and challenges?

AKAHLOUN: I worked as a secretary for three men in the economic and commercial section. Things were quiet, because the Uruguayan economy was sluggish. Our section chief, Steve Watkins, was a bright officer with a sympathetic nature. I thought his talents were underutilized. Periodically, I worked in the ambassador's office, which

ELEANOR LOPES AKAHLOUN

I relished. Upstairs there were more opportunities to practice Spanish and to follow political events.

In 1972, President Juan Maria Bordaberry gave military leaders free reign in their counterinsurgency efforts. They crushed the Tupamaro guerrillas and then repressed university students, labor unions, as well as all political opposition. Congress was dissolved in 1973, and the country became known as a "prison state." This was the tense atmosphere that greeted us upon our arrival.

When Julio Maria Sanguinetti was elected president in 1985, the right-wing military dictatorship of twelve years ended. Before the political upheaval, Uruguay was considered the most advanced, stable, free, and democratic nation in South America. Students from all over Latin America came to study at the Uruguayan universities. For its size, the country possessed a significant number of intellectuals and artists. The artwork produced was very sophisticated. Ahmed's gold-and-silver-leaf frames for his paintings were made using a special technique imported from Italy. By the time we arrived, the culture was still refined, but the wealth had disappeared. Nevertheless, the quality of food remained high.

This reminds me of the Tinkal Bar, a family-owned restaurant next to the U.S. Embassy. It served the best *chivitos* in town. The national dish was generally served on a bun and layered with a thin slice of filet mignon (*churrasco*), ham, bacon, lettuce tomato, melted mozzarella cheese, and a fried egg. Then it was topped off with grilled onions, red peppers, black or green olives, mayonnaise, and ketchup. Absolutely delicious. At the time, there was not much dialog about high cholesterol. We were addicted to our *chivitos* and ate at the Tinkal frequently. We knew the owners well. The wife was very sweet. Her husband was a gentle soul who never forgot to smile and always wore a white chef's hat. Both of them were short, and their heads barely cleared the top of their counter. Jose, their ten-year-old son, helped out. The floor of the Tinkal Bar was not littered with layers of discarded napkins and an assortment of bottle caps typically found in many other places, and it soon became one of our favorite restaurants.

Q: How much of this did you know before you went, or did you just discover it? You've cited some tangible examples of bottle caps, the buses that can't get up the hill. By the time you arrived in the mid-1970s, the country was already declining economically. Is this what you expected when you went to Uruguay?

AKAHLOUN: Somewhat, but "seeing is believing." The extent to which the country had overdeveloped shocked me. Let me explain the terminology. Uruguay was South America's first welfare state. It was known for its pioneering efforts in public education, health care and social security and was considered the "Switzerland of South America." Around the fifties, a stagnating economy put strains on the system. Tax revenues declined, but spending increased. This produced large government deficits and accelerated inflation. It was an ideal climate for a guerilla group to have some influence. When the military came into power, it restricted funding to social welfare, specifically public schools, hospitals, and clinics. The standards of education and care for the mass population sharply declined. We made the best of the subdued environment by relying on our sense of humor and keeping active.

Every Sunday we walked to the *Tristan Narvaja Feria,* an enormous flea market covering several city blocks. The streets were roped off and everything imaginable was sold there, including fresh vegetables, dairy products, flowers, and lots of valuable old pieces. The *feria* was happy hunting grounds for antique collectors. We spent most of our time buying paintings and visiting the stalls selling beautiful woolen sweaters. Abbey, an embassy wife, and I joined *Sakura,* a Japanese club. At age thirty, I was playing softball with sixteen- to twenty-five- year-old Uruguayan National champions and felt the age difference with every swing of the bat. Every year there was a tournament in Buenos Aires. We pumped ourselves up to win a trophy, but each time we came back empty handed.

Q: We have been discussing Uruguay's economic circumstances in the 1970s, the rudimentary things you observed—people repairing cars, not getting new cars, the feria and the artist, and softball. At the time, Uruguay's thinking was rather provincial. How were you and Ahmed treated?

AKAHLOUN: Ahmed fared slightly better than I. In practically all instances—shopping, walking down the street, or riding the bus—adults and children gawked at me. There was a small, largely marginalized

African Uruguayan community, but my mannerisms and clothes were different. I heard them whispering, "She must be Brazilian." Sometimes, it was annoying, but I tried to place myself in their shoes and made allowances. When it reached a breaking point, I stared back and replied in Spanish, *Buenos días. ¿Cómo está usted?* (Good day, how are you?) They were caught off guard and either promptly looked away or politely responded. In the Foreign Service, we often put on blinders and fix our gaze straight ahead when we stand out among host country nationals. Sometimes unusual behavior or physical appearance attracts unwanted attention. It was helpful to remind myself that I was the foreigner and not the other way around. Turning against the local culture would be counterproductive. Generally, I found it amusing and was not offended because no one was outwardly malicious.

There was a fair degree of racism evident though. *Charrua* Indians, the indigenous Uruguayans, were killed off when the Spanish arrived. And legend has it that the last four were sold off to the circus in France. People very much valued their European ancestry, and darker skinned Uruguayans were relegated to the bottom of the social structure. As you can imagine, Ahmed and I stood out like sore thumbs.

Soon Ahmed began studying under Clarel Neme, a noted Uruguayan painter, and received his first break in November 1973 when he exhibited at the American Embassy. He sold ten of his eleven paintings. I faintly remember an art exhibit in Buenos Aires, but the details escape me. He also designed Christmas cards for the local and expatriate communities. The front was a collage of ten Uruguayan stamps, individually glued, and inside appeared a simple message, "Merry Christmas, Uruguay 1973." The cards were reasonably priced and sold well.

Q: Did you do much traveling?

AKAHLOUN: Oh yes. One memorable trip involved a retreat to a rustic *estancia* (ranch) south of Montevideo. As far as security was concerned, there was no problem. We went with the ambassador's wife, her bodyguard, the Gunny, who was the Marine Sergeant in charge of the Security Guard Detachment at the U.S. Embassy, and his girlfriend. The weekend was very exciting and entertaining.

We stopped at a gas station and spotted a 1928 Ford on sale for $1,800. Ahmed got behind the wheel, but he didn't go very far. The car was not in mint condition nor was the ranch. It had no electricity and no central heating. We used lanterns and space heaters and slept on the floor in sleeping bags. Because it rained heavily, we spent the majority of time indoors, playing poker, and toasting marshmallows. We sang songs, told stories, and laughed until tears flowed. The ambassador's wife, a gracious, creative, and talented woman, brought her guitar along and serenaded us. When the rain finally stopped, we rode to Colon (population 380) on horseback. It took us one and one half hours to reach the center of town, consisting of one bar, a post office, and a few scattered, rundown bungalows. The next day, we suffered the consequences. With all our aches and pains, we felt like invalids.

Shortly after we returned home, Ahmed developed gallstones. The abdominal and back pains were so intense that Dr. Jorge Stanham, the embassy contracted physician, recommended removal of his gallbladder. After the surgery, there were no more *chivitos*. Despite the operation, however, the pain persisted. Dr. Stanham then realized he had misdiagnosed Ahmed's case but was never able to pinpoint the underlying cause of the ailment. It was a rough patch of road, but Ahmed rebounded. While convalescing, he continued painting and held another sold-out art exhibit, which did wonders for his morale. Soon, we went to Brazil for carnival. This was February 1974.

Rio de Janeiro has exceptionally warm and friendly people and is definitely one of the most vibrant cities in the world. The *Corcovado* (Christ the Redeemer Statue) welcomed us with enormous outstretched arms. So did Sugarloaf Mountain, the sandy white beaches and the crystal blue waters of Ipanema and Copacabana, as well as the smooth sounds of *Bossa Nova*. It was electrifying.

Q: *Sounds like a nice place to be. Did you regret living in Uruguay, instead of a big, diverse place such as this one?*

AKAHLOUN: Not at all. There are positive aspects to all assignments. Sometimes the surface needs to be scratched to discover the inner beauty.

My friend, Mary Ann Salamie, a secretary at the American Consulate in Rio de Janeiro, invited us to come up for carnival. It was one of those too-good-to-be-true moments. Fortunately, her Copacabana apartment was relatively close to the parade route, but obstacles emerged.

Ahmed was not wild about crowds and ultimately decided to skip the entertainment. Mary Ann had to work at the consulate at the last moment. I was willing to risk going alone and hatched a plan. I woke up early and took the 4:00-a.m. bus to the reviewing stand for dignitaries, which I thought would be the safest place for me. My intent was to act natural, evade security, avoid the ticket line, and once inside head for an inconspicuous spot. The game plan worked. I ended up sitting on the edge of the sidewalk in front of the grandstand and watched the entire parade. Back then, heightened security measures were not in place. Besides, I blended in nicely, and my Spanish and limited Portuguese Creole turned out to be an asset. I was in heaven.

At the time, as is the case today, Rio de Janeiro's Carnival was enormous fun. The outfits were skimpy but less revealing than those currently worn. The event, part of a weeklong pre-Lenten celebration, is of mammoth proportions. Hundreds of participants dressed in beautiful costumes dance, sing, play drums, and march in the streets or ride on elaborate floats. Prior to the main parade, there are competitions among the various samba schools or social clubs, and only the best ones are selected to participate in the big event. Throughout the week, formal balls are held and street dancing and musical contests take place. The festivities consume the entire city—day and night.

Sociologically, I think Carnival is significant because it helps people escape from the mundane realities of life. The celebration brings together different elements of Brazilian society—African and European, rich and poor. Wealth and power appear to be set aside, and poverty seems to be temporarily forgotten. People fantasize by slipping on costumes. It is something unexplainable. I found the music, drums, and Samba dancers hypnotizing. Ahmed was not bothered by my gallivanting. He had faith in my ability to keep away from trouble. Besides, he was gearing up for his upcoming art exhibit.

As soon as we came back to Montevideo, he started painting. He worked diligently to live up to the high expectations of Pete Seeger, Director of the *Alianza* (the U.S.–Uruguayan Cultural Center), who scheduled a one-man show for July and extensively publicized the affair. Ahmed delivered. The vernissage went well. He sold three-quarters of his paintings, received favorable newspaper reviews, and gained an entrée into Uruguay's art circles. After this, he busied himself designing his 1974 Christmas cards. The theme that year was a gaucho (Uruguayan cowboy) riding a horse and lassoing a steer. Once again, he chose a secular theme that suited his audience. Sales were more than adequate.

Q: You frequently went to Buenos Aires, Argentina. What recollection do you have of the city and the people?

AKAHLOUN: Buenos Aires was only a thirty-minute flight away. It literally was just across the Rio de la Plata. Culturally and emotionally, the Argentines seemed more European than Latin American. Most of the residents in the city were of Spanish and Italian origin. The people were very proud and regarded Uruguay as one of the country's provinces. On the whole, we found the Argentines to be somewhat boastful yet sociable.

We went to Buenos Aires mostly for shopping and entertainment. Calle de la Florida, a famous downtown pedestrian street, had many sophisticated shops, selling antiques and fur coats. Leather coats and shoes were great buys. The restaurants served excellent steaks with *chimichurri* (an olive oil and spice mixture) that was rubbed on the meat and lots of *dulce de membrillo* (quince jelly), which was delicious. In addition, we enjoyed the cultural events and the flamenco dancers at the nightclubs. Although Argentina offered much, we preferred the warmth and charm of Brazil, which is why we returned a second time. It was over the 1974 Christmas holiday. We took a twelve-day trip to Rio de Janeiro, Iguacu Falls, and Asuncion. Coincidently, the Gunny and his girlfriend were planning a visit to Brazil, and they asked us to join them. The Gunny, as you recall, was the marine commander of the small unit that protected the U.S. Embassy. He was the same person who accompanied us to Minas.

On December 20, 1974, we set out in the Gunny's white gas-guzzling Ford Galaxy. The drive through the mountainous tropical terrain was enchanting. Heavily congested Sao Paulo, with its industrial pollution and guarded gated communities, was the exception. The disparity between the haves and the have-nots was shocking. This also applied to Rio de Janeiro. In spite of tremendous poverty, somehow the people in the favelas (slum areas) found reason to smile. I realize it is a generalization, but I have no memories of encountering any obnoxious Brazilians.

The journey was fatiguing, but the Cariocas transferred their vitality to us. The city sparkled with holiday lights and vibrated with energy. It was a special time. New Year's Eve is the second most popular festival in Brazil and attracts tourists from around the world and Brazilians from all states. Mary Ann planned a full schedule. Christmas Eve we dined with her friends and ate the national dish, *feijoada* (a rich stew of black beans and various cuts of pork and beef served with rice, collard greens, and deep-fried plantains). At midnight, we went to a folk mass at the Notre Dame Chapel in Ipanema. Christmas Day we attended a Latin mass with Gregorian chant music at the historical Sao Benito Monastery. Its Baroque church was astonishing. There was ornate, hand-carved wood dripping in gold everywhere. This set the stage for the moving *Revillion* (New Year's Eve) celebration on Copacabana beach, honoring *Yemanja*.

Q: *Yemanja . . . that doesn't sound Christian to me, but I guess it was a fusion?*

AKAHLOUN: Yes. The history behind *Yemanja* (Goddess of the Sea) is enthralling. She rules over the moon, oceans, women, children, fishermen, sailors, and witches. *Yemanja* is linked with the Virgin Mary in the Catholic faith. Captured slaves, mainly from the Kingdom of Benin and Yoruba in western Africa, were shipped to the Caribbean and Central and South America to work in mines and on sugarcane plantations. In their new home, they were converted to Roman Catholicism and strictly forbidden from worshipping their traditional gods. They preserved their African beliefs and practices by substituting saints' names for many of their *orishas* (spirits or deities). Originally, the captives honored *Yemanja* for bringing them safely across the water. These days, on New Year's Eve in Rio de Janeiro, thousands of people gather along the beach and toss flowers into the water or place gifts in small wooden boats that float out to sea. The offerings are to curry favor for the year to come, as well as to thank *Yemanja* for past favors.

This was truly a magical experience. The festivities began early in the week. Every inch of the city—beaches, streets, concert halls, and clubs—were packed with people. Parade day, there was an avalanche of streamers, newspapers, and rolls of toilet paper thrown from skyscrapers. Everyone was joyfully singing and dancing. Elaborate floats carried samba bands and dancers wearing splashy costumes. Nothing broke the spell—not even exploding fireworks. It was unbelievable.

Late afternoon, we arrived at the Copacabana beach and mingled with the friendly masses. Worshippers of the various temples began preparing their spots, where the rites were to take place. Each area was cleared and divided into inner and outer sanctums. In the center, white flowers, candles, saints, glasses, grass dolls, and other sacred objects were organized in some mysterious way. Trenches were dug and flickering candles placed inside. Fires were lit. When everything was prepared, the priests, male and female, arrived and ceremoniously sat down. Crowds gathered around them, and the rituals began.

The priests seemed to possess supernatural powers. One of them opened a bottle of champagne and sprayed the people. Several times he lifted a saber high in the air and violently plunged it into the ground. Apparently, he was trying to destroy the evil forces encircling his devoted followers. He seemed to be a spiritual being, divine messenger, faith healer, fortune teller, and guardian all wrapped together. It was spellbinding.

Hordes of people, mostly wearing white or a mixture of white and blue clothing, carried lit candles and flowers and moved along the beach front. Drummers played hypnotic, rhythmic beats to summon each spirit to the ceremony. Women and some men began dancing wildly and singing songs, praising *Yemanja*. Soon, they were possessed. Some of the women were smoking and drinking, and I wondered if this had influenced the process. But most of them seemed to be naturally transfixed. The spirit seized them differently. Some fell to the ground as though they were having an epileptic fit, others fainted, and several staggered, falling into a peaceful trance with their eyes rolling up under the eyebrow. All of them were treated with respect and carried into the inner sanctum of the priests, where they received a blessing of their particular saint.

Q: *The trances and the calling of the spirits are very similar to the Haitian phenomenon. But it is somewhat different in Brazil. What forms of African spirit worship are prevalent?*

AKAHLOUN: Primarily Candomble and Umbanda are practiced in Brazil, and the umbrella term used for these two forms of worship is

Macumba. But central to all of them is dance, trance, and fortune-telling. During the ceremony, those who wanted a cleansing formed a line. The worshippers were individually embraced and smoke from a cigar was blown on both sides of their faces. This was to cleanse them from sins. At midnight, the priests led their followers to the water. Gifts of flowers, candles, food, wine, boats, statues, and other items were thrown into the sea. Some people stared at the waves, and others impatiently waded into the water, desperately hoping *Yemanja* would accept their gifts. If so, it meant happiness and prosperity for the coming year. On the other hand, if violent waves hurled them back, tradition held it was a bad omen, signaling that *Yemanja* was angry.

Q: And the year you were there, were the gifts accepted by the sea?

AKAHLOUN: As a matter of fact, they were. The year 1995 turned out to be a promising one for us. At the end of the ceremony, the fires died out, but the crowds were slow to disperse. They lingered on the beach, paying homage to the Goddess of the Sea. At daybreak, we staggered back to Mary Ann's apartment and collapsed. After New Year's, the Gunny returned to Montevideo, but we made our way to Iguaçu Falls.

We spent $27 for a twenty-four-hour bus ride to see these waterfalls, which are one of the great natural wonders of South America. The money saved on transportation was used for luxury accommodations at the elegant Colonial Das Cataracas Hotel. We splurged, but it was worth it. The pink hotel in the Brazilian Iguaçu National Park was literally minutes away from the falls. Viewing them from the hotel platform was dramatic. Ahmed aptly described the scene as "a little piece of heaven on earth." The hotel was surrounded by nearly four acres of nature. The exotic hotel garden was filled with palm, lemon, and banana trees and an array of flowers. I remember the bright-colored toucans, perching on our shoulders, the fluttering butterflies around us, and the roaming Ostriches. It was paradise. We reluctantly left the following day.

Asuncion, Paraguay, was our next stop. But first we had to endure a fatiguing 225-mile bus ride on rough country roads in a decrepit Paraguayan bus. There was no air-conditioning. The air of the steamy-hot *pampas* (grassy plains) was motionless and suffocating. The boiling heat made sleep impossible for us and the Paraguayans. They sat by their lonely farm houses, fanning themselves in hopes of finding relief. There was no electricity. They lit kerosene lamps. I felt we were stuck in a time warp until we reached Asuncion. After two days, we flew to Uruguay.

Q: Now it is early January 1975, and you are back in Montevideo.

AKAHLOUN: Right. And Ahmed once again reached for his paintbrushes. About twenty-five paintings needed to be finished and framed for a March–April exhibit at the U.S. Embassy. His efforts paid off, as the event turned out to be profitable. Subsequently, I received a letter from Washington, advising that my Nairobi request for an onward assignment was being considered, but it looked dubious because of timing issues. The Department requested me to submit three other possibilities. I obliged but still pressed for Kenya. I wrote to my former African Bureau contacts in the Department who advocated for me. Simultaneously, I was promoted, which helped the situation. A month later, when the Nairobi assignment became a reality, I sent letters of appreciation to everyone.

Q: Why Nairobi? What caught your fancy about Kenya?

AKAHLOUN: Ever since working in the Office of East African Affairs, the region fascinated me. You may recall we were earlier assigned to Ethiopia, but the assignment was broken. Traditionally, a country such as Montevideo was followed by one considered to be a hardship post. This term is used in the Foreign Service to describe a place where living conditions are difficult due to climate, crime, health care, pollution, or other factors. Employees assigned to these areas receive a differential of between 10 and 35 percent of their salary. Kenya at the time did not fall into this category.

Technically, we were assigned to Montevideo because of the needs of the service, not by personal choice. This argument worked to our advantage. Nairobi was also East Africa's international hub and had an appreciation for artists. We hoped Ahmed's artwork would continue to flourish there as it had in Uruguay. Lastly, professionally it was a good move, as it was a larger post and afforded me more challenging work. From all perspectives, Kenya was the best option for us.

Q: At that time, Kenya was certainly not classified as a hardship post. In the seventies, the country was, perhaps, the most desirable posting in sub-Saharan Africa. When did you leave Uruguay?

AKAHLOUN: We departed Montevideo in August 1975. Before home leave in Onset, Massachusetts, and leaving for Kenya, we stopped in Washington for consultations at the State Department. This time there were no anti-Vietnam demonstrations. Earlier, on April 30, 1975, while we were still in Montevideo, Saigon was overrun by the North Vietnamese. During my consultations, a dark cloud seemed to hover over Washington. At that point, the war was the longest in U.S. history. The casualties were high. More than fifty-eight thousand American soldiers died, and over three hundred thousand were wounded in the fight against Communist North Vietnam and Vietcong guerillas in South Vietnam. The conflict split families and pitted the older generation against the younger one and drove a wedge of mistrust between many Americans and their political and military leaders. I looked forward to unwinding at home with my dear family and friends and getting a much-needed respite from politically charged Washington, D.C.

Guia Reyes, my friend from the Philippines, surprised me with a wonderful visit. Other old acquaintances traveled to Onset as well. We toured Provincetown, took the ferry over to Martha's Vineyard, tried our luck at deep-sea fishing, and went go-carting. I appreciated the warm hospitality my parents extended to all my visitors and thought about their support over the years. They always placed my interests first. I was indebted to them.

Q: After home leave, did you consider visiting Cape Verde?

AKAHLOUN: The thought of seeing the Cape Verde Islands never left my mind. Pan Am had no direct flights to the islands, but it did fly to Dakar, Senegal, where we intended to overnight before continuing on to Nairobi. I wondered if we had any relatives in Senegal. Only one person would know, and that was Ti-Frank (Francisco Andrade), my dad's five-feet, three-inch godfather. With my father's assistance, a meeting was arranged, and I brought along my tape recorder.

Since my last visit home to Massachusetts, Ti-Frank had not changed much. His face wore few wrinkles, and his green eyes still sparkled. He appeared twenty years younger than his actual age. Ti-Frank recounted his life's story with surprising detail and humor. At age twenty-five, he sailed on the *Barkentine Savoia* from Fogo to New Bedford, which arrived in April 1914. He paid $35 for the voyage and said everyone had a bed. According to the ship's manifest, the vessel carried 264 passengers. When I asked him if we had any relatives in Senegal, he laughed and said, "Of course, Cousin Jose Lopes." I nearly fainted. Before leaving Onset, I contacted Jose who worked as a regional catering manager for Pan Am Airlines in Dakar. He wanted to meet us. I was so excited that I hardly sleep that evening. On September 2, 1975, Ahmed and I fastened our Pan Am seat belts and were whisked away to West Africa.

ELEANOR LOPES AKAHLOUN

CHAPTER SEVEN

SAFARIS AND SURPRISES

KENYA, 1975–1977

In Kenya, our lives were forever altered. We had close encounters with all types of wildlife in the East African game parks—even an unexpected stork.

Q: So off you went on another adventure—this time from Boston to East Africa via Senegal in West Africa.

AKAHLOUN: Once we landed in Dakar, Senegal, we heard someone shouting, "Mr. Akahloun, Mr. Akahloun." It was Cousin Jose who had found his way inside the cabin of the airplane. His warm personality immediately put us at ease. He helped us through customs, drove us to our Croiz du Sud Hotel, and retrieved us later in the afternoon for lunch. Jose's wife was gentle and sweet. Lydia, their twenty-six-year-old daughter and her son lived at home. No one knew English except for Jose who spoke five languages—Creole, Wolof, Portuguese, English, and French.

My desire to communicate with the rest of the family was so strong that expressions used as a child and dormant in my subconscious randomly came out. We gestured a great deal, but ultimately we understood each other. We ate outside in the patio of their four-bedroom home, which had the luxury of a garage. The meal reminded me of the homemade dishes my grandmother cooked. We were in Dakar about a day and a half before heading off to Kenya. It was thrilling getting closer to my old country roots.

After lunch, we looked at photo albums and then piled into Jose's white van for a shopping expedition. In the market, we purchased two *Ashanti* (fertility) dolls, which traditionally were thought to be the last resort for remedying infertility. After being married for six years, Ahmed and I were still childless. Medical and natural treatments to produce offspring had thus far failed, and we were beginning to accept the idea that we might never have children. These wooden carvings had a top-heavy, flat, round head and a disproportionate, cylindrical body. Odd looking, I thought, but I hoped they would have some magical power.

On the following day, September 3, we took the ferry to the notorious slave-trading Island of Gorée. African men, women, and children were brought here against their will, sold into slavery, chained and shackled, naked except for a cloth around their waist, and held in a slave-holding warehouse until they were shipped to North America, the Caribbean, or South America. Historians differ as to the exact number of newly enslaved Africans who passed through Gorée. However, between the mid-1500s and the mid-1800s, the estimated figure is twenty million. A dark and atrocious era in human history.

Although the island was about twenty to thirty minutes by ferry from Dakar, reaching it was a harrowing experience. It was not the best time to visit because of a forecasted tropical storm. Since we were leaving the following morning, our choices were limited. We set off under threatening skies but remained optimistic. Soon torrential rains and fierce winds engulfed us. I have never seen such monstrous waves. It was petrifying because our boat nearly capsized. Later the sea calmed down, enabling us to safely reach the island. In 1903, 1908, and 1909, my grandfather made three daring trips across the Atlantic Ocean. I can now fully appreciate the danger associated with these long, treacherous transatlantic voyages.

Q: You were fortunate. When you arrived in Nairobi, can you remember what you saw and how you felt? Sometimes that first day is very vivid.

AKAHLOUN: Nairobi was brighter, the sky bluer, the earth redder, and the grass greener than I had imagined. The "City in the Sun" lived up to its reputation. It was strikingly clean and cosmopolitan. Vibrant flowers grew along the side of the roads and inside traffic circles and parks. The entire city resembled one enormous garden. I was stunned by the beauty and overjoyed to be there. Departing the airport, I immediately noticed a splash of color everywhere. Women walked to the market with beautiful batik dresses as they balanced buckets on their heads. Mothers used colorful cloth slings to carry their babies on their backs. Instantly, I thought Ahmed would have more than enough inspiration for his paintings.

The climate was absolutely marvelous. Nairobi is situated close to the equator and has an altitude of about 5,500 feet. The days were warm and sunny, and the evenings were crisp and cool. It is said the word "Nairobi" originates from the Masai phrase *Enkare Nyirobi* (the place of cool waters).

At the time, there were about six golf courses around the city, English-style homes, amateur theater, tennis and cricket clubs, and even a race track. The Nairobi National Park was about five miles away from the center of town where you were able to feed giraffes, cuddle baby elephants, or pet cheetahs, as Ahmed did. Back then it was the only place in the entire world, where you could drive into a game reserve within the city limits, watch a breathtaking sunrise, and look out onto plains dotted with wildlife. During this time, Kenya was attracting many tourists. Historically, when the British settled in the country, they found rolling green hills, savanna, snow-topped mountains, deserts, and deep valleys. They wanted to create a community with the same comforts of their own English countryside, so they built an infrastructure that we were presently enjoying.

Q: Now let's proceed to your office in Nairobi. Previously, you had worked in the economic section. In Nairobi, what was your assignment?

AKAHLOUN: At the outset, there was a choice of being either in the economic office or the political section. Whatever was convenient for the State Department was fine with me. After all, the system had gone out of its way to accommodate me. I ended up working for Economic Officer John Eddy. After four months, I was transferred to the executive office, and Ralph E. Lindstrom, the Deputy Chief of Mission (DCM), became my new supervisor. I felt sorry leaving Mr. Eddy but was grateful for the opportunity to advance my career. Our ambassador,

Anthony D. Marshall, was reserved, but he was very dedicated and mixed well with the embassy staff.

There were about 125 U.S. businesses operating in Kenya. To promote American trade opportunities and support the country's economic development, Ambassador Marshall established regular meetings at his residence with these groups. He also met frequently with Kenyan President Jomo Kenyatta and was friendly with Attorney General Charles Njonjo.

Nairobi entertained several political extremists, some of whom were anti-American. After the ambassador received a death threat, the chief of station and the security officer recommended he be given maximum security—a guard with a machine gun riding in the front seat and a follow car. Ambassador Marshall refused to accept this because he believed it would draw too much attention and send the wrong message. They compromised. He carried a gun for about three months.

Q: What about the office dynamics?

AKAHLOUN: The relationship between Ambassador Marshall and the Deputy Chief of Mission was cordial. I believe much of the credit went to Mr. Lindstrom, a Foreign Service career officer with impeccable qualifications—educated at Harvard, received economic training at Princeton, and attended the Naval War College. He displayed unbelievable patience and flexibility. After being Chargé d'Affaires, ad interim for an extended period of time, Ambassador Marshall arrived, and Mr. Lindstrom assumed his regular duties. The busy office suited me just fine. I kept abreast of current events taking place inside and outside of the embassy. Working closely with the Foreign Service Nationals and the Ministry of Foreign Affairs, I often gained access to privileged information. Ambassador Marshall and Mr. Lindstrom appreciated my contributions and treated me well. I loved my work.

The ambassador's office was a fine place to observe the difference between committed and self-serving Foreign Service officers and their particular managerial styles. The sincere ones acted with decorum and constructively engaged people, regardless of their status. The latter tended to exploit others and advance their careers by being aggressive and stepping over others for personal gain. For the record, the vast majority of the officers were sincere, committed, and conscientious.

Q: You went from a relatively small embassy in Montevideo to a rather large one in Nairobi. How big was the mission? And where was it situated?

AKAHLOUN: We were located at the Cotts House, a commercial building on Mama Ngina Way, close to Parliament and the Jomo Kenyatta Conference Center. It was a sizable post. State, the U.S. Information Agency (USIA), Agency for International Development (AID), Peace Corps (about 208 volunteers), and the Foreign Agricultural Service (FAS) were represented, as well as the Library of Congress (LOC) and the International Executive Service Corps (IESC), a nonprofit organization focusing on supporting private enterprise in developing countries. As a former businessman, the ambassador strongly endorsed this group.

Q: Kenya was the communications and transportation hub of East Africa and had frequent visitors, ranging from State Department officials, CODELS (Congressional Delegations) and private American tourists. The Mau Mau movement was in the past. An independent Kenya had been established and evidently doing very well. What was the situation with the American Embassy at that time?

AKAHLOUN: U.S.-Kenyan diplomatic relations were good, but President Kenyatta was aging and growing weaker. Washington was concerned about the country's post-Kenyatta stability. The embassy reported extensively on leading political figures and their activities and alliances. Tension between the Kikuyus (largest ethnic group) and the Luos (the second largest one) was closely monitored. Although we believed the country would undergo a peaceful transition, there was no guarantee.

Kenyatta was a remarkable person who belonged to the Kikuyu tribe. He was generally well-regarded and popularly known as *Mzee* (old man in Swahili). Around the age of ten, he entered the Church of Scotland Mission at Thogoto, about twelve miles north of Nairobi, and paid for his school fees by working as a houseboy and cook for a nearby settler. After completing his education, he became an apprentice carpenter and held a variety of jobs. In 1922, he joined the East African Association (EAA), a group campaigning for the return of Kikuyu lands wrongfully seized by British settlers. This launched Kenyatta's political career. The Kikuyus and the Masais were forcefully removed from their fertile land or heavily taxed if they stayed put. They were allowed to farm but were accountable to the Europeans. The influx of the newcomers to the Highlands caused severe land shortages. Kenyatta was overall disillusioned, as his vision for Kenya was one of equality.

He left Kenya for England in May 1931, where he eventually studied social anthropology at the London School of Economics (LSE) and married a British governess. After almost fifteen years of living outside the country, he returned home and eventually assumed leadership of the Kenya African Union (KAU), traveling around Kenya and campaigning for freedom. After the Mau Mau uprising in 1952, Kenyatta was arrested, sentenced the following year and spent seven years in prison. The country became independent in December 1963, and Kenyatta became its first president the next year. He suffered a major heart attack during our assignment and later died on August 22, 1978, roughly a year after our departure.

We lived in Kenya from 1975 to 1977, when President Kenyatta was well into his eighties. In November 1974, he was elected president for a third term. By then, some of his appeal had waned due to his poor health, government corruption, the widening gap between the rich and poor, unfair distribution of land after independence, major political ethnic tension, and skirmishes with his neighbors.

Q: At the time, what were some of the other issues occupying the section and the ambassador?

AKAHLOUN: There was a great deal of political unrest and turmoil in the region. We monitored the volatile situation and reported back to Washington. Uganda in 1976 suddenly began claiming all Kenyan territory west of Lake Naivasha on the basis of colonial-drawn boundaries. Earlier, Ethiopia's Emperor Haile Selassie had been overthrown by the Soviet-leaning Derg (military council) and now there were border and territorial conflicts between Ethiopia and Eritrea. At the same time, Somalis stepped up their decade's long secessionist campaign in the Northern Frontier District of Kenya, historically a region almost exclusively inhabited by ethnic Somalis. Travel to most of these countries was restricted. We flew, however, to Ethiopia on a U.S. military flight, which I will discuss later.

Because of this open hostility, Kenya was increasingly concerned over the possibility of warfare and approached the U.S. government with a request to purchase military equipment. The proposed sale generated a great deal of back and forth with Washington, but in August 1976 the agreement for several Northrop F-5E and F-5F jets was finalized. This strengthened Kenyan-U.S. bilateral relations. As a result, the embassy received several high level visitors, including Secretary of State Henry Kissinger and Secretary of Defense Donald Rumsfeld.

Another important event that occurred in December of that year was the groundbreaking ceremony for the new U.S. Embassy. Incredibly, the chancery was later bombed in 1998. The attack killed approximately 213 people, one of whom was a close colleague of mine in Uruguay. The U.S. Embassy in Dar es Salaam was also blown up. An estimated four thousand in Nairobi were wounded, and another eighty-five in Dar es Salaam. What an enormous tragedy.

Q: *Returning to your assignment, by and large, it was a period of harmony, relative prosperity, and the country was a new and growing African state.*

AKAHLOUN: Basically, that was true. When we arrived, people said, "Oh, you should have been here in the late sixties." For us, the country was still an East African garden spot with friendly people but with detectable signs of trouble.

Poverty was a major issue. One incident that occurred about a week after our arrival is etched in my memory. We were living downtown on the ninth floor of the Agib House, close to the embassy in a transient apartment until permanent housing became available. One morning around 4:15 a.m., we heard a terrifying noise. At first, I thought I was dreaming, but it sounded like an explosion. There was no phone, so we could not communicate with anyone. We peeked out the window. About four or more men were breaking into the downstairs home furnishing store by smashing a large display window. We watched helplessly as they snatched everything in sight, and threw the stolen goods into their van. With the speed of lightening, they drove away. We were traumatized. I whispered, "Where are the guards? And Ahmed asked,

"What happened to the alarm system?" Undoubtedly, the petrified guards realized their nightsticks were no match for the robbers' weapons and concealed themselves.

Ten minutes later, a lonely policeman, slowly pedaling his bike, appeared. As he passed us, he looked straight ahead, as though in a trance, and never bothered to glance at the broken glass. He kept riding down the deserted street and gradually disappeared in the darkness. The scene reminded me of a silent Charlie Chaplin movie. Two police vans arrived fifteen minutes later. There were no sirens. The policemen quietly got out and began interrogating the trembling guards. We thought the theft revealed some social instability and resentment between the rich and the poor, which was indicative of rising crime levels spurred on by poverty and extreme inequities between the upper and lower classes.

Q: *Were these tensions mostly self-contained in the local Kenyan society, or were foreigners working extremely hard seen as wealthy people and part of the problem? You had the privilege of being in a diplomatic status. Were you ever personally confronted?*

AKAHLOUN: I think Kenyans were somewhat disdainful of seemingly rich foreigners. As a diplomat, I was never in any personal danger but took necessary precautionary measures. I could not help noticing that wealthy people, expatriates, and tourists frequented places where the average Kenyan felt unwelcomed. Waiters at exclusive hotels and restaurants catered to the rich—gave them preferential treatment.

Kenya was intriguing, especially Nairobi. Refugees from neighboring countries poured into the country. The New Stanley, an upscale hotel, was a lively place. Ahmed and I sat under the shade of the acacia at the Thorn Tree cafe, observing a parade of humanity. There was a mishmash of people—artists, safari groups, politicians, diplomats, business executives, and refugees. The British, Asians, Germans, Arabs, French, and other nationalities congregated at the hotel, which was considered a beehive for international espionage. It was a great spot to sit and people-watch.

I never tired of seeing the tall, lean Masai men, wrapped in their traditional blood-red shukas. Their clean-shaven heads, elongated earlobes, colorful beads, and their staffs fascinated us. Asian women, dressed in shimmering gold and turquoise saris also paraded around.

The New Stanley connected Ahmed to the local art community. We met several people there, including the wife of the Pakistani Ambassador who became Ahmed's student. She was an openhearted, sensitive person, searching for identity. The lessons provided a welcome relief from what she described as her "burdensome role" as the ambassador's wife. She felt at ease in our house. When she ran out of money, Ahmed gave her free art lessons.

Q: Were some of these people a subject for Ahmed's work?

AKAHLOUN: Occasionally, but mostly he painted landscapes. His paintings reflected the vivid East African colors—the intense blues and greens of the Indian Ocean, the yellows and browns of the hills and savannahs, and the radiant light of the Kenyan sky. He began painting on large thirty-six-by-forty-eight-inch surfaces and developed his own technique of thinning oil paint and applying it with traditional brushes, as well as sponges, cloth, and hypodermic syringes. The canvasses took on an alluring, transparent watercolor texture. Soon he was exhibiting at the American and French Cultural Centers in town and had a six-week show at the 1976 UNESCO Conference held at the New Stanley Hotel. He made quite a name for himself. He also appeared on *Mamboleo,* a popular television program spotlighting aspiring artists and politicians. Normally, guests spoke ten to fifteen minutes, but Ahmed had plenty to say. His segment lasted twice as long. The enthralled interviewer lost track of time and his show.

Q: It sounds like he achieved a measure of success.

AKAHLOUN: Yes, thank God. One year after arriving, Ahmed presented me with a ticket home to the U.S. It was a Christmas gift. He covered all the expenses and even added one night at a swanky London hotel. That year it was the coldest winter in Massachusetts in sixty-nine years. I picked up the flu but recuperated quickly and was able to interview Ti-Frank again. As usual, he was knowledgeable and amusing. As a construction worker, he labored seven days, ten to twelve hours, and brought home $35 a week. He earned twenty-five cents a day picking cranberries. He also mentioned buying $10 worth of groceries that had to be delivered because it was too much to carry. Ti-Frank was now around eighty-five years old, but his mind was razor-sharp. During our stay in Onset, I reflected on how far we had come from the early penny-pinching days of our Kenyan assignment.

When we first arrived in Nairobi, life was not so comfortable. We didn't have much money nor did we own a car, but we wanted to visit Mombasa. We decided to ride the East African Railway (originally Uganda Railway) and experience some of the country's colonial past. The railway began as early as 1896 and linked Uganda and Kenya with the Indian Ocean at Mombasa. In the 1890s, an estimated thirty-two thousand laborers from British India were brought to East Africa to work on the project. Once the undertaking was completed, passengers were needed to help defray construction costs. A push for white settlers ensued. This resulted in the confiscation of African farmland, the cultivation of coffee and tea to help entice the pioneers, and the introduction of missions and churches to spiritually fortify these newcomers.

From the train's window, I saw my first Baobab and was very excited. The ancient tree begins blooming for the first time at about twenty years. It has a strange upside-down appearance, as if it were pulled up by the roots, tipped over, and plunged back into the earth. Along the way, we caught glimpses of giraffes, Thomson's gazelles, and other wildlife. Our overnight train finally reached Mombasa, where we sufficiently entertained ourselves and promptly ran out of money. It was just the two of us on the trip and no one else around to rescue us.

Coming back to Nairobi, we opted for second-class—rather than third-class—accommodations. But this meant skimping on food. We chuckled, because we could only afford one meal and asked for an empty plate and extra silverware. The waiter looked at us disgustingly. We were foreigners and presumably wealthy. Luckily, after Ahmed became successful, our days of sharing one meal ended. After returning to Kenya from Massachusetts, Ahmed bought a 1976 White Ford Corsair, employed Oscar, a Somali refugee, as his studio helper, and acquired additional students. Gosh, this reminds me of an earlier incident prior to owning a car.

I had a fondness of wearing heavy dangling earrings that caused my right earlobe to split. It needed mending. Our Pakistani friend recommended a Doctor Haq, a reputable plastic surgeon, practicing at the Radiant Health Clinic. I should have immediately said, "No thanks." Hubby let me decide. "Do what you think is best, honey." After deliberating, I phoned the doctor who confidently said, "Yes, madam, I certainly can accommodate you." "There is one obstacle," I explained, "We do not have a car." "Madam, there is no worry. I will fetch you, and we will drive there together." This was an opportune time to back out. Against my better judgment, I didn't.

A few days later, the doctor arrived in his chauffeur-driven, silver Mercedes. I entered the limousine, and my entire body sunk into the comfy and cozy red-leather seat. We chatted about an hour and a half, and then the limousine stopped somewhere in the wilderness. I blurted out, "This is the place?" Regaining my composure, I calmly said, "Oh, we have arrived." The Radiant Health Clinic certainly was not glowing. The paint of the gloomy, two-story building was badly chipped, the concrete walls were crumbling, and its roof sagged.

Inside, it was hot, smelly, noisy, and filthy. I was lucky to find a chair with a bottom still intact and anxiously sat down. Upstairs, things were even more chaotic. Young and old patients, bandaged and unsupervised, wandered around. Two attendants in the courtyard below fumed. They shouted at the patients, cursed the phones, and generally seemed to resent the world. A young man with one leg in a cast, wrestling with a broken wheel chair, slammed into objects and other patients in the upstairs balcony. The injured leg was awkwardly elevated on a loosely attached table. The contraption threatened his life and those around him. Just then, the doctor announced, "Madam, theater number one is ready."

I froze—couldn't move a muscle. My blood pressure was sky high, but no one bothered to check it. Dr. Haq led me into the operating room, and I hopped onto a table with my street clothes. I prayed, "Oh God, please get me through this one." The two nurses were having a bad day. The doctor repeated simple instructions several times. When he asked for surgical thread, one assistant produced a thick wire from a rusty can. It was the kind Ahmed used for hanging paintings. This is no exaggeration. Dr. Haq angrily walked across the room and fetched the right material. Midway, there was a tremendous crash. One helper dropped a tray of instruments on the floor. The frustrated surgeon roared like a lion. After lambasting the guy, he continued stitching my ear, which, actually, mended nicely. This experience will stay with me my entire life. Foreign Service employees learn to cope with unpredictable events. We develop a one-track mind that says, "I am here and maybe I shouldn't be but I am, so let's make the best of it."

Q: *Before I forget, I believe Barack Obama's father was part of the Kennedy "airlift" in the early sixties, when a number of Kenyans were brought to the U.S. for university training. Now, here you are several years later in your retirement, campaigning for his son's election as President of the U.S. You say the Americans were popular. How would you explain this popularity?*

AKAHLOUN: I am guessing some of this probably stemmed from Kenyatta's association in England with prominent black leaders and intellectuals from the global community. He attended the Fifth Pan-African Congress in Great Britain in 1945 together with Kwame Nkrumah, who would lead the struggle to turn Britain's Gold Coast colony into Ghana, and other political and social reformers. The meeting affirmed the goals of African nationalism and unity and was patterned after four previous ones held between 1919 and 1927. American W. E. B. Dubois, a sociologist, historian, author, editor, and Pan-Africanist, played a major role in organizing these earlier gatherings. He is considered one of the greatest African American intellectuals and civil rights activists.

Q: *There's an irony here. People were meeting in the colonial metropolis center and coming out of the experience as activists, making social changes, and it was happening in the colonial capital.*

AKAHLOUN: Yes, it is interesting. After World War II, when Kenyatta returned home, the country was more international. The British used Nairobi as a base, preventing the Italians in Ethiopia from penetrating deeper into East Africa. Kenyans, conscripted into the British Army, fought with American and European soldiers and became exposed to the outside world. Different nationalities settled in the country, and it became a sanctuary for refugees. Perhaps this is another reason for his cosmopolitan attitude.

Q: *Now, there you were in the seventies less than twenty years after the movement had produced a country. And you are saying there was a great openness, hospitality toward refugees. Kenya had a universal character. Do you remember it that way?*

AKAHLOUN: Yes, I do. Although the country had this global appeal and was relatively prosperous, Kenya was falling behind somewhat economically and tension with Uganda and Tanzania had grown. Political differences culminated in the 1977 collapse of the East African Community. This transpired shortly before Ahmed and I went on safari to Kenya's Masai Mara Game Reserve. As a result, we were unable to enter Tanzania's Serengeti National Park, because the border was closed. This was extremely disappointing, but our safari was fabulous.

Let me provide some context. Economic Officer Bob Benzinger at the U.S. Embassy was an exceptional photographer who loved safaris. When he invited us to Masa-Mara, we jumped at the chance and sealed the deal by offering our services to carry his bags, polish his boots, and wash his dishes. In other words, we were enthusiastic about accompanying him.

With our Kenyan tour guide behind the wheel, off we went for a thrill of a life time. When we reached the Great Rift Valley, heaven suddenly opened. The splendor of the powerful sight swept us away. On the horizon, there were a series of high white clouds, towering mountains, and beyond that rows and rows of ridges. Hundreds of feet below, the savannah stretched endlessly. It was one of the most enchanting sights I have ever seen. After a long descent, we reached the valley floor. The scenery was mostly dry, flat grassland with yellow thorn trees, gravel, driftwood, and patches of stone laced with quartz. We began passing wildlife—herds of gazelle, zebras, and giraffes—and soon we were deep into the reserve.

Then we witnessed something phenomenal. There were thousands of white bearded wildebeests migrating from the Serengeti National Park to the greener pastures of the Masai Mara Game Reserve. All of this exploded before our very own eyes. Nowhere in the world does one find this massive migration of animals. By chance, we were there at the precise moment it was happening, and we were literally spellbound.

I had read about the spectacular event in *National Geographic Magazine*. Annually, over two million animals migrate during the dry season—roughly July through the end of October—in search of food and water. Not all of them withstand the long trek, especially the Mara River crossing. Shallow water allows the majority of the herd, which includes a few Thomson's gazelles, zebra and elands, to cross safely, but it depends on the amount of rainfall. If the water is deep and fast flowing, the very young and the wounded fall prey to crocodiles, hyenas, and vultures. Nothing is wasted in the animal kingdom.

For over an hour, we sat inside the land rover, eyes glued on the fascinating stream of wildebeests. Then we decided to head into the bush to get a better look at these quarter-of-a-ton beasts. Bob was too busy pressing his camera's shutter button to realize we were now uncomfortably close to the animals. They were peaceful, but we knew large concentrations of them at the riverbed easily triggered stampedes. Besides, dusk was fast approaching. Our guide urged us to leave. When he tried to turn the jeep around, we got stuck in the mud. Instinctively, I reached for my rosary. We got out of the vehicle, and the men kept pushing and pushing until we were finally free.

Q: *The sun is setting, you're close to the wildebeests, and you're in the mud. Once free, did they approach the vehicle?*

AKAHLOUN: No, thank God. The unpredictable animals went about their business. We got back on the road, and hastily returned to camp. Believe me that was too close for comfort. There were other exciting safaris as well.

Ahmed and I and some embassy friends were privileged to see a variety of wildlife at the Tsavao West National Park. In addition, we were treated to game viewing at night from an open-air wooden deck of the famous Treetops Hotel in Aberdare National Park. The lodge, built in trees, was raised on stilts and had its own water hole where we caught sight of a rare mountain bongo antelope. We also stayed at a popular lodge close to Mount Kenya. Ironically, the top of the mountain was covered with snow even though it was so close to the equator.

At Lake Nakuru in the Rift Valley region, we saw another amazing sight—thousands of tall flamingos with long necks seemingly painting the shores of the lake pink. Presently, the numbers are decreasing, and some say this is attributed to local factories releasing untreated waste into the water, which is triggering a significant bird migration. Sprawling cities and farms, which results in widespread loss of natural habitat, and the poaching for exotic pelts and horns are also threatening Kenya's wildlife. For example, Grevy's Zebras that resemble mules, black rhinoceros, and cheetahs are some of the animals now on the endangered species list of the International Union for Conservation of Nature (IUCN).

Q: What are some other memorable adventures? You've got something. Let's have it.

AKAHLOUN: Well, this story may sound far-fetched, but it is factual. Shortly after arriving in Nairobi, the embassy announced a five-day trip to Addis Ababa, beginning December 31, 1975. Some type of U.S. military training exercise was taking place in Ethiopia, and a few seats on the aircraft were open. We signed up to go and waited and waited for what seemed an eternity. Finally, we received the tremendous news— space was available for the Akahlouns.

The inside of the old herculean C-130 military transport plane was refurbished, and I found it surprisingly modern and comfortable. The pilot gave us a tour of the cockpit and my eyes doubled in size when I discovered we were flying on automatic pilot thousands of feet above ground. The plane's belly seemed to scrape the snow-capped mountains. The sky was a brilliant blue. It was magnificent.

Emperor Haile Selassie had ruled the country for half a century. Revolutionary forces in 1974 removed him from power and placed him under house arrest. Apparently, the new Marxist regime promised much but delivered little, and the high hopes of the Ethiopians were dashed. Uprisings occurred frequently. The Derg, the ruling military junta, detained and killed thousands of protesters and rivals assumed to be plotting against them. Curfews were imposed, and security was tight. At the same time, Eritrea was fighting for its independence. Not the most opportune time to visit, but there we were in the thick of the political tension—again!

Movement around Addis Ababa was tightly controlled. The day after we arrived, Ahmed went to the Marine House to socialize with some of the marines who guarded the embassy, and I rested at the hotel.

It was well beyond curfew time, and I had not heard from him. A worst-case scenario crossed my mind, and I grabbed my rosary. A few hours later he phoned and said he was caught up in a demonstration. Because the streets were sealed off, the van he was riding in was forced to turn back. What a relief. He was safe. The next day, we went to an early dinner at the Agency for International Development (AID) Director's residence.

One guest, Mrs. Haile DeBass, thought I looked Ethiopian and asked about my background. "I'm Cape Verdean American," I replied. "Is your name Penny? I'm Joyce," she said. I was astounded but began piecing things together. Before my assignment to Ethiopia was changed to Nairobi, a mutual friend in Onset had given me her name and telephone number. Ironically, we now were randomly meeting in Addis Ababa. Her maiden name was Lopes (same as mine), and we were both born at Toby Hospital in Wareham. After high school, she moved to Washington, worked for the U.S. Department of the Navy, and met an Ethiopian Military Attaché. At the age of eighteen, she married him. For nine years, she had been living in Addis Ababa, and they had two children. Sadly, the political situation in Ethiopia was too unstable for Joyce and me to establish a friendship. I returned to Nairobi and never saw her again. However, the chance meeting proved beyond the shadow of a doubt that despite the vastness of the world, we humans are one family.

Q: Meeting a Cape Verdean, born in the same hospital, on the other side of the earth is a fine illustration of that. Did you get to see some of the old half-buried churches and other Ethiopian sights?

AKAHLOUN: Regrettably, we were confined to the capital. I did manage to venture outside the hotel briefly and bought some Ethiopian Coptic crosses. Love them. Fairly recently, I contracted a company to do some home improvement work and an Ethiopian representative came out to the house to take measurements. He noticed my collection of these brass and silver crosses and asked if I had visited his country. I replied, "Yes, and the people are very dignified and cultured." It turned out he arrived in the U.S. with two degrees—one in political science and the other in library sciences. His father, a former high-ranking government official, was imprisoned when Haile Selassie was ousted.

Q: I think, at that time, Ethiopia was officially one of the poorest countries in the world. Terrible poverty and misfortune.

AKAHLOUN: In spite of this, Ethiopians are infamous for their royal demeanor, tenacity, and resiliency. Judging from the stories he told me, he instilled these qualities in his children who now have professional careers. There are many highly educated Ethiopians, particularly in Northern Virginia who left their country due to political strife and now enjoy a much better life in America.

This dogged persistence and optimism calls to mind President Obama's inspirational memoir, *Dreams from My Father*. Perhaps, I shouldn't be speaking about politics, but after retiring from my U.S. government job, I am now free to actively participate in political activities. It is unimaginable to think that Ahmed and I in the seventies could not easily make contact with the U.S. Yet in 2008, in Barack Obama's tiny ancestral village of Kogelo in Alego, Siaya District, West Kenya people were watching American politics being streamed live on cable television and filled with joy to see him being elected president of the U.S. I understand there was no electricity there prior to Obama's first presidential election, but I could be wrong. We never visited the region.

Q: Extraordinary. There was a special event that occurred toward the end of your tour. Care to share it with us?

AKAHLOUN: With great delight. In early 1977, I noticed I was no longer my exuberant self. A mere cup of tea made me queasy. I switched to a milder brand without any noticeable results. I thought I was developing an allergy and decided to stop drinking tea altogether. Next, fatigue set in. This was strange because I was thirty-three, healthy, and energetic. I rationalized. "Well, lately, you have not been exercising." So I picked up my tennis racquet and went to the court, but the energy level was still low. The next strategy was to focus on sewing projects. I remember kneeling down on the floor to cut out a pattern, standing up, and becoming woozy. I thought the high altitude was playing tricks on me.

Then I spoke to Ahmed. After explaining my symptoms, he reached for our medical encyclopedia, flipped through a few pages, and began laughing. I thought to myself, "Gee whiz, I am suffering, and he is amused." "Honey, you are pregnant!" he shouted. I was skeptical because during our eight years of marriage, nothing had worked. And it was not for lack of trying. Given all of this, I was doubtful but decided to see Dr. Khehar, a local obstetrician.

The next morning, Ahmed called and said, "Honey, the results will be ready at noon." I held my breath, said some prayers, and tried to concentrate on my work. He soon waltzed into the office carrying a bouquet of gorgeous flowers. "Honey, honey, its official, you're pregnant, you're pregnant." We jumped for joy. Ambassador Marshall and Mr. Lindstrom rushed out of their offices to see what the excitement was about. Ahmed blurted out, "Say hello to the new mom!" They smiled and congratulated us. That day activities to further U.S.-Kenyan bilateral relations were unofficially suspended.

We gleefully made our rounds throughout the embassy, broadcasting the news of the century. Everyone was celebrating, but two weeks later—about the end of February— Dr. Khehar gave us distressing news. The doctor discovered I was spontaneously aborting and ordered complete bed rest. My emotions plummeted. I followed his instructions and was confined to bed flat on my back for fourteen days. Changing my mind-set to motherhood was the biggest test of my life.

At the time, Arlene, one of Ahmed's students, needed a place to live. She temporarily moved in and organized the household, served me meals in bed, and was literally a godsend. Ahmed was also very attentive. Pus-Pus, our Siamese cat, faithfully guarded me. Physically, I was inactive, but my mind was still engaged. "Get up. Go to work. Get your projects done." Keeping a daily journal and reciting three rosaries each day put things into perspective. Sometimes, we have no choice but to be still and listen to our bodies.

After my confinement, I resumed work on a part-time basis. This temporary work schedule was possible because of a sympathetic boss and a hefty sick-leave balance accumulated over the years. I was lucky to have the support of Ahmed, friends, and colleagues. But the one person who motivated me the most was Leila—my unborn daughter.

We spent eight years dreaming up appropriate names. If blessed with children, they would be called Leila and Omar. The birth order made no difference. They would be loved to the same degree. I felt Leila's presence deep inside and even envisioned her appearance and

ELEANOR LOPES AKAHLOUN

temperament. I used to rub my belly and talk to her, "Leila, sweetie, you must be very patient with Mommy. You are very, very precious. We must work together as a team. With your help, we are going to overcome this. We will be successful." Pus-Pus occasionally inserted a "meow, meow" and then contentedly fell back to sleep. Seriously, this is exactly what transpired. It sounds surreal, but it is true.

Q: What was Ahmed's reaction to all of this?

AKAHLOUN: He was a doting husband full of humor. He had a lot on his plate, as he was preoccupied with my health and Leila's and his busy art career. In January, he became the art exhibition supervisor at the French Cultural Center, which was a pretty big deal. He was also preparing for his own March–April exhibit at the center. Despite the press of business, he served the proud "mother-to-be" breakfast in bed nearly every day. I was being catered to and thoroughly relishing the attention.

When folks at the embassy asked how Leila was doing, I proudly turned sideways and stuck out my belly. The ambassador and my boss received the same treatment. It became a ritual. Everyone good-naturedly tolerated my antics. Because of the wonderful support network in Nairobi, I dreaded leaving Kenya. However, our tour was drawing to a close.

Q: When did you transfer? And what was going through your mind?

AKAHLOUN: We departed in July 1977. Many things concerned me. Despite a shaky beginning, our fine Kenyan physician had seen us through. Now, I was confronted with finding another doctor willing to care for a nearly seven-month pregnant woman coming from Africa. There was also a medical risk of traveling such a long distance so far along in pregnancy. A colleague highly recommended Dr. John W. Walsh, an old-fashioned obstetrician who had a private practice in Bethesda, Maryland. After an exchange of letters, he agreed to take me on as a patient. I was blessed.

Although Tunisia was our onward assignment, we were not due there until January 1978. I had to think creatively and balance career aspirations and growth as well as the demands of impending motherhood. A short-term assignment to bridge the gap between leaving Nairobi and giving birth was necessary. Mary Kincaid, my trusty career counselor, came up with a solution. "Penny, are you up for language training?" I replied, "Of course, Leila is very accommodating." "Great," she said. "Let's give you eight weeks of French before you go to Tunisia. See you in Washington!"

CHAPTER EIGHT

Overcome By Gratitude, Wonder, And Joy

WASHINGTON, D.C.

The State Department, Foreign Service Institute (FSI), 1977

Back on home shores, I summoned extra reserves of energy and courage to help with my studies and to see my pregnancy through to full term. The love between mother and baby is one of nature's strongest attachments. It makes parents want to shower their children with love and affection and to protect and nourish them.

Q: Did your return trip from Kenya go smoothly?

AKAHLOUN: Yes, but I arrived in Washington exhausted. When I stepped into Mary Kincaid's office, my tummy entered first and the rest of me followed. In shock, she asked, "Penny, how in heaven's name are you going to do this?" I giggled and said, "I am expecting a miracle." We shared a good laugh. After the briefing, I wobbled out of the office.

Next, I visited my new obstetrician, Dr. John W. Walsh. Fortunately, the physician-patient chemistry was present. I had heard he was Jacqueline Kennedy's physician. When I inquired, he responded diplomatically by saying, "I guess I wouldn't be betraying anyone's confidence by confirming that Jacqueline had a difficult time with her pregnancies." Later I learned the doctor delivered two of her children,

John F. Kennedy Jr., and Patrick Bouvier Kennedy who was born prematurely and died two days later in August 1963. After President Kennedy's assassination in Dallas, Texas, that same year in November, Dr. Walsh accompanied Mrs. Kennedy on board Air Force One, which flew the president's body back to Washington.

I was relieved to know we were in the hands of a sensitive and caring person who happened to be a clinical professor of obstetrics and gynecology at Georgetown University. It was not hard to like Dr. Walsh. As nervous first time parents, he thoughtfully presented us with an autographed copy of his book, *Expectant Motherhood*. Amazing, huh?

As time progressed, my energy level increased, and I was granted an additional three weeks of French training. Meanwhile, I grew rounder and rounder and Leila kicked harder and harder. It was time for another pep talk. "Leila, sweetie, Mommy must complete this eleven-week course. We can do it." She gave me a hard thump but cooperated, and I finished my training. Now it was time to shop for baby supplies. I bargained for more time, "Leila, honey, we only need ten more days to prepare for your arrival." Astonishingly, on exactly the tenth day, October 17, 1977, I gave birth to her at Georgetown University Hospital. What unspeakable joy and happiness. We brought her home and placed our little angel into a makeshift bassinet—an empty dresser drawer, covered with soft white and yellow blankets. It was her first official lesson on being flexible.

There is an old Cape Verdean custom—no longer widely practiced in the States—where baby and Mom remain in the house one month after the child's birth. The tradition is a wonderful bonding exercise between mother and child. I came up slightly short. After three weeks, it was necessary to venture out and have Leila's passport picture taken. Apparently, it was an agreeable outing; she kept falling asleep in my arms.

As with all pregnancies, mine was filled with physical, emotional, and psychological challenges. In spite of this, there was discovery, growth, and enrichment. I was a well-supported expectant mother who lovingly rubbed her belly, developed a strong connection with her unborn child, and steadfastly clung to her faith. After giving birth, there was time to reflect on the strenuous journey—the threat of miscarriage, transfer from one continent to another at nearly seven months' pregnant, the dread of finding a new doctor, the intensive language training, the

ELEANOR LOPES AKAHLOUN

worry of complications at birth, and other concerns. Because Leila and I went through so much together before she was born, it seemed as though I was now reuniting with a cherished, trustworthy friend. Our love blossomed even before we met. While this was my enjoyable experience, I am mindful others might be less enthusiastic about becoming parents. I believe the decision should be left up to each individual based on the lifestyle they choose to adopt.

At the tender age of four weeks, Leila became an official traveler. We flew from Washington, D.C., to Massachusetts. Ahmed's biological Mother, Momma Habiba, journeyed from Morocco to meet my parents in Onset and her new granddaughter. Although Leila became the center of our Universe, the celebration soon ended. Two weeks later we left for our new assignment, and the delicate work of juggling the needs of an infant, a career, and marriage began. Fortunately, Momma accompanied us to Tunisia and stayed one month to assist with the transition.

CHAPTER NINE

HEADING IN THE
WRONG DIRECTION

TUNISIA, 1977–1979

Tunisia was a tiny country that packed a powerful punch. The demands of parenthood, cultural differences, and political disturbances threw the family for a loop. We struggled to turn our lives around.

Q: How strenuous was it to get your footing in Tunisia?

AKAHLOUN: Life sometimes is an easy stroll in the park, and other times it is a climb up a steep rocky hill. Tunisia was a lovely country with pleasant people and a reasonably high standard of living. Unfortunately, we were not fully prepared for the ups and downs that were to come our way. It is nearly impossible to completely know how we will adjust to a new environment until we arrive and begin the arduous task of settling in. It was a rude awakening.

Finding suitable domestic help challenged us. Either the applicants were younger and inexperienced, or older with appropriate skills but possessed less patience. Looking back at our lack of adjustment, it was not entirely the fault of the Tunisians. I was overprotective of my newborn baby and somewhat hypercritical. I thought everyone should measure up to the exceptional care Momma Habiba provided upon our arrival. It was distressing leaving Leila, who had taken so many years to conceive, in the hands of others. At the office, I was anxious about her welfare. At home, I was worried about the affairs of the office. After one month, when our second helper was let go, Momma returned to babysit for us. Soon we found the right person, Khedija, a young girl with a radiant smile and a wonderful spirit. She had no appreciation for children's bibs, and Leila's clothes were always covered with food stains. But she loved our ray of sunshine, and that was all that mattered.

Unfortunately, Tunisia was not a very warm, hospitable environment for us. As time progressed, we noticed more dissimilarity between the Tunisian and Moroccan cultures. The Tunisians spoke Arabic and French, as in Morocco, but the country was more European-oriented. Historically, Tunisia had been influenced by the Phoenician, Roman, Byzantine, Arab, and Ottoman empires. Frankly, we thought we would be more at home, but it was not the case. This depressed Ahmed and affected his artwork, although the village of Sidi Bou Said did provide some inspiration. It is a stunningly beautiful village high on the slopes that overlook the Mediterranean Sea. It was very picturesque. The villas and cafes had whitewashed walls with blue arched doors, and grilled bay windows painted the same shade. Colorful flowers and palm trees were plentiful. Ahmed's paintings captured all of Sidi Bou Said's charm, and they sold well at his art shows.

Q: Was President Habib Bourguiba in full control of the country then?

AKAHLOUN: Not completely. The Tunisians feared that both Algeria and Libya were going to destabilize the government as several border towns were being raided. There was also concern that Algeria's radical Islamic movement would spell over into Tunisia and become a destructive force within the country. Because President Bourguiba staunchly opposed all forms of Islamic fundamentalism, suspected leaders were rounded up and thrown into jail. In 1978, a union strike was repressed by the government and dozens of people were killed. The strikers were not necessarily fundamentalists—but demonstrators opposed to Bourguiba's suppressive actions. The political situation was worrisome.

I believe President Bourguiba, who was more culturally attuned to France and Italy, was playing a subtle political game. He was a moderate Arab leader who was against Algeria's fundamentalism movement. Yet, he wanted to demonstrate to his people that he was also independent of western influence. This is possibly one of the reasons he permitted the Arab League to move its headquarters to Tunisia in 1979. Three years later, the Palestinian Liberation Organization (PLO) was driven out of Lebanon by Israeli forces and relocated in Tunis. Bourguiba had incredible sustaining power. He became President of Tunisia in 1957 and was removed from office because of ill health in 1987.

The American Embassy tried to maintain order by providing Tunisia police and military security assistance. My boss, Deputy Chief of Mission Barrington King, spent a great deal of time working with military officials and the Tunisian Ministry of Foreign Affairs on these issues. To his credit, our political relations improved. I was happy for him when he later became the U.S. Ambassador to Brunei.

Aside from the tenuous political situation, there were other reasons preventing us from firmly establishing roots in Tunisia. We lived in an attractive house in a middle-class neighborhood, but there were maintenance-induced headaches associated with the property. One time we smelled leaking gas fumes that were overpowering. I was concerned about everyone's safety, especially Leila's. Tunisians from the maintenance shop of the embassy's General Services Section came out to investigate several times, but they were condescending. This applied to the landlord as well. No one took responsibility for fixing the problem. Everyone said, "No, no, no. Nothing is wrong. Everything looks fine." I was merely the lady of the house and was not to be taken seriously. Nor did they respect Ahmed. He was a Moroccan—not a Tunisian. The foul odor mystery took months to unravel. Finally, it was discovered the problem was sewer-related, and the affected pipes were drained. At this point, everything seemed to be a struggle, with little rhyme, reason, or solution.

Tunisian society was challenging to navigate. Even our helper Khedija experienced difficulties with cultural expectations and norms. Let me explain. Prior to leaving the country, we tried to help her secure another job. She was raised in the countryside and not very cosmopolitan. Even though she lacked a formal education, she was sweet, conscientious, attractive, and had good common sense. A former employer, Mrs. Babcott, urged her to apply for a nurse-trainee position at a health clinic in town. Khedija interviewed but was rejected. Apparently, her physical appearance did not meet the standards. She was too plain—wore no makeup and pulled her curly hair back in a bun.

Q: Did they actually say that? They wanted her to alter her physical appearance to gain employment as a nurse?

AKAHLOUN: According to Khedija, they did, and she was crushed. I protested, and Mrs. Babcott intervened. After she agreed to wear lipstick, she was hired. Someone long ago commented that "problems come in bunches like bananas." There is some validity to this statement. Shortly afterward, Khedija developed a rash on her face, which alarmingly became more pronounced. We rushed her to the clinic and learned she was suffering with rubella (the German measles). What a predicament. Within a few days, she was beginning her new job. We brought her home and nursed her until she was on her feet again.

As the breadwinner of the family, I was under substantial pressure. Demands at the embassy, training new help at home, and monitoring Leila's movements consumed me. Additional help on the home front would have been useful. However, most men in the Arab culture perceive parenting and child-rearing as the mother's responsibility. This is true of other ethnic groups around the world as well. Their involvement oftentimes is limited, as was the case with Ahmed. Moreover, he was struggling with other issues—coping with an inhospitable environment, a stalled art career, and a sense of loneliness and homesickness. These feelings frequently strike "stay-at-home" spouses who must figure out how to constructively utilize eight hours of the day when there is little or no structure. It also pained him that he could not contribute financially to the household or assimilate into Tunisia's social or art circles. As the pressure mounted and his suffering heightened, he began drinking more and using alcohol as an escape mechanism.

Some assignments get started on the wrong foot, and this was certainly one of them. There were many stumbling blocks—finding and keeping suitable child care, political demonstrations, Ahmed's frustrations, the hazards and aggravation of living in a poorly maintained house, and the list goes on. My parents' declining health also weighed heavily on my mind. They wanted us closer to home. In addition, the tour of my supportive boss was ending. The chain of events was overwhelming, and the downward spiral needed to be stopped. In desperation, I requested the tour be shortened, but the decision to leave was not taken lightly. In all my years with the Foreign Service, this was my only curtailment.

While we were overall miserable with life in Tunisia, there is a valuable lesson to be learned here. Cultural adjustments are a two-way street. Chances are the Tunisians were equally irritated with our mindset of unhappiness, and they reacted in the same negative light toward us. There were also delightful times, such as visiting Morocco. Leila was nine months then and took her first baby steps in the family's apartment in Rabat. Our trip coincided with the Muslim holy month of Ramadan, so I decided to fast from sunrise to sunset as well. I prayed for renewed strength, patience, and spiritual enlightenment. It was "soul restoring" to be surrounded by our loved ones.

Q: You managed to juggle these competing, two full-time jobs—a baby and a career.

AKAHLOUN: And a husband. That makes three full-time jobs. After eighteen months, we left Tunis. It was in July of 1979. I distinctly remember because Leila was climbing out of her crib and swiftly becoming quite proficient at it. The Department was sympathetic. I think people thought, "Well, if Penny wants a curtailment, there must be a reason for it." Mary Kincaid, my career counselor who was still with Human Resources in the Career Development Office, proposed I go to Washington, D.C., for consultations and take home leave. She arranged for a transfer to Ottawa, Canada, as a special assistant to the Science Counselor, Dr. Clyde McClelland, a brilliant officer widely admired and respected. "Wow!" I thought, "We are moving in the right direction. This is an excellent career move. It would give me more responsibility, afford Ahmed better job prospects, and allow me to be closer to Massachusetts." But first, Washington, D.C., consultations awaited us.

Speaking of these briefings, in the past, the Department of State was not considered a "baby-friendly" establishment. Working moms improvised as best possible, and it was taxing. For instance, once I towed Leila—poor thing—from one end of the building to the other, because I was trying to find some privacy to change her. I ended up in the transportation and shipment supervisor's office praying she would remain quiet and not disturb the office routine. While tending to her soiled diaper, we made arrangements for delivering our air freight and household shipments to Ottawa. Thankfully, times have changed.

These days, the State Department's strategically located baby-changing stations and other parenthood initiatives make striking a work-life balance much easier for employees.

Luckily, I had acquired an extensive network of friends inside and outside of work who were accommodating and very adept at helping me juggle a career, motherhood, and marriage. Going home to visit my folks was a chance for us to relax and catch our breath. Onset was a place where we felt safe, protected, and loved.

People bathing in the Ganges River in Varanasi
(formerly Benares), India, October 1967.

At our May 31, 1969, stateside wedding, Saint Margaret's
Parish Hall, Buzzards Bay, Massachusetts.

With my parents at the wedding reception.

At the traditional marriage in Tangier, Morocco on
June 5, 1969. Ahmed's grandfather, Abdesselam Ben
Mohammed Zefri, presided over the ceremony.

February 1973, in our cozy Washington, D.C., Kalorama Road apartment, being interviewed by the New Bedford *Standard Times* for an article entitled "Her Childhood Dreams Come True."

Ahmed in his Montevideo studio preparing for an upcoming *Alianza* art show on July 8, 1974.

Ambassador Ernest V. Siracusa, Ahmed, and me at the exhibit.

With Ahmed and Leila, nine months old, at
our villa in Tunis, Tunisia, 1978.

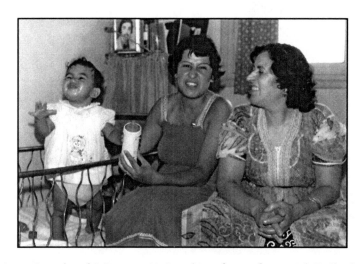

Aunt Souad and Momma Aini making funny faces with Leila the summer of 1978 in Rabat, Morocco, where she took her first baby steps.

Aisha, our domestic helper, her brother, and Leila the day we departed from Tunis, Tunisia, 1979.

In 1980, perched high on her father's shoulders, Leila gets a bird's eye view of Ottawa's Winterlude Festival.

Leila making a new friend.

One year after this photo I turned forty and gave birth to Omar.

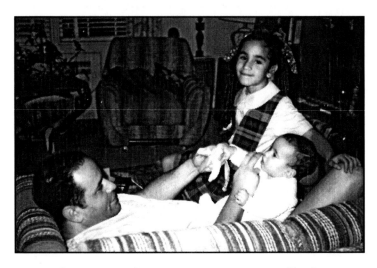

Leila, Omar, and Poppy in 1983, at our Buckingham
Village apartment in Arlington, Virginia.

Omar is still in diapers, but big sister gives him some packing lessons, 1984.

My father and Leila in 1984 nursing Omar, who
was suffering from chicken pox.

His health on the mend, Omar was all bundled up and
barely visible as he went for a ride in his baby stroller.

In 1985, Ahmed and Leila at her first Holy Communion,
Saint Thomas More Cathedral, Arlington, Virginia.

Omar and his grandfather lend a helping hand during one of my oral history interviews with Ti-Frank, my dad's godfather, Onset, Massachusetts, August 1985.

Wearing traditional Moroccan dress for a family portrait, Arlington, Virginia, 1986.

President George H. W. Bush Sr. during his December
1990 visit to Uruguay. Leila was quite excited because
the president's hands landed on her shoulders.

Leila and her fun-loving classmates in 1990 at
the Uruguayan-American School.

Omar makes his First Holy Communion, Stella Maris Christian
Brothers' College, Montevideo, Uruguay, May 1991.

The children in Montevideo on August 31, 1992,
celebrating their dad's 48th birthday.

My father busy at work tending his award-winning garden,
the summer of 1993 in Onset, Massachusetts.

Grandpa at age 77 with his troops heading to Cumberland Farms to
redeem empty soda bottles worth two cents apiece, Onset, 1993.

CHAPTER TEN

THE GREAT WHITE NORTH

CANADA, 1979–1982

A quick flight across the border, and we arrived at our next "overseas" post. The stress and strain of the Tunisian assignment was behind us. We now anticipated brighter and sunnier, albeit colder, days ahead in Canada.

Q: Were you impressed with Ottawa?

AKAHLOUN: Very much so. The moment we arrived in Canada, we sensed we were on the road to regaining our equilibrium. We felt the tour would be a gratifying one. Ottawa was a well-kept, organized city with lovely flowers and rich green lawns and parks. Radiant sunshine. Clear blue sky. No pollution. In many aspects, it reminded me of Kenya, but it was less congested—only about seven hundred thousand people. Although the standard of living competed with that of Washington, D.C., the way of life was uniquely Canadian. The entire city seemed to be a village, filled with friendly French and Anglo Canadians, enjoying a comfortable life.

The U.S. Embassy was situated at 100 Wellington Street. We had a superb view of the Parliament Buildings across the street. Every day, we listened to the sounds emanating from the Peace Tower Carillon. Everyone within a mile or so from the Hill in downtown Ottawa heard the music produced by accomplished carillonists or *carillonneurs* and their fifty-three perfectly tuned bells. Listening to the concerts was mesmerizing. The Changing of Guards was also impressive. Members of various military units, wearing red coats and big, black, bear-skin hats, paraded up the street. They played brass instruments, pipes, and drums. At the top of Parliament Hill, the guards were ceremoniously exchanged. It was exciting. We also saw plenty of Royal Mounted Police, the "Mounties." Tourists carrying cameras mobbed them.

During my time there, the embassy was a classic three-story limestone structure built in the early 1930s. Initially, our mission opened as a legation but was upgraded in 1943, the year I was born. Our staff was already outgrowing the present location, and there was talk about constructing a larger more modern building. The new chancery, which President Bill Clinton dedicated in 1999, is on Sussex Drive at the edge of historic Byward Market.

Embassy Ottawa had a massive reception area. The marine guard station occupied one corner, and there was not much else in the room other than a grand stairwell. The mission was sizable. My desk was in the same room with two other secretaries, who worked for the economic counselor and about two commercial officers. The Science and Technology Office (S&T) was not part of this section. Dr. McClelland's office was in a separate area, and there were just the two of us doing the work.

Upon arrival in Ottawa, we checked into the downtown Embassy Hotel at Cartier and Cooper Streets. The refrigerator was empty, so I went grocery shopping. The exchange rate was favorable—roughly one U.S. dollar to eighty-four cents Canadian currency. Soon I discovered St. Vincent de Paul's thrift shop, which sold sweaters for thirty-five cents. I stocked up. We also purchased secondhand furniture there. We opened our first charge account at Sears.

Unlike most overseas assignments, there was no State Department–sponsored housing in Ottawa. We had to find one within our government-authorized allowance. House hunting was completely alien to us. And we were clueless as to how to maintain one. Over the years, we grew dependent on the General Services Office (GSO), which looked after U.S. Embassy property. They even changed our light bulbs. Now we were left to our own devices to find and upkeep a home.

After a nearly two-week search and looking at ten possibilities, we found our dream place—a townhouse at Stone Hedge Crescent in the French-speaking Gloucester area. I was sold on the olive green dishwasher and refrigerator, which complimented the gold carpets.

ELEANOR LOPES AKAHLOUN

Moreover, it was a newer community with beautiful townhouses and separate homes landscaped with big lawns and beautiful flower gardens. As an added bonus, the neighborhood was family oriented and racially mixed.

There was one drawback; we did not have a domestic helper. I was it. Chief-bottle-washer-and-cook. The help we had grown to depend on overseas was non-existent. The commute to the embassy was an easy twenty-minute drive on the Queensway. In winter, it was a different story. Essentially, we lived in the country, surrounded by cornfields and three barns—an old lopsided one across the street and two picture-perfect red ones on either side of the development. We walked a short-distance to the farmer's market to buy fresh produce. There were plenty of children at the swimming pool in front of our unit or at the playground. It was a wholesome environment. The doors of the 110 units were painted firemen's red, yellow, orange, and olive green. I think the vivid colors helped alleviate cabin fever during the long bitter winters. This gives you a glimpse of why the picturesque neighborhood attracted us.

Oftentimes the winters in Ottawa were filled with a bright blue sky. Some days, I took advantage and went for invigorating walks. My lunch-hour strolls were therapeutic. Canada offered us a relatively high standard of living, except for one aspect—our temperamental car. In mid-September, our 1975 Fiat—otherwise known as "Nellie Belly"—arrived. The security officer in Tunisia, who sold the vehicle to us, grossly misrepresented the car's reliability. We barely survived the winter. The Fiat was in and out of the repair shop. From day one, it was allergic to the frigid weather and refused to start. We towed the car to the garage and installed a block heater that warmed the engine during freezing winter weather. We plugged a cord into an electrical outlet overnight. Each unit had its own power source. After two weeks, we picked up Nellie Belly from Performance Motors and went to gas up. No way. She had a European fuel cap, requiring a special key. Three garages failed to unlock it. The next day, Ahmed replaced the cap.

As the temperatures plummeted, our unpredictable car gave us more headaches. Twice a day, I bundled up, walked to the embassy parking lot, and warmed up her engine. Despite the coaxing, we were lucky if she turned over by the end of the day. As a rule, we needed a jump start. When this failed, the tow truck took her away. This happened frequently.

In winter, when snow and ice thickly blanketed the ground in minus-forty degree weather, the situation became impossible. We changed routines. No longer did I drive to work. Each morning, I woke up at the crack of dawn, winterized myself, and walked down a narrow snow-cleared path to the Fiat. The thick ice on the car lock was melted with a cigarette lighter, and the door was then pried open. On good days, Nellie Belly started and the defroster was switched on. I then ran into the house, dressed Leila, buckled her into the car seat, scraped the windows (while making funny faces and playing hide and seek), unplugged the block heater cord, drove to the babysitter's, deposited her, and returned home. After this, I parked the car and walked to the highway to catch the bus (only one bus to town; my timing had to be well synchronized). In the evening, the practice was reversed. Ottawa's winters were notoriously brutal, especially for Ahmed, given the moderate climate of Morocco in which he was raised. Even for me, as a New Englander, the weather was unforgiving and definitely wreaked havoc on Nellie Belly.

For my thirty-sixth birthday, Ahmed decided to chauffeur us to Onset. He preferred driving, and I enjoyed being a passenger. It was a highly satisfactory arrangement. The twelve-hour drive was long, and tiring. Once we arrived, Nellie Belly was also exhausted. The left brake had locked, and both rear tires had worn out. It cost $125 for repairs—a fortune at the time. My journal indicates we spent a total of $28.70 on gas and highway tolls. At least, that part of the journey was cheap.

In June 1980, someone rear-ended our Fiat at the Queensway Innes exit when it stalled. The car was totaled. Thank God, Ahmed walked away unharmed. People said he had nine lives. Toss him in the air, and he consistently landed on his feet. The insurance company gave us a fat check for $1,800, and we said good-bye to Nellie Belly. We immediately purchased a replacement vehicle that appreciated Canadian winters.

I think it is no secret that Canadians genuinely know how to celebrate winter, and we joined in on the fun. On sunny days, we sometimes walked through snow-covered fields to the babysitter's house. We also participated in Ottawa's traditional Winterlude carnival. The frozen Rideau Canal turned into a gigantic skating rink. There were jugglers and clowns who painted children's faces. Leila sat on her father's shoulders so she could get a better view of the ice carvings and snow sculptures. Next to our house, we flew down icy hills on saucer-like sleds. I would never do that again—too risky. Snow never dampens the Canadian zest for life. There was no such thing as hibernating. Not even blizzards kept them off the highways. I found that out the painful way.

Unfortunately, one day I was driving to work in a terrible storm. Visibility on the icy Queensway was very poor. Suddenly, my car spun around and faced the opposite direction in the path of an oncoming vehicle. The headlights were getting closer and closer. I stayed calm, prayed, and kept turning the steering wheel until the car was facing the right direction. God and good luck was with me that day.

Q: You were working with Dr. McClelland who was leading the effort to collaborate with the scientific community and to benefit from Canadian technology. Let's discuss the activities of the Office of Science and Technology (S&T).

AKAHLOUN: The main objective of our section was to foster scientific and technological cooperation between the Canadian and U.S. governments. Dr. McClleland assigned me substantive work, and I was grateful to have these career-enhancing opportunities. Some of our activities included obtaining overflight aircraft clearances, gaining marine scientific research vessel approval, and monitoring the country's space and nuclear programs.

When the March 1979, Three Mile Island Nuclear Power Plant accident occurred, Canada began scrutinizing its nuclear policy. Parliament formed a science committee to study how the country could better safeguard its reactors. The Canadians also wanted to look into the moral and ethical implications of such a disaster. Pressurized heavy water Canada Deuterium Uranium (CANDU) reactors were already being exported overseas.

Q: These are the reactors that Canadians developed by themselves? Did they borrow American technology?

AKAHLOUN: The Canadians invented the reactors using their own technology. Nuclear waste management was a hot topic and tougher internal safety regulations were needed. Many questions were being tossed around. "What was the best safeguard measure? Should it be disposed deep within the Canadian Shield? Stored closer to the surface at nuclear sites? Or saved in a central spot?" The Canadian government and the scientific community debated the pros and cons at length. To keep up with the latest developments, Dr. McCelland attended several conferences, seminars, and symposiums in various parts of Canada. In his absence, I closely kept track of developments taking place in Ottawa. As a result, I was able to help him draft various reports, which we then forwarded to the State Department.

One key project was Canada's Remote Manipulator System Arm (RMS) program. The robotic mechanical arm was being designed to deploy and retrieve space hardware from the payload bay of U.S. space shuttles. After the first space walk in 1969, the U.S. decided to build a new space transportation system. Sometime later, the National Aeronautics and Space Administration (NASA) requested help from the Canadians who were experimenting with their own robot for handling nuclear waste. Canada agreed to construct a portion of the space shuttle project. A Memorandum of Understanding was drawn up and work began around 1975. The Canadians designed, built, developed, and tested the Canadarm. Its first flight was with the U.S. space shuttle Columbia back in November 1981. Shortly after this, astronauts Commander Joe H. Engle and Pilot Richard H. Truly came to Ottawa, and we had the honor of meeting them. Over the years, the Canadarm performed well and exceeded all expectations. Its final flight was in 2011 when NASA's space shuttle program officially ended.

Incidentally, I read an article in the *Washington Post* about the long-broken Hubble Space Telescope that was carried into orbit in 1990. The Canadarm captured and anchored down the telescope, enabling space-walking astronauts to make repairs so that the instrument could peer into the universe's atmosphere. The telescope is now expected to function possibly until 2020. The article dredged up old memories. It is gratifying to know that the U.S. Embassy's role in the venture was of some value.

Another portion of our work involved marine scientific research in Canadian waters. Our job was to ensure everything went smoothly with ocean research. In July 1979, the government began requiring a license for foreign commercial fishing and scientific research vessels, which collected biological and oceanographic bottom and water samples. This is around the time when ecologists noticed the Georges Bank was being depleted of fish. A bilateral agreement existed but was not strictly enforced.

Now, advanced twenty-four-hour written notice to the Department of Fisheries and Oceans for all ships entering and departing Canadian waters was necessary. This clearance applied to port calls as well. A comprehensive report of all marine scientific research activity in Canadian waters over a lengthy period of time needed to be compiled and submitted. Dr. McClelland assigned me the project, and I was overjoyed. Our Embassy Ottawa files contained limited information, but the Bureau of Oceans and International Environmental and Scientific Affairs (OES) kept complete records, including information on vessels sailing to Southern Vancouver Island and British Columbia. For the most part, we were in compliance with Canadian regulations. Going forward, our contacts exerted tighter control, but they were still cordial.

Q: Earlier you raised the subject of managing up and saving face. I think you wanted to use your Canadian experience as an illustration. Care to elaborate on this now?

AKAHLOUN: Gladly. For me, the science and technology field was unfamiliar and rather complex. Dr. Clyde McClelland envisioned a "maximum-initiative" role for his aide and gave me plenty of rope to hang myself. As mentioned, in addition to performing secretarial tasks, he assigned supplemental reporting and analytical responsibilities. We worked closely together. After one year, he suddenly retired. "Oh, Dr. McClelland." I said, "You cannot leave. What will happen to S&T affairs?" "Penny," he responded, "You are competent, and I trust you will take excellent care of the office. You will be just fine until our new science counselor arrives." It turned out to be a three-month gap. A long cold winter.

Q: I see this story unfolding. Who was the acting science counselor?

AKAHLOUN: Political Officer Mr. Nee was in charge. Yet, he allowed me to handle the day-to-day matters of the office until Dr. McClelland's replacement, Dr. Getzinger, arrived. Meanwhile, I searched newspapers for science-related articles and sent telegrams and airgrams on issues of potential interest to our State Department counterparts. Mr. Nee was pleased because his workload did not increase, and I was thrilled because the office was functioning as well as could be expected. However, the economic counselor, who already had two secretaries working for him, was unhappy.

He frequently walked over to my desk and asked why I was wasting time reading newspapers. "Sir," I politely replied, "The Canadian space program is reorganizing. Fifty-four million dollars is being slated for new research projects. Washington needs to know about these developments. I am preparing a report." (Later, the State Department sent a cable complimenting the embassy on its submission.) The economic counselor was fuming. The situation grew worse, and I became more exasperated. Ultimately, I decided it was time to "manage up." That is, take the matter to another level.

I marched into Mr. Nee's office and proposed I speak with higher management to explain the contentious office dynamics. He agreed, and I set up an appointment with the acting Deputy Chief of Mission. "Sir, thank you for seeing me," I said. "Yes, what is it, Penny?" he responded. I continued, "You know, Mr. So-and-So is a highly experienced and well-intentioned economic counselor, but he does not officially report on Canadian scientific matters." Then, I looked directly into his eyes and said, "Like you, I am a professional." He was caught off guard. "Yes, Penny, I know. Yes, yes, I know." I had gotten his attention. "Upon retiring, Dr. McClelland asked me to look after the office, and that is precisely what I am doing." He smiled. "Penny, we will handle this, and I appreciate your raising the issue." From that day forward, my economic section woes disappeared.

Q: The economic counselor behaved better because the Deputy Chief of Mission (DCM) spoke with him. Going above the head of the person you report to is a nuclear option. There is some risk involved speaking to a higher authority.

AKAHLOUN: I certainly don't advocate it, but the circumstances were unique. In this instance, the two men were friends. I was confident the DCM would handle the situation diplomatically, and there would be no serious repercussions. After my talks with the economic counselor failed, I took action as a last resort but only after analyzing the situation

ELEANOR LOPES AKAHLOUN

from every angle and addressing my concerns directly with the officer first. Rather than complaining, I presented the facts in a positive light. I tried to save face for him. My intention was not to seek revenge or to be malicious but rather to have him change his behavior so my work could continue unhampered. In the end, I received a Meritorious Honor Award, a salary increase, and earned the economic counselor's respect. Most important, both our careers and professional reputations were intact, and there was no lingering animosity between us.

Q: You also worked on a special task. Let's hear more about that?

AKAHLOUN: Mr. King, my former supervisor in Tunisia, had urged me to volunteer for activities outside my portfolio to better position myself for career advancement. I internalized his advice. In Ottawa, I became the Embassy's Federal Women's Program Coordinator. This was in 1981. To celebrate Women's Equality Day, the State Department requested its overseas missions to send a report on the status of women. Mr. Knee, the Political Officer, received the request and approached me. "Penny, you are the embassy's women's coordinator, you want to have a go at this?" I was ecstatic. The project turned out to be addictive and time-consuming. I plowed through over thirty-eight references, worked nearly two months, and ultimately produced a nine-page report on the Worldwide Status and Rights of Women in Canada. The history is quite captivating.

Canadian feminism, like other countries in the west, began in the late nineteenth century. It centered on voting rights, holding elected or public office, and access to an education and training. During the depression and the Second World War, the focus was on the women's role in the workforce, the need for equal pay for equal work, violence against women, and concerns about women's reproductive rights. In the early 1990s—well, after my tour ended—the movement became more of a grassroots operation linked to antiracism, anti-imperialism, and anticapitalism themes.

Canada's ethnic minorities held various viewpoints on their feminist leanings. For instance, some aboriginal women found the "feminism" label to be antifamily and thus offensive. Women of color felt that the fact they always worked outside the home in support of their families and struggled against racism and a male-dominated society was being ignored. In essence, the ethnic groups believed the white, Anglo Canadian women's perspective differed from their own unique experiences. I found it intriguing to analyze the divergences in opinion and the special issues facing different groups of women.

The 1966 U.S. Feminist Movement dramatically influenced Canada's efforts. The following year, the country established a Royal Commission on the Status of Women (RCSW). In 1971 a new Canadian cabinet position, Minister Responsible for the Status of Women, was created as a result of this commission. Canada was the first industrialized nation to take such an initiative. An intensive lobbying campaign for equal rights developed and women began networking throughout Canadian provinces and territories. Prime Minister Pierre Trudeau later introduced a proposal giving women more rights. But most feminists were not satisfied and insisted on deeper concessions.

Reaching an agreement pleasing to all Canadians was tough. Considerable infighting in the provinces and territories took place. For instance, Rene Levesque, the Premier of Quebec, advocated for his French-speaking province's sovereignty, the Maritime Provinces sought control over offshore resources, such as fisheries, and the Prairie Provinces wanted more power concerning mining issues. In the process, women's issues took a back seat. Coast-to-coast protests ensued. After extensive negotiations between the federal and provincial governments and widespread consultation with all segments of the population, a Charter of Rights and Freedoms became entrenched in Canada's constitution.

Q: Tell me more about the revised Constitution and the Charter of Rights.

AKAHLOUN: This is somewhat complicated. Essentially, the Constitution Act, 1982, was introduced to transfer the Canadian constitution from England to Canada, and it contained several amendments. Queen Elizabeth II on April 17, 1982, signed a proclamation to complete the process of patriation (a colloquial term) granting Canada sovereignty. For the first time, Canada's constitution included a Charter of Rights and Freedoms, which profoundly altered the lives of its people. Gender equality, native rights, multiculturalism, and bilingualism in federal institutions were introduced. In addition, all government documents were to be written in both French and

English. But one critical element was missing—the signature of the government of Quebec. In the sixties, the Province had developed a strong nationalistic outlook and wanted to become independent.

French President Charles de Gaulle visited Montreal in 1967. This is when he appeared on the balcony of city hall and uttered those famous words, *Vivre le Quebec libre!* Loosely translated, "May Quebec live long and free!" Which is not what most Canadians wanted, but it energized Quebec. As of 2014, the province has not formally approved the act, although official consent was never necessary. The issue is still a heated topic of discussion in Quebec.

Q: Who were the women you interviewed? Were these exchanges mainly to obtain information for your nine-page report?

AKAHLOUN: Yes. The interviews were report driven. I met with Maureen O'Neil, Canada's UN Representative on the Commission on the Status of Women and other officials as well. Later I obtained an appointment with Judy Erola, the Canadian Minister Responsible for the Status of Women. At the Department, I coordinated with Julie Jacobson in the International Women's Programs Office, Bureau of International Organizations. These accommodating women were indispensible during a future visit of Nancy Clark Reynolds who was Ms. O'Neil's U.S. counterpart.

Q: You were in Canada at the historic moment: the redrafting of the Constitution to accommodate gender, race, language, and indigenous people. You were the tip of the spear in reporting these developments to the State Department. What was your contribution to the visit of Nancy Clark Reynolds?

AKAHLOUN: I was an escort officer. It is curious how this occurred. In May 1982, Ms. Reynolds, the U.S. Representative to the United Nations Commission on the Status of Women, met Judy Erola, the Canadian Minister for Women's Affairs, at a UN meeting in Vienna. They wanted to ensure that Nairobi's UN international conference scheduled for 1985 would not be a fiasco like the 1980 gathering. In Copenhagen, women's issues were hijacked by well-organized political groups. Canada and the U.S. decided early in the game to pool resources and develop a joint strategy to prevent this from happening again.

One month later, I received a letter from the Canadian government officially inviting Ms. Reynolds to Canada and forwarded the message to Washington. Ms. Reynolds accepted the invitation and proposed a June 14 and 15, 1982, date. To ensure that I followed protocol within the embassy, I consulted with the ambassador's office, as this type of visit was usually handled either by a political or cultural affairs officer rather than by a person of my rank. On the note designating me escort officer, the Chargé d'Affaires ad interim, scribbled, "Penny, see that it happens this way." I took what he wrote to heart.

After making the necessary logistical and protocol arrangements, the day arrived. I greeted the charming and energetic Ms. Reynolds at the airport and whisked her away for a series of meetings and a luncheon on Parliament Hill. This was followed by a House of Common's question and answer period and other briefings. She met with over two-dozen Canadian officials and representatives from nongovernmental organizations. I took notes at the meetings, did the follow-up reporting, and ensured everyone involved received recognition. The outcome was heartening. The bilateral visit was well received. The Ottawa *Citizen* published a favorable article entitled *Planning Starts to Keep UN Conference on Track*. After my tour finished, the Canadian–U.S. proposals were finalized. In de facto, Canada and the U.S. led the way for a successful Third World Conference on Women held in Nairobi, Kenya in 1985.

Q: What about Anglophone–Francophone relations? In later years, they say the French community in Montreal became somewhat less friendly. You lived in a French-speaking neighborhood of Ottawa. Back then, was this an issue?

AKAHLOUN: There was a certain amount of turmoil politically, but on a personal level, I found people very pleasing and friendly. In fact, one day, Leila and I were going downtown to the library. A French Canadian bus driver, who saw me struggling with her stroller, quickly left his seat and lifted her inside. Once we reached our destination, he carried the stroller down to the sidewalk, and cheerfully waved good-bye as he drove away.

At the embassy, and our Stone Hedge Crescent neighborhood, people mixed well. In general, the Canadians were open, welcoming, and warmhearted. However, there was some friction between Anglophone Francophone Canadians, particularly in certain regions. Montreal prospered economically while other areas struggled. For instance, Quebec's unemployment rate was substantially higher than the Canadian average, and many of the people were poorer. Differences over language, economics, and politics definitely existed.

Q: Now, let's get a little bit of the chronology. You went to Canada in 1979. How did the family adjust to the new surroundings?

AKAHLOUN: We were there three years—from August 1979 until July 1982. Ahmed found various jobs, including managing the embassy's commissary and his Peruvian friend's coffee shop. Simultaneously, he sold paintings. A year after we arrived, he saved enough money to purchase sturdily built dining and living room furniture for $690 and a $1,000 six-piece bedroom set, which is still being used today. The money was well invested.

As for Leila, the harsh winters initially caused her frequent bouts with lingering colds and bronchitis, but later her condition improved. She got along well with other children, especially her friends at the babysitter's house. In the morning when I dropped her off, her tiny playmates would run up to our car as fast as they could to greet her. It was a joy to witness.

Leila loved books. On weekends, rain, sleet or snow, we attended enriching programs of storytelling, films, and puppet shows at Ottawa's Public Library. The children's section, in the shape of a mini amphitheater, was brightly decorated and had gold carpeting. September 1980 she received her first library card. Because of these visits and flash card study exercises at home, she was reading at age three. Six months later, she was printing her name. During one library visit, we selected a book about the Muslim culture. One page showed men praying at a mosque. "Mommy, where's Poppy? Where are all the women?" she asked. She was extremely perceptive and entertaining.

Once, on the eve of her third birthday, she received a rare slap on her bottom for misbehaving. That evening she reprimanded me. "Mommy, you don't have to spank me. Just talk to me. I will listen." Then she gave me a kiss and said, "Now we are friends again." It was a valuable parenting lesson and one never forgotten.

Q: *Your father had some health problems during this time frame. A painful aspect of Foreign Service life is separations from family members for long periods of time. How did you manage family obligations and your career demands?*

AKAHLOUN: During the three-year Canadian assignment, we visited Onset a total of eight times to check on my parents. My mom had minor foot surgery but was in acceptable health. My father suffered from osteoarthritis on his wrist, elbow, and knees, which caused him significant pain, swelling, and difficulty in walking. He had completely lost the cartilage on the right knee and the bones were rubbing together. Over the years, construction work damaged many of his joints. He first started working at the age of thirteen. The physical labor and prolonged exposure to the outdoor elements damaged his body. His physicians at Massachusetts General Hospital recommended the arthritic knee be replaced.

In December 1980, I went home to consult with the doctors. It was bitterly cold there but mild in comparison to the record-breaking weather we escaped in Ottawa. The heavy snow and strong winds formed gigantic snow squalls completely covering cars. Enormous icicles hung everywhere. I was more than delighted to be home.

We brought along Leila's homemade vocabulary and math flash cards. My father, mother, and Auntie Katie taught her new words and played Pokeno, a favorite card game of ours, with her. She was nursing a persistent cold, and we decided it was best for her to avoid traveling back to Canada. Dr. Lovejoy was reasonably certain my father's heart was strong enough to withstand the operation, but he was going to conduct further tests. I headed back to Ottawa only to return two weeks later when the doctor cleared him for surgery.

Q: *So the knee replacement procedure was performed. That, undoubtedly, required extensive recuperation. You were there to assist.*

AKAHLOUN: I did my best. In two months, we shuttled between Canada and Massachusetts—in the dead of winter—three times. The operation lasted three and one-half hours. That evening I slept on a chair next to his bed and kept one eye open watching him. There was no need to fret; I saw Mr. McGeehan, his Irish roommate, sprinkling holy water on my father. They had instantly bonded. My dad's engaging personality readily attracted people.

He started therapy immediately after the ordeal and exercised faithfully. Despite his aches and pains, he never gave up. Later, he underwent more operations—one on his left wrist and another on his elbow. A pinched nerve was causing numbness in his hand. Each time he healed quickly. My father was the personification of the expression "tough times never last but tough people do."

Meanwhile, Leila was turning into a budding conversationalist. Two weeks after my father's operation, we were on a bus returning to Ottawa. An hour into the ride, she stood up and started chatting with two passengers behind us. I was listening to the conversation but did not turn around. She shook hands and said, "Hello, how are you? How's your husband?" The women snickered, "We don't have any." Leila persisted, "Why? Well, then how are your children?" When I tried to interrupt, she bent down and smothered me with kisses and said, "Mommy, please be quiet or else you will have to get off the bus. Eat your apple and look straight ahead, okay?" I finally convinced her to sit down. Embarrassed, I turned around to greet the strangers and apologize. I was in shock. They were Catholic nuns!

Here is another funny story. One time at a restaurant, I ordered a soft drink with my meal. Leila turned to an elderly man seated at the next table and said, "Hi, do you want some of my mommy's coke? The stranger smiled. "No, thank you. I'm not allowed to have sugar." Leila replied, "There's no sugar in there. Sugar is in a bowl, not a can. There's only caffeine inside."

In the fall of 1981, we wanted to enroll her into a junior kindergarten class at Pine View Catholic School. Home interviews were required, so we made an appointment with the teacher, Carole Policky. When she arrived, I don't think she was expecting two hours of continuous amusement. She asked Leila about her special friends. Leila replied, "Oh, I have a boyfriend. His name is Greg, and he lives in the corner." Pointing, she said, "It's the house that you cannot see." Another time, they spoke about the neighborhood park, and Leila volunteered, "I know the name of the people who stole the big wheel off the ship on the playground. Their names are 'teenagers.'" That evening, she was admitted to Pine View, and Ahmed gave Ms. Policky a painting as a reward for her patience during the prolonged visit.

Q: Overall, Canadians appeared to be tolerant and respectful of their cultural diversity. Were there ever instances of your being treated unfairly?

AKAHLOUN: Absurdly, the only time I was blatantly discriminated against in Canada was by an American—a U.S. Embassy Marine Security Guard. It was early in the tour, on a Saturday morning. I went to the embassy to retrieve some personal papers. Ahmed, Leila, and I waited outside for a long time. When he unlocked the door, I smiled, apologized for the disturbance, and lightheartedly said he was sleeping on the job. He immediately took offense. "I have better things to do than open the door for you so that you can get something from your office." I thought he was joking and asked if he was serious. "Yes, I am," he said. Then he shouted to Ahmed and Leila to sit down in a corner and wait. When I tried to reason with him, he angrily shoved me. Fortunately, for the guard, Ahmed was unaware of his aggression. I controlled myself and hastily fetched the item. On the way out, I thanked him again, but he completely ignored me.

The next morning, I sent a heated memorandum to the Gunny, the administrative counselor and the regional security officer, demanding an apology. I stated that the sergeant's "insulting, disrespectful, discourteous, and adolescent behavior was not becoming of the proud Marine Corps uniform he wore." Moreover, I wrote, "If he 'cracked' under the pressure of merely unlocking a door for embassy personnel, I seriously questioned his judgment in the event of a terrorist attack." I refrained from reporting him directly to the ambassador because he was still young and immature. Everyone makes mistakes. Nevertheless, he needed to learn how to treat people decently, regardless of skin color. So I lodged a strong complaint but stopped short of notifying the front office.

The next day, Ahmed and I gathered in the administrative counselor's office. The sergeant apologized and defended his actions by saying he mistook me for a Canadian citizen. Dissatisfied with this explanation, I drafted another message. "Regardless of whether or not I was Canadian, it was wrong to behave in such a rude manner. If the sergeant had doubts, he should have requested my identification."

I pointed out that "a painting of my husband's had been raffled off at the Marine House the evening prior to the July 12 distasteful incident. It was dubious that the question of my husband's citizenship or the fact that he was married to an American secretary working at the U.S. Embassy had not surfaced at some point." Ultimately, I recommended he be reprimanded but left everything in the hands of his superiors. The point was emphatically made, and we moved on with our lives. The embassy handled the situation as best as possible, but I was livid over the way the marine insulted and demeaned my family, and I promptly turned into a gladiator. With considerable effort, I later regained my composure and put the ugly episode behind me. For the record, I have the highest regard for the U.S. Marine Security Guards who, throughout my career, have been friendly and supportive.

Q: This was quite unfortunate. Wrapping up, you were in Ottawa three years. You gave us a good sense of what you did at the office and what was happening in the Canadian society. In 1982, you saw and actually participated in a major step forward in setting the UN agenda for the Nairobi conference on women. Leila thrived and your father recuperated from his operations and you got Dr. Getzinger started in his new tenure as Science Counselor. Is there anything else you wish to mention?

AKAHLOUN: Yes. I neglected to point out our pilgrimages to Montreal's St. Joseph's Oratory of Mount Royal, a renowned site for Catholics in search of healing and support. One entire wall of the shrine is covered with crutches and other items left by those who were "miraculously" cured of ailments. I have a special connection with the Oratory. During my first visit at age ten, I had a severe asthma attack. My parents took me to the doctor, but my condition deteriorated. The next day, my asthma disappeared after climbing on my knees the ninety-nine steps reserved for petitioners. Thus far, thank God, it has not returned. Many of my prayers were answered at this shrine. Leila flourished, Ahmed's health improved, and my father healed in record time. After recuperating, he came to Canada, and our first stop was St. Joseph's Oratory. I fondly remember him and Leila walking hand-in-hand to the playground, stopping along the way to pick pretty wildflowers growing in the field. These are treasured memories.

Also, during the assignment, I considered applying for one of the Department's upward mobility programs, which offered employees training opportunities to enhance their skill set in order to assume more challenging roles and opportunities within the State Department. Many Foreign Service officers, including my supervisors, had encouraged me to maximize my potential.

Q: *So the idea was planted some time before. But during this reporting period and this exciting series of events, it became more of a reality.*

AKAHLOUN: Absolutely. When I first met Dr. McClelland, he asked, "You're coming from Tunisia, where you worked in the ambassador's office. Do you feel you are stepping backward by working for me?" An assistant to a science counselor was perceived as less prestigious than being a secretary to the Deputy Chief of Mission, but it was never an issue. My parents and grandparents set a good example for me. They persevered despite adversity, sustained their self-confidence, and clung to their dreams. I was eager to work for Dr. McClelland, excited to take on a more substantive portfolio under him, and elated to be posted in Ottawa near my family in Onset. In November 1981, when the timing seemed right, I submitted my paperwork. Although my application landed on the upper-third of the administrative and personnel register, the program was abruptly cancelled.

Q: *Just before you would have been selected.*

AKAHLOUN: Can you believe it? It was disappointing, but I gave myself a pep talk. "Penny it was not meant to be. Don't be discouraged." My Canadian tour was drawing to a close when my onward assignment as Personnel Assistant in the Office of Civil Rights and Equal Employment Opportunity (M/EEOC) arrived. At the time, I felt somewhat intimidated. But, Dr. Getzinger reassured me. "Penny, don't worry. If the State Department offered you the job, it means you are more than qualified." The position, however, was being established, and no one knew how long the process would take. With that uncertainty, in July 1982, we departed Ottawa for Washington, D.C.

CHAPTER ELEVEN

THE FAST LANE, U-TURNS, AND DETOURS

WASHINGTON, D.C.

The State Department, Office of Civil Rights, and Equal Employment Opportunity (M/EEOC), and Career Development and Assignments, Office of East Asian Pacific Affairs (PER/CDA/EAP), 1982–1989

Because of Canada's proximity to the U.S., the transfer was smooth. Then we suddenly found ourselves on an emotional roller coaster ride. The surprising twists, turns, drops, and loops left us breathless and at times petrified.

Q: Q: After home leave, you traveled to Washington, where you were to work on equal employment issues at the State Department once the job materialized. Tell us what happened next.

AKAHLOUN: In August 1982, I began working temporarily in the executive office of the Bureau of European Affairs. Although the move from Ottawa was relatively flawless, I felt exhausted and drinking tea upset my stomach. One month later, Ahmed took me to see the doctor where I learned I was pregnant—at forty years old! I was utterly bewildered but overjoyed. Once again, the obstetrician recommended bed rest for the beginning stages of the pregnancy. I was at high risk because of my age. We headed for Onset, where my parents devotedly looked after me for three weeks. The Office of Equal Employment Opportunity of Civil Rights (M/EEOC) officially placed me on its roster in December.

Director Andre Navez and the entire office handled me with kid gloves. Back then, having children at the ripe old age of forty was somewhat unique. I napped in the medical unit during lunch break. Almost overnight, my belly ballooned. I suspected it was a precious baby boy, even before the sonogram confirmed it. Omar, which means "life" in Arabic, would be his name. We were thrilled to be having another bundle of joy. As my energy level increased in the second trimester and the pace of work picked up, the forty-five-minute naps became less frequent.

I spoke to Omar in the womb, as I had done with Leila. "Omar, honey, Mommy needs to work until the last moment, so she can spend more time with you later. You can arrive after Friday when Mom goes on maternity leave." Omar was obliging. Saturday morning the onset of delivery began, and by Tuesday, I went into labor. At 2:00 a.m. on Wednesday, June 8, 1983, I woke up Ahmed. "Honey, time to go." It was only a fifteen-minute drive from Buckingham Village in Arlington, Virginia, to George Washington University Hospital in Washington, D.C. Yet sometimes seemingly clear-cut situations can become very complicated. At the hospital, the nurse looked at me and flatly said, "You are not in labor." I was too composed for my own good. Next, a physician examined me. Instead of admitting me, she gave me two choices: take a monstrous pill (not happening) or walk around the block at 3:00 a.m. to induce delivery (and risk a mugging). The whole thing was insane.

Ahmed was enraged, threw his hands in the air, and said, "What type of service is this?" His Mediterranean temper was on the verge of being unleashed. Before he exploded, I said, "Honey, it is fine. We can come back. The drive is not long." So we left. At home, the contractions grew stronger. I practiced a couple of breathing exercises a friend shared six years earlier when Leila was born. Somehow that got me though the next few hours. Then my water broke. Omar wanted out. "Omar, sweetie, you cannot come yet. We must go to the hospital. Be patient." We woke up Leila and took her to the neighbors downstairs on the first floor.

ELEANOR LOPES AKAHLOUN

Reaching the car was a slow, painful process. We climbed down two flights of stairs, walked through the courtyard about a hundred feet, and then crossed the street, where the car was parked. The entire time the urge to push was overwhelming, as Omar was bearing down. Ahmed flew to the hospital. We arrived at 7:00 a.m. The attending nurse said, "We need a urine sample." I headed for the bathroom but stopped midway. In desperation, I said, "No, no. The baby is coming!" Next she said, "Hop up on the table." And then she panicked. "Oh, my god. You are crowning. Hold on!" The nurse summoned the "on-call" obstetrician, and they rushed me into the delivery room.

Omar was born within thirteen minutes of my arrival at the hospital. That's right—thirteen minutes. The delivery went well, and the physician and nurses apologized profusely. Ahmed witnessed the birth and was the first one to cradle Omar in his arms. I was wheeled into the recovery room, where Mother and son became acquainted. He had a tremendous appetite, and I was grateful he was healthy. Afterward, they took him to the nursery. My twenty-six-year-old roommate had a C-section and was still feeling groggy while I was full of life after my natural childbirth. Two hours after delivery, I walked to the nursery to ensure Omar was receiving proper supervision.

Right from the beginning, Leila was an ideal helper and sister. She yearned for a baby brother and earnestly prayed for one. She considered him a gift from above. There was plenty of time to nurse and take things leisurely. This was something I wanted to do with Leila, but six weeks after her delivery we found ourselves in Tunisia. Now I had accrued enough leave to be a proud stay-at-home Mom for a longer period of time. Omar and I observed the Cape Verdean tradition of staying indoors for a month, and then we went to Onset. Everyone fell in love with his cute smile and round "button" nose. Despite being at home for a total of three glorious months, the maternity leave ended far too soon. Back in Washington, I engaged in one of our one-sided conversations. "Sweetie, it is time to think about your future. Who is going to watch you when Mommy returns to work?"

One Sunday morning, Leila, Omar, and I were on our way to mass at the St. Thomas More Cathedral. Silently I thought, "Dear God, we must find someone to babysit Omar; time is running out." Just then, a woman named Maria Sharma passed by with her daughter. Something motivated me to speak with her. I found out she lived in the neighborhood and looked after children. The next day we visited her impeccably clean house, and I noticed she bonded with the two children already in her care.

Omar had a temper tantrum. He screamed and hollered. Maria said, "He's *malcriado* (badly behaved). He never acted up this way before. I suspect it was partly because he was always in my arms, being caressed and nursed. After he calmed down, they connected and the deal was sealed. We became one family. We called Maria "Momma" and her husband "Daddy Sharma." She was born in Brazil, and he was originally from India. He owned the Rajaji Restaurant on Connecticut Avenue near the former Woodley Park Hotel. Their eleven-year-old daughter, Indira, ran errands for us. It was a too-good-to-be true situation. After four months, Momma moved to a house on McKinley Road, seven miles away. I panicked but not Momma. She drove from her house and picked up Omar every morning at 7:20 a.m. sharp and babysat him for a number of years.

She adored him. Sometimes in severe weather Omar spent the evening. Also, while I was training for the Functional Specialization Program (FSP), he periodically slept over. The program was a career development avenue for State Department employees to accomplish their professional goals. Without Momma, it would have been almost impossible for me to simultaneously care for a young child, and fulfill the demanding requirements of the upward mobility program. She was really worth her weight in gold.

Q: Now the State Department's earlier career-enrichment program you had been interested in was cancelled. You worked in the Office of Equal Employment Opportunities and gave birth to your son at age forty. How did you make a conversion in your professional life? Tell us about the mechanics of that?

AKAHLOUN: Well, in 1983, the Department announced it was opening sixteen positions for the newly created Functional Specialization Program (FSP), also known as the Upward Mobility Program. It would offer Civil and Foreign Service specialists the opportunity to switch their primary skill code to one of three areas: personnel (now human resources), budget and fiscal, or general services. Employees accepted into this new program received a yearlong Washington, D.C.–based training that included classroom instruction, on-the-job rotational assignments, and briefings. If successful, the individuals were assigned overseas and after a year of satisfactory performance their skill code was changed, and they climbed up the State Department ranks.

At the time, Omar was less than a month old, and I was thoroughly enjoying my period of hibernation. One day, my career counselor showed up at my door with the Department's announcement. "Penny," she said, "you would be perfect for this. Why don't you apply?" I looked at Omar, snuggling up to my chest, and said, "Omar, not to worry. This is not happening." I thanked Mary for her thoughtful gesture and she left. Two issues held me back. Number one, I am deeply devoted to my children who are my pride and joy. I felt it was premature to leave Omar who deserved the same strong bonding Leila had received. Secondly, my academic base needed strengthening. The timing was off, but my interest persisted.

A year later, Career Development Officer Maria Melchiorre approached me and said, "Penny, I have another assignment for you, which could be career enhancing—a personnel technician in Career Development and Assignments, Office of East Asian Pacific Affairs (PER/CDA/EAP). This was a job in the Human Resources Bureau (HR), formerly the Personnel Bureau. Maria was my guardian angel. She is yet another illustration of the value of sisterhood and the importance of women helping, encouraging, and supporting each other as they navigate the workforce. Thankfully, I transferred into the new position. The other technician in the office was Shirley Wilson who quickly became a lifelong friend. There were thirteen technicians (seven Civil Service and six Foreign Service) who had responsibility for over ten thousand Foreign Service employees. Each technician handled approximately twenty-five to thirty overseas posts and fifteen bureau divisions.

We supplied technical advice and guidance to Foreign Service personnel going overseas and initiated their travel documents, including home leave and separate maintenance orders. We also answered post queries on employee entitlements. For the functional bureaus within the Department, we processed various personnel actions: leave without pay, return to duty, extensions, and separations. During the day, there were countless interruptions. There was always a backlog. On weekends we came into the office to catch up on our filing. We spent considerable time resolving problems and conflicts between what the employees wanted and what the State Department dictated.

Allow me to give you an example. One case involved an individual who was departing Washington, D.C., for Bangkok within twenty-four hours. Suddenly, the employee's life turned upside down. Her medical clearance was revoked. Because her apartment was already rented, she was living in temporary quarters. In desperation, she turned to me for help as clients trusted and confided in their technicians. After an extensive search of the regulations, I found an obscure Foreign Service grant that allowed her some financial assistance. Outcomes such as this one were gratifying.

In preparation for my career move, it was necessary to develop a strategic plan. The first step involved formal training at the Foreign Service Institute (FSI). I took writing, speed-reading, and speech dynamics classes. During my periodic absences, my colleague Shirley Wilson covered for me. Office Manager Specialist Carolyn Lee was also tremendously helpful. These two wonderful ladies were a pillar of strength to me, and I am truly indebted to them. The second element was honing my speaking skills by briefing junior officers and secretaries at their respective orientation sessions about the role of personnel technicians. The third part of the strategy was keeping abreast of current events. This sounds simple, but free time was a luxury. Family and work commitments consumed my days and nights and left little energy for pursuing other activities. The final phase was selecting someone to mentor and coach me.

There is an interesting story behind my tutor, a labor/political officer whom I worked with in Tunisia. He and his superior openly bickered. One day, Mr. King, my supervisor, passed by my desk and noticed I was working on a document for the officer. He asked, "Penny, what on earth are you doing?" I replied, "Jerry asked me to type this paper for him." "What?" he said, "Show it to me?" I replied, "Sir, with all due respect, I cannot. This is a confidential matter. Trust me. I would never do anything unethical or damaging to you or the Department. I am just trying to be helpful." He angrily walked away. While the specifics have fallen through the cracks, I know whatever I was working on at the time required utmost secrecy. The officer I was loyal to came back a few years later and assisted me. By chance, we met again in Washington. We spoke about my interest in the program, and he volunteered to help. So I met him for lunch regularly. During these mentoring sessions, we discussed domestic and international political, economic, and social events. You see, when Mary Kincaid showed up with the Functional Specialization Program (FSP) announcement in 1983, I was not emotionally, physically, or intellectually prepared to undertake the journey. Now, I felt more self-assured and motivated to move forward.

Q: *So you had the benefit of a new plan called the Functional Specialization Program. You had to adapt it to your own lifestyle and the scarcity of time. You were clever enough to find the resources needed, even though time was not ample. What was the procedure?*

AKAHLOUN: Foreign Service applicants submitted an SF-171, showing pertinent experience in one of their chosen administrative specialties. Awards, language scores, and dates of medical clearances were listed. The latest performance appraisal report and a one-page statement, explaining your interest and what you hoped to accomplish, were included. Each applicant was ranked against certain qualifying factors: analytical, planning and organizing, oral and written communication, and problem-solving skills. I handed in the package in the fall of 1985 and prayed. Sometime later, I was invited to the Oral Assessment Center. My intuition told me, "Penny, you need to get a sense of what the test site is like."

The day before the exam, I took the shuttle bus to Rosslyn. I told the receptionist the truth—I was terrified of taking the orals and wondered if it was possible to see the testing area. She was very obliging. "Sure, go ahead," she said. It was late in the afternoon, so the rooms were empty. I saw everything, especially where the examiners sat. This eliminated tremendous stress.

No expense was spared to improve my chances. I went out and purchased a woolen suit for $126 that happened to break the bank. In 1986, this was an extravagant sum of money for us, but the sophisticated gray tweed outfit was a great investment. I also wore a frilly white blouse, black-and-white heels, and classy jewelry. Looking professional boosted my self-esteem.

On exam day, something significant occurred. I carried a black leather briefcase with shoulder straps. It doubled as my handbag. For good luck, I tucked a small bible inside. When I opened it, my eyes immediately fell on a powerful message: "Fear not, for I am with you. Do not be dismayed. I am your God. I will strengthen you; I will help you; I will uphold you with my victorious right hand" (Isaiah 40:10). This was no accident. I believe by heavenly design the scripture was there to comfort me.

As for the test, the first portion was a written forty-five minute exercise. I chose to write about the pros and cons of imposing international trade barriers. It was very technical, but my experience overseas as well as my mentoring sessions adequately prepared me. I knew the subject matter but was very slow in getting the facts down on paper. Time ran out. Turning in a paper three-quarters finished at the outset of any examination is catastrophic. I hoped the assessors would be lenient and not severely penalize me for an incomplete essay. I kept positive and focused on round two—the orals.

As I entered the room, three poker-faced men stared at me. Fortunately, they thawed out as the interview progressed. They asked me about my interests, academic background, and accomplishments which made me stand out from the rest of my high school or college classmates. The probing questions were designed to determine motivational, leadership, and social skills. When asked what prompted me to switch careers, I stated, "It would provide a better opportunity to positively contribute. As a Foreign Service Personnel Officer, I intend to foster closer cooperation between Americans and Foreign Service Nationals, be sensitive to everyone's needs and impartially resolve conflicts. By building a strong team spirit, employees would be happier and more vested in the U.S. Embassy's goals." My answer was well-rehearsed.

After an hour or so, they said, "Well, this segment is over." I was taken aback and blurted out, "Oh, is that all?" They smiled. The lead examiner asked, "Would you like more questions?" Instantly, I regained my composure and said, "No, no, thank you very much." The final section was the planning/organizing and analytical skills test, the "in-basket," which everyone cringed at taking. It was dreadful.

Here is the scenario. Each of us pretended to be a newly arrived junior officer at an embassy, but we were leaving town in three days. There was ninety minutes to go through stacks of paper, prioritize them, and decide who should be assigned what and the course of action recommended. In other words, we had to sort out a multitude of thorny issues and schedule appropriate follow-up meetings with embassy personnel upon our return. Later, I was surprised to learn my score on this section was a 95. On April 7, one day after my forty-third birthday, Career Mobility accepted me into the program. Classes began July 21, 1986.

Q: What took place during that one-year of training?

AKAHLOUN: The program was rigorous. We began by formulating action plans, took the Myers-Briggs Type Indicator test, analyzed our skills, practiced time and stress management techniques, identified professional development barriers, learned to give positive feedback, and to deal with criticism. Daily logs and monthly reports were submitted. Once a month we gave talks to our classmates on self-selected topics. All of our activities were graded in the form of quarterly performance reports. We interned in various State Department bureaus as well as other foreign affairs agencies, including the U.S. Information Agency (USIA), the Agency for International Development (AID), and the Office of Personnel Management (OPM). These rotational assignments varied in length. I worked eight weeks in the Office of Foreign Service Personnel (PER/FSN). Most days, it was like being in a pressure cooker, but the intensive training proved beneficial. Among other things, we learned to view problems through multiple lenses. We became "critical thinkers."

Q: You were already employed by the State Department, but your status needed to be changed. You passed an exam, completed your training, and now had to be tenured. How did this work?

AKAHLOUN: For Foreign Service employees, it was mandatory to go overseas in order to receive the new skill code. Failure to comply resulted in automatic withdrawal from the program. Thankfully, I had successfully completed all of the program's coursework and internships and was now ready for an overseas assignment. The end was in sight, or so I thought. Only our medical clearances were pending. While undergoing my physical, I was visualizing a life beyond briefings, rotational assignments, speeches, and reports. My days of rising as early as 4:00 a.m. to study for my courses and then prepare myself and the children for school would soon be history.

Meanwhile, my classmates chose me to deliver the graduation speech. Families, friends, the Foreign Service Director General, and other officials assembled on the eighth floor of the State Department's Ben Franklin Room on June 26, 1987. During the ceremony, I remember Omar fidgeting, removing his suit jacket and kicking off his shoes. He was bored stiff and quite restless, which was predictable for an active four-year-old child. His father and sister were making huge efforts to restrain him.

In my heartfelt remarks, I thanked everyone for their support and encouragement and spoke about three categories of people. "The first group went out and made things happen, the second sat back and just watched things happen, while the third group didn't know anything was happening." I commented that the audience belonged to the action group, and I urged them to continue believing in us. We were matching forward triumphantly and were determined to be shining examples of what Career Mobility embodied. In reality, however, I wasn't certain of going anyplace. My fate was up in the air. A few days prior to graduation, the Medical Unit placed a hold on our clearances while awaiting further test results. Shortly thereafter, we received the earth-shattering news. Ahmed and I had flunked our exams, and we could not be assigned abroad. My career plans of advancement were disintegrating right before my eyes. I was devastated.

Q: You passed a number of medical clearances prior to that, correct? So this was pure bad luck.

AKAHLOUN: It certainly was, and I was in a state of shock. My life flashed before me. I was forty-four with twenty-two years of government service in the Philippines, Morocco, Kenya, Tunisia, Canada, and numerous assignments in Washington, D.C. Despite this experience, without an overseas posting and subsequent shift in job function, I would remain a secretary earning grade-four pay indefinitely. Again, I thought about my husband of eighteen years and our two children, ages four and nine. I had sacrificed too much, come too far, fought too hard to give up now. I desperately wanted a better life for them and a more challenging career for myself. Where there is a will, there is a way. Defeat was not an option.

Two days later, I met with an agitated Career Mobility director. She chose strong language to express her dissatisfaction with me and said in no uncertain terms I was being dropped from the program immediately. I quietly remarked that this was unfortunate, considering the thousands of dollars the State Department had invested in me. I asked if she objected to my speaking to Ambassador William Lacy Swing, the Director General of the Foreign Service, before taking decisive action. She fumed and fussed but consented. I knew Ambassador Swing when he headed the Office of Career Development and Assignments, and I was a personnel technician. A couple of times, he received complimentary messages about my work and went out of his way to congratulate me. I requested an appointment to discuss a "personal and private matter," and he readily agreed to see me.

Ambassador Swing listened sympathetically. He agreed it was a waste of resources to terminate me. "What do you propose we do?" he asked. I responded, "Sir, there is a workable solution. A vacant classification management specialist position exists in the Office of Foreign Service Personnel (PER/FSN). I can occupy it while waiting for the medical clearances to come through." I explained that I had recently finished a lengthy rotation in the office and was familiar with the work. The position, however, was Civil Service and needed to be converted to Foreign Service. I stressed the assignment would be a win/win situation for everyone. With his concurrence, I was willing to speak to the office director. He smiled and said, "Okay, Penny. Go for it." I gave him a big hug. Prompt action was necessary to prevent Career Mobility from squashing my plan. Through creative thinking and flexible decision-making, I joined PER/FSN as one of four position classification management specialists in July 1987. I was very lucky.

Back in our apartment, Leila and Omar were sharing a tiny bedroom where Omar practiced the daredevil sport of diving from his crib onto Leila's bed. An exceptional real estate agent, who turned into a wonderful friend, Miki Markoff, found a condominium for us in Springfield, Virginia that enabled us to move out of our congested two-bedroom apartment. I shared my thoughts with Leila about the new place. "Princess, now you and your brother will have separate bedrooms. We have a washer and dryer, and we will no longer need to walk two blocks to the Laundromat." Full of wisdom, she said, "Mommy, they weren't problems, they were just challenges." Today, that pep talk still resonates with me. The children were enrolled at Rolling Valley Elementary School, and Ahmed began working at a nearby Holiday Inn as a night auditor.

Nevertheless, I was anxious to go overseas and serve as a Foreign Service officer—something I had strategically set my sights on, spent many grueling months training for, and overcoming nearly insurmountable obstacles. Here I was in limbo; stuck with a temporary stateside position and on the verge of being released from the program unless our medical clearances were received. One way of boosting my morale was to recall an inspirational speech I once delivered where the Chinese language was able to provide positive reinforcement. I showed the audience the word crisis, which is composed of two Chinese characters. Separate them and one represented danger and the other stood for opportunity. Reflecting on this changed my perspective, and I became more optimistic.

Q: *What type of work were you doing?*

AKAHLOUN: The office advised our missions on complex Foreign Service National position classification and personnel management issues. I briefed the audit teams that performed wage/salary surveys and analyzed and classified American Embassy positions. These sessions familiarized me with the "survey world" and boosted my public-speaking skills. My geographic area covered twenty-one countries, eight major agencies, and several smaller ones, which employed about four thousand Foreign Service nationals. I primarily covered Central and South American posts but occasionally various Caribbean and African missions were added. When I entered the office, a new worldwide category of workers was being created—the Personal Service Contract (PSC) employees. Thousands of them had been previously contracted by embassy commissary associations at different grades and benefits. Standardizing their positions required a monumental effort.

My supervisor was a former Foreign Service officer who converted to Civil Service. Some of his people skills were wanting, but we got along fairly well. There was some office tension between Civil Service and Foreign Service employees. My officemate had a slight air of superiority and was unhappy sharing her workspace. One day, I was eating lunch at my desk. With an offensive tone of voice, she said, "Penny, you're slurping. Can you drink that without making a lot of noise? It bothers me." That was a wake-up call for me. From then on, I watched my back.

Q: Were you curious as to what the teams did at the other end in Latin America?

AKAHLOUN: Positively. One was going out to Guatemala, but my boss prevented me from accompanying them. This made no sense. The auditors needed extra help, and the experience would give me a clearer picture of the overseas operation. Some battles are worth fighting, and this one fell into that category. In confidence, I spoke with a contact in the executive office of the Western Hemisphere Bureau (now Bureau of Inter-American Affairs, ARA/EX). She suggested speaking to the director, which I did. He rejected the idea because of the expense involved. He was thinking numbers. So I decided to "fight fire with fire." I crunched some figures, showing the amount of work a third person could accomplish verses two people and how much time and money would be saved. I presented the information to him and kept a low profile. Shortly thereafter, my supervisor announced I was joining the team for two weeks. And that is how I became an enthusiastic member of the Guatemalan survey team. Fortunately, there were no serious reprisals when I returned. Aida Castellanos, the post's de facto personnel officer, dispatched a cable to Washington thanking the Department for my input. Ultimately, my boss wrote me a decent efficiency report.

After what seemed an eternity, the nightmare ended. The medical clearances came through, and my status was no longer in jeopardy. I was assigned to Montevideo, Uruguay as a Regional Personnel Officer. The welcomed news lifted a heavy burden from our shoulders. The move would rid Ahmed of the punishing night auditor job at Holiday Inn. Additionally, commuting to work overseas would be far less tiresome. Once we moved to Springfield, I woke up before sunrise, prepared breakfast, got Leila ready for school, took Omar to the day care center, and drove seven miles to the "commuter line." There I waited for anyone destined for downtown Washington, D.C., to pick me up. Drivers needed at least three passengers to use the express lane. After being dropped off at Constitution Avenue, I trekked up the hill to my office at Fourteenth and K Streets. This was my routine for two years.

The scripture that sustained me through this trying time was Isaiah 40:31–"Those who wait on the Lord shall renew their strength; they shall mount up with wings like eagles, they shall run and not be weary, they shall walk and not faint." Although I was virtually worn-out, I had no intention of collapsing.

CHAPTER TWELVE

THE NEVER ENDING ROLLER COASTER OF LIFE

URUGUAY, 1989–1993

My struggle to balance lifelong career aspirations and family life finally seemed attainable. I was a Regional Personnel Officer overseas and seemed to be on a nice merry-go-round ride, at least for a while. Then I had to hop off.

Q: When did you transfer from the U.S. to Uruguay?

AKAHLOUN: We arrived mid-July 1989. Montevideo, the capital, was cold and damp, but we had packed twelve suitcases filled with ample winter clothing. Thankfully, this time around, the political situation was much less volatile than it was during our first tour.

Q: What were some of the major issues at the embassy at the time?

AKAHLOUN: The country was suffering from rampant inflation. We immediately began conducting private sector wage and salary surveys. Although we were not paying the salaries of the national employees in U.S. dollars (done when countries are experiencing hyperinflation and major economic turmoil), inflation was accelerating. Montevideo's rate was around 120 percent and peaked the following year at roughly nine points higher. Washington listened to our appeals and granted a salary increase. Paraguay suffered from similar circumstances. Although based in Uruguay, I managed the human resources program for both countries.

The embassy in Montevideo had approximately 260 employees (61 Americans and 199 Foreign Service Nationals and contract workers) plus five agencies. In Asuncion, there was a combined 135 American and local employees and eight agencies. Paraguay had the distinction of being the smuggling capital of the world. Presently, it is still the hub in the global illegal trade of drugs, weapons, fake clothing and handbags, pirated DVDs, counterfeit electronic gadgets, and other goods that are easily purchased for remarkably low prices. Authorities turn a blind eye, and the market continues to boom.

Our second Uruguayan tour surpassed our first assignment there. As Regional Personnel Officer, the work was more stimulating and challenging. I felt I was making more of a contribution to the embassy and advancing my career at the same time. Moreover, I was grateful that the State Department retained me on its Career Mobility rolls. Uruguay was a small country conducive to raising a family. Leila was twelve years old, and Omar just turned seven. During the first visit, Ahmed's art career prospered, we savored Rio's carnival, celebrated New Year's Eve on the beaches of Ipanema, and experienced other memorable events. The second time, however, was more satisfying because we were deriving pleasure from the world of parenthood.

Q: You were in the country from 1989 to 1993 and continued to work in the personnel field. Did your status change during this time?

AKAHLOUN: Indeed. The conversion took place in July 1990, and I became a Foreign Service Specialist. Another highlight that year was President George H. W. Bush Sr.'s visit in December. He was embarking on a five-nation trip to Latin American to gain support for the Persian Gulf War led by the U.S. in response to Iraq's invasion and annexation of Kuwait. President Bush also was promoting his Enterprise for the Americas Initiative (EAI), a plan to open up trade and investment in the region.

Weeks before his arrival, Embassy Montevideo mobilized in preparation for the presidential visit. Survey, pre-advance, and advance teams descended on us. I was assigned assorted tasks, including medical control officer, which meant coordinating with the staff of the White House physicians. The goal was to locate the best hospitals and doctors and formulate a "minute-by-minute" medical emergency contingency plan for the president. I found that the Uruguayan doctors were competent, but the hospitals lacked proper equipment, and so the White House modified their plans accordingly. Meanwhile, Ahmed interpreted for the White House Communication Agency. At the end of the trip, the team rewarded him with a beautifully framed certificate of appreciation. President Bush was sincere, likeable, and accommodating. At the embassy, he posed with nearly thirty-five youngsters and teenagers. Somehow, Leila landed in the middle of the pack with Bush's hands resting on her shoulders. I have the photo to prove it, plus another one, showing Omar's head peeking out from behind President Bush's coattails.

Q: How did Leila and Omar adapt to their new environment? What were some of their activities? And what about your husband?

AKAHLOUN: Thank God, the children adjusted nicely. Our house was a block from the Uruguayan–American School (UAS), so we had many opportunities to participate in their scholastic activities. Both of them attended the school's gymnastic program and later competed against the Uruguayans. Leila won silver on the balance beam and two bronze medals for the floor exercise. Omar was invited to join one of Uruguay's national clubs. According to his coach, although he was the youngest member of the team, he had more potential than many of the older gymnasts. Our house and yard turned into a gymnasium. After work one day, I drove into our driveway and Omar greeted me on the front lawn. "Hi, Mom, how are you? How was your day?" "What are you doing, sweetie?" I asked. "Oh, nothing much," he answered. But throughout this conversation, he was upside down practicing a headstand with straight legs and feet and toes pointed to the sky. It was an effort coaxing him into the house for dinner.

A year after we arrived, he took piano lessons, as his sister had done in the U.S. He received a *sobresaliente* (outstanding) grade on his very first exam. Professor Niño, his piano teacher, who was well into her eighties, deserved a prize for her endurance. Omar was a less-than-eager student. His Cub Scout activities engaged him somewhat, but his real passion was sports. Each year, he won the school's field day races for his age group. The teacher was hard pressed to convince his classmates to participate. "What's the use, Omar's going to win again," they said. These were happy occasions, but there were unpleasant ones as well. One in particular involved Omar's accident with our dog.

This is what happened. Against my better judgment, we acquired a rather rambunctious German Sheppard named Abdul. One day, Omar and the puppy were playing in the backyard, and Abdul accidently clawed him. Leila discovered him in the bedroom, concealing his bloody face. Ahmed phoned me to say they were rushing him to the British Hospital. At that very moment, I was walking out of the office to consult with the doctors at the hospital concerning President Bush's forthcoming visit. When I arrived, big sister was comforting her brother and carrying a tote bag filled with water and snacks. She had the situation well under control. I could not have done a better job. We waited two hours for the plastic surgeon who mended Omar's cheek (sixteen or so tiny stitches). Throughout the procedure, Leila was by his side, holding his hand. Suffice it to say, the dog was promptly given away.

As for Leila's activities, she was the volleyball and handball team captain. She also played softball and basketball and won several trophies, but one escaped her—"athlete of the year." She never stopped dreaming until she acquired that one as well. The same diligence applied to her academic studies. Her sophomore year, she was inducted into the National Honor Society. As a member of the Uruguayan-American School's Knowledge Bowl team, she went to Chile, and we tagged along. What a great trip. She also was an International Thespian and participated in an acting and poetry competition held in Bolivia.

The transition for Ahmed was more uneven. The negative effects of drinking exerted an emotional toll on him and the family. After struggling to regain his equilibrium, he eventually was successful and worked at the embassy as a mail room supervisor and a courier escort. He also painted and found side jobs translating French and Arabic documents. As mentioned, he served as an interpreter during President Bush's visit and volunteered for the school's yearly International Day fair. Students flocked to his display booth to learn about the Moroccan culture. Young and old were mesmerized by his tales and his manner of dress—a camel-hair djellaba, black cape, embroidered turban and his signature piece, a curved, silver dagger.

Another fulfilling activity which defined our time there was my involvement in establishing an English-speaking Catholic Church. This deserves explaining. At an official function, Monsignor Paul Gallagher, a British-born *nuncio* (ambassador) representing the Mission of the Holy See in Uruguay, asked me to join his committee. The Dutch Ambassador and the U.S. Embassy's information officer were already recruited. I was more than content attending the local Spanish masses at the cathedral, but he convinced me that my calling was to assist him build a church.

We moved heaven and earth, and soon thirty people began attending Sunday mass at the Christian Brothers' Stella Maris School. (As a footnote, the survivors of the rugby team's plane crash in the High Andes in 1972 were graduates of Stella Maris.) Father Gallagher was replaced by Monsignor Joseph Marino who became a family confidante. I was a Sunday school teacher and one of the church lectors. At one point, I organized a Christmas play, which leads me to the point that a diplomat's life is not a bed of roses. We are definitely not exempt from life's hardships. Thieves targeted homes belonging to foreigners with the expectation that they would find valuables and electronics not readily available on the Uruguayan market.

One dark, stormy evening, Ahmed drove us to a play rehearsal and then went back home. Once he arrived, he could not open the front door. So he walked around to the back entrance. When he entered the kitchen, he heard a tremendous crash and realized the house was being burglarized. He stunned the robbers who smashed a window in the den and fled. They stole a television, a silver teapot, and some goblets. In their haste, they left a bag filled with valuables, including our sterling silverware. It was frightening because the criminals could have attacked Ahmed.

One year later, another home invasion nearly ended my life. It was a warm, breezy summer afternoon and a gorgeous day for an outing. So we went for a drive. Returning home, we noticed an opened bedroom window. Upon entering, we discovered missing items and called the Gunny, who lived across the street. He came running over brandishing his weapon ready to shoot the bad guys who had already fled. We summoned the police. Two hours later—probably more—a policeman arrived on his bicycle. Ahmed let him inside, but I was puttering around in the back bedrooms and was unaware of our visitor. As I walked toward the front of the house, I saw a gun pointing at my face. I threw my hands in the air and said, *Para, yo soy la dueña de la casa!* (Stop, I am the owner of the house!) The officer thought I was the intruder and was ready to pull the trigger.

Q: That's a pretty close call. By now, you must have been entertaining thoughts of your own onward assignment.

AKAHLOUN: After Uruguay, State Department protocol dictated I be assigned to a hardship post, but many of them had no high schools, which meant Leila would be sent to boarding school for her junior and senior years. This was a no-brainer as we wanted her as close as possible for as long as possible. China looked promising, but I had reservations about the Beijing International School (ISB), which thus far had only graduated ten high school students. Dr. Bentz, the head of the Department's Office of Overseas Schools, informed me Leila could supplement her education by taking extension courses, but he felt ISB's standards were high. Also, a deputy personnel officer position was becoming available, which would be a step up career-wise. As time passed, the thought of moving to China became more appealing because of the disturbing events taking place at the office in Montevideo.

Sadly, my relationship with my supervisor in Uruguay, the administrative counselor, deteriorated. The man was extremely intelligent, charming, and witty. Yet he suffered mood swings. Although he primarily operated with a "closed-door" policy, we communicated fairly well for nearly two years. He could be very intimidating, and several employees came to my office in tears, complaining about his harsh treatment. Many found it difficult to work with him. During my time at the embassy, one Foreign Service officer retired prematurely and another one lodged a formal complaint with the employee relations office in Washington, D.C., over the poor performance evaluation he had received.

Our dealings turned sour over a position classification incident. The ambassador wanted his political assistant's position upgraded. After a desk audit, I asked for more information. My boss was annoyed and said, "Just do it." However, the duties did not warrant a higher grade.

ELEANOR LOPES AKAHLOUN

I was not willing to compromise my principles or lose my creditability. Communication was then severed. After meeting with the ambassador, he himself produced a five-page justification that resulted in the position's legitimate upgrade. The administrative counselor gave me an awful evaluation—the worst one of my life. Despite everything, he never reduced me to tears.

As much as possible, I tried to keep a positive outlook. From past experience, I knew hard times did not last forever, and it was possible to pull through even in the most dreadful circumstances. Faith, family, and friends upheld me. When things overheated at the embassy in Montevideo, I flew to Paraguay and scheduled meetings there for spells of one to two weeks. I maintained my sense of humor and put things into perspective. Life's journey has many bumps, roadblocks, and detours, especially for Foreign Service personnel. Our lifestyle imposes undue stress and strain. We need to learn new languages, cope with cultural differences, different food, climate, medical conditions, crime . . .

Q: There are people who become accustomed to these drawbacks, and we call them Foreign Service officers.

AKAHLOUN: Happily, most individuals in the Foreign Service adjust nicely, but there are exceptions. Initially, Ahmed was very upset about the situation, but I insisted that his personal relationship should not be negatively impacted. The same applied to Leila and Omar. They were to be polite and respectful. I was opposed to raising embittered children. For my fiftieth birthday, on April 6, 1993, I asked for a day of annual leave, but the request was denied. Instead, the family brought flowers and balloons to the office, and we went to lunch and celebrated. They were intent on making the event a happy one, and they succeeded. Unfortunately, a month later on Mother's Day, Ahmed fell sick.

We were departing in seven weeks for home leave in the U.S. followed by our onward assignment to China. After church, Father Marino came to the house. He and Ahmed enjoyed many intellectual and humorous discussions together, involving international political, economic, and social issues. They seemed to resolve all the world's crises. I asked him to drop by, because Ahmed was doubling over with pain, and I thought Father Marino's presence would surely cheer him up. When Ahmed failed to get better, I then called Dr. Jorge Stanton

Jr., the embassy's medical adviser who suggested hospitalization. Ahmed was admitted and required further tests. After a few days, his condition was still not improving and Dr. Stanham recommended a medical evacuation to the U.S. I trusted his judgment, as he was a competent, caring physician, and a loyal friend.

As for Leila and Omar, it was the end of the school year, and the calendar was crammed with recitals, banquets, and other activities. Leila was also studying for her final exams. It was essential that their routine continue. Luckily, they were well-adjusted, thoughtful, and considerate. Multiple families offered to care for them. Leila made the final decision, and we agreed with her choice. This is another plus factor for the Foreign Service, when tragedy strikes, families rally around each other. I accompanied Ahmed back to the U.S. and then returned to Montevideo to pack out.

Back in Montevideo, I closely monitored his situation. In between the many school activities, we packed boxes. We did the best we could under very trying circumstances. When I worried and began to despair, Leila and Omar filled my days with joy and laughter. There were also many individuals who spread sunshine and good cheer. I cherish the many inspirational words and caring deeds of Dr. Stanham, Father Marino, Juan Luis and family, Juanita Snyder, Renate and Patricia Regules, Cynthia Farrell Johnson, Linda and Bruce Pearson and their sons, Rick Gray, Perla Bimson—my personnel assistant, and Rico—an embassy chauffeur. The list is long.

In retrospect, Uruguay was a fruitful assignment. The children acquired an academic and spiritual base. They became fluent in Spanish, played sports, earned various medals and awards, and showed signs of becoming reasonable and responsible adults. Leila passed her finals and finished the school year on the honor roll. As for religious activities, Omar made his first Holy Communion and became an altar boy. Leila received her confirmation and was a church lector.

As for Ahmed, he was well-liked. He dazzled the Uruguayan-American School with his Moroccan presentations and endeared himself to the community with his humorous stories and warm heartedness. I received a skill code change, a promotion to FS-3, and helped set up a church community. There was much to be thankful for, but it was a bittersweet departure. My husband and partner was missing.

ELEANOR LOPES AKAHLOUN

We left Montevideo the evening of July 3, 1993. The airport terminal was very crowded, but the administrative counselor, who had shunned me for well over a year, spotted me. Incredibly, he walked over, smiled, and gave me a big hug. Then he spoke. "Pen, good luck to you." He might have said something else, but I was shell-shocked and honestly cannot remember the entire conversation. I wished him and his family the best. And I meant it. I wasn't harboring a grudge. Living abroad we make scores of small and big adjustments every day. The pressure of work, the loss of routine, doing without favorite things, and other inconveniences over a period of time can have adverse effects. Most people cope well and others find it more traumatic. Each of us has at least one grain of goodness inside. Perhaps this was his attempt at making amends before we parted ways. Who knows? We are all unique and motivated by different forces. But at that moment, my primary thoughts were focused on my husband and children and the unknowns that lay ahead. We boarded the plane and literally took off into a world of uncertainty.

We landed in Washington on July 4 in the middle of a record-breaking heat wave. Temperatures, reminiscent of steamy Paraguay, soared to 110 degrees Fahrenheit. It was a scorcher. I deposited Leila and Omar at the Riverside Inn and dashed to the hospital. Ahmed was upbeat, but his lifestyle of heavy drinking and smoking had taxed his body and damaged key organs. The following day, the children visited him. Uppermost in his mind was their welfare. He thought it was best for them to go to China, and I wholeheartedly agreed. It was the hardest, most heart-wrenching decision of my life.

After our stay in Washington, D.C., we left for Massachusetts. It was great to be in the company of my family and friends and have the opportunity to spend quality time with them again. Before departing for China, we spoke on the telephone. Ahmed said, "I'll be with the kids in spirit. Take good care of them." "Don't worry," I responded, "I will call you from China. I love you." His last words were, "Okay, honey."

En route to the Far East, we stopped off in San Francisco. The following day, we flew to Tokyo, which took around eleven hours. After a six-hour layover, we proceeded to Beijing (Peking then) and landed with our twelve suitcases at 9:00 p.m. It was a long, grueling, and tiresome journey.

CHAPTER THIRTEEN

EXPLORING
THE MIDDLE KINGDOM

CHINA, 1993–1998

We pushed forward determined to make the best of a dismal situation. Thankfully, a powerful energy from above surrounded and protected us. Our five years in the Middle Kingdom turned out to be a treasure trove of adventure and awe-inspiring experiences.

Q: China has undergone incredible growth in recent years. You were there at the beginning of this expansion. What was your reaction when you arrived?

AKAHLOUN: That evening on Wednesday, August 25, 1993, it was hot and muggy. The heavily polluted air contained a peculiar aroma, which smelled like burnt rubber. This was caused by the pervasive burning of high-sulfur soft coal. We used the old two-lane airport road with signs in Chinese characters, reminding us of the foreign world we had just stepped into.

Our U.S. Embassy designated sponsor, an individual or family responsible for helping newly arrived personnel settle in, met us at the airport and drove us to our new residence, Sanlitun 2-1-42. We reached there around midnight and were greeted by armies of cockroaches, scampering everywhere. It was overwhelming. The roaches were coming from a favorite hangout—the kitchen garbage chute. We later taped it up to prevent the critters from further invading the apartment. I looked at Leila. Leila looked at me. And Omar stared at both of us. As convincingly as possible, I said, "It's going to be all right, kids." The refrigerator contained a meager supply of food and no water. And none of the beds were made. I politely thanked the sponsor who was hurriedly backing out of the doorway, as he apologized for his wife's "no-show." Alone, in a filthy apartment, I wondered what I had gotten myself into.

The next morning, I briefly went to the embassy and met the wife who interrupted her work just long enough to take me grocery shopping. She was knowledgeable, however, and introduced us to Aiyi, our domestic helper. When I returned home, Leila and Omar excitedly greeted me and led me to the kitchen window. What did I see? A Moroccan flag! The Moroccan Embassy was across the street. We sensed Ahmed was with us in spirit.

The Chinese government confined foreigners to diplomatic housing compounds. Sanlitun was the smallest one with two six-story buildings. We were the only American diplomats living there. It was less-than-glamorous living. No grass or flowers, just cement, and a bare minimum of anemic trees out back. Omar and his buddies played all their games on concrete. Newfound friends—Peter La Montagne, an embassy economic officer, and his wife, Lynn—lived about three blocks away in a separate Sanlitun area. In other sections of the city, there were three fifteen-story apartment complexes—Ta Yuan, Qijiayuan and Jianguomenwai—where more American diplomats and expatriates resided. All of these compounds shared one thing in common—gate guards who locked up Chinese domestics without proper identification. It was normal for westerners, especially journalists, to be shadowed. Most of the officers were also under surveillance. Our apartment was likely bugged, as when it rained we heard static emanating from the walls. That seemed to be a dead giveaway. Listening devices were probably planted everywhere.

Whenever we left our diplomatic compound, it was an adventure. There were two entrances, each with Chinese security guards. When we first arrived, they were undisciplined and exercised little discretion. Frequently, the guardhouse door was left open, and we saw more than was necessary. I covered Omar's eyes to shield him from the female visitors and inappropriate posters on the walls. My image of Chinese guards being regimented and vigilant was shattered. A few months later, the authorities did some housekeeping. They substituted the unruly guards for more professional ones and banned extracurricular activities.

That first afternoon we ventured out and explored our neighborhood. China is a fascinating place for "people watching." We sat at the corner of a wide boulevard and saw a parade of humanity. The sights were mind-boggling. A man with no more than an ounce of flesh on his skeleton peddled a flatbed tricycle laden with an oversized set of living room furniture. The sofa and love seats were piled high. Under all that weight, it was surprising he remained upright.

Security cameras were suspended from tall traffic light poles. The road was about six lanes wide. Two or three of them were saturated with bicycles. At the time, bikes outnumbered cars. It appeared one out of every third person was riding them. The other lanes were reserved for taxi cabs, buses, trucks, and cars. We saw some horse-drawn carts and men pushing wheelbarrows. They usually removed the debris from the *hutongs,* ancient neighborhoods, which were being demolished. Beijing was a study in contrasts. There was also a man on a tricycle, presumably heading to market, hauling a pig. Its pink body swayed, its feet dangled, and its lifeless eyes bulged. This is no exaggeration.

Q: Interesting. What happened next?

AKAHLOUN: An ancient Chinese proverb says, "An invisible red thread connects those that are destined to meet, regardless of time, place, or circumstance. The thread may stretch or tangle, but it never breaks." This is very true. The first order of business was to get the children established in school. On August 27, 1993, we attended the International School of Beijing's (ISB) orientation. After roll call, a stranger shouted, "Are you Penny Akahloun?" I thought, "Am I hearing voices? Who knows me here in China?" A woman approached me and said, "I've been looking for you." I asked, "Have we met before?" She replied, "No, but I met a friend of yours, Susan Pizarro, your American neighbor in Uruguay. My name is Marion Hird." I was astonished. The world is such a small place. Susan and I worked together at the embassy, and her daughter, Suzy, and Leila were classmates. After their tour in Uruguay, the family was reassigned to Hong Kong.

It was difficult to overlook Marion Hird's kindness. She was an easy person to like, and we became fast friends. At the time, Kraft

Foods was transferring her husband, Bill Hird, to China to open a dairy factory. She was now taking a solo trip to scout out the place, and Susan Pizarro happen to be on the same flight. They began chatting, and Marion confided she was anxious about uprooting her youngest daughter, Jennifer who was entering the eleventh grade. Susan laughed. "I know someone assigned to Beijing, Penny Akahloun. Her daughter is at the same grade level. My Suzy and Leila were friends. Jennifer will love Leila." From that moment, Marion was on the lookout for me.

Inconceivably, the Hirds moved into Capital Mansions, a skyscraper fifty stories tall and less than three-quarters of a mile away. In a city of ten million people, what are the chances we would end up as neighbors? Jennifer and Leila bonded and are still best friends and so are their moms. It sounds like fiction, but this is actually what occurred.

The next day, we visited Tiananmen Square, located in the heart of Beijing and a fair distance from our compound. The exact date was Saturday, August 28, 1993. It was somewhat of a bold move as we spoke no Chinese and the average Chinese lacked English. I was unable to do any studying in Washington because the classes conflicted with the International School of Beijing's schedule. My priority was to ensure the kids were registered on time and properly situated. The embassy gave newcomers flash cards, such as *Trouble Giving Directions? Need to Place a Call? Let these cards do the Talking for You,* which contained basic phrases, numbers, and places of interest. We also had a map. That was it. Leila was the sign language interpreter and navigator, and she did an excellent job getting us safely to and from the iconic square.

The sheer vastness of Tiananmen Square was the first thing that struck me. It seemed to dwarf the surrounding buildings, even the Great Hall of the People and the Mao Mausoleum. From the adjacent monuments and memorials, you had a sense of the country's communist past. Visiting the Forbidden City, which was the imperial palace during the Ming and Qing Dynasties, you came away with a deep appreciation of ancient China. Witnessing all of this was both a somber and awesome experience. It was like stepping back in time but still being connected to the present.

Many things raced through my mind. I thought about the 1989 student uprisings. The brutal crackdown, the army killing hundreds in the square and thousands throughout Beijing, tanks crushing the demonstrators, and the tragedy of it all. Unbelievably, we were standing at the same place. It was an eerie, edgy feeling. There were many cameras trained on the square, and the People's Liberation Army (PLA) soldiers and undercover agents were on patrol. A few people gingerly strolled around. By then, the government had succeeded in publicly erasing the incident. Throughout my tour, people never talked about the event. It still is a politically sensitive issue.

While taking in the sights, a strange sensation of Ahmed swept over me. I had a premonition that something was wrong. Returning home, I phoned him, but there was no answer. Next, I called my friend Carolyn Lee, who was keeping an eye on him, but she could not be reached either. Finally, I spoke with my parents who had nothing new to report. It was a gut-wrenching feeling. I was overcome by a sense of emptiness and of being swallowed up by darkness. I knew something profound had happened. Our spirits had been tied together for twenty-four years. Neither time nor distance could alter that.

Early Sunday morning, Carolyn phoned and told me about Ahmed's passing. She said she had visited him the previous evening. He was very peaceful and told her to tell Leila and Omar he loved them. Jokingly he added, "You don't have to tell Penny, she knows that already." The timing coincided with my strange emotions at Tiananmen Square. I shared the devastating news with the children, and together we attended mass at the Philippine Embassy to pray for his soul and to ask for strength to carry on. During the service, the priest spoke about St. Augustine's trials and tribulations. This is exactly what he said, "We must walk and sing and stand up, as St. Augustine did. Let us keep walking and go from good to better. The dead will live in the light and in our hearts." The powerful message moved me to tears. Ahmed was absent physically but not spiritually.

For the sake of not further distressing the children, I grieved in solitude. While we would not forget the past, we would move forward. Brighter days were ahead of us, and we needed to claim them. At that point, returning to the U.S. was impossible—Leila and Omar were beginning school the very next day. We were without domestic help, and I had not worked a full day at the embassy.

Two days later, Aiyi came on board. I liked her. She was perky, smiled a lot, and connected with Leila and Omar. Aiyi was the first and only domestic helper I hired throughout the tour. She kept the household functioning, especially during our whirlwind entry into

China. Nevertheless, there was one drawback. Like many maids expats preferred to hire, she was not affiliated with the government's Diplomatic Service Bureau (DSB), a branch of China's Ministry of Foreign Affairs, and therefore worked for us "unofficially."

In the meantime, we received many greeting cards and letters of condolence—mostly from Montevideo. Here is an illustration of how Ahmed shaped the lives of others. A political officer wrote that until he had met Ahmed, he was "prejudiced against Arabs," mainly because he had "never known any." He went on to say that Ahmed was "a genuinely good person, as well as being one of the funniest guys I ever met. As a result, I have had to rethink a lot of things. I treasure my lunches with my special friend . . . He always had some witty observation to make about the latest current events." The messages were heartwarming.

Eventually, I had to go back to Washington, D.C., and tend to affairs related to Ahmed's passing. Leila was fifteen and Omar was ten. Leaving them behind was sheer torture. I did so only after consulting with teachers and school officials and was reassured a safety net was in place. Once they settled down, I made my move and left for Washington on September 26, 1993, one month after arriving in Beijing. The two of them remained alone in the apartment with Leila supervising, but their teachers periodically checked on them.

Stateside my dear friends, Carolyn Lee, Miki Markoff, Lois Gore-Thompson, and Beatrice Beyer provided tremendous support. The most agonizing task was informing the family in Morocco of Ahmed's passing. His mother, Momma Habiba, was overcome with grief. News of this magnitude is best communicated personally, yet I had no choice other than conveying the message over the phone. A voice deep within me said, "Take the kids to Morocco soon." After two weeks, I wrapped up administrative matters and flew back to Beijing.

While I was away, Leila and Omar fared well. Years later, I discovered a letter written by Leila to my mother. "Mom is in the states now, and I am in charge. It's a lot of responsibility, but I can handle it . . . we have four hours of homework per night . . . going to Kobe, Japan, in October for a volleyball tournament (where she ended up bringing home an "All Star" trophy) . . . and the Netherlands for the Hague's Model United Nations (MUN) conference next year . . . I like studying Chinese and practicing with Aiyi." The international baccalaureate curriculum at the International School of Beijing (ISB) was grueling, but it ended up being a great decision to enroll them there. They received a fantastic education in China.

I want to digress somewhat and give you some school history, as it exemplifies China's fast-paced growth. In the early seventies, the U.S. Liaison Office in Beijing, a precursor to the U.S. Embassy, began what was called "The Little Red Schoolhouse," wedged in the hallway of the Sanlitun diplomatic apartment compound. That first school had eight students and two certified teachers. In 1980, the U.S. merged its school with the British and Australian Embassies. The Canadians and New Zealanders joined in. These five nations officially founded the International School of Beijing which was now located on U.S. Embassy grounds. Gradually, children from other embassies enrolled, and China's Ministry of Foreign Affairs in 1988 officially registered ISB as a "school for diplomatic children." The campus then moved to the Lido complex of offices and housing units and began accepting applications from Beijing's expatriate community.

When we arrived in 1993, the school's enrollment was approximately six hundred students, and it already had a waiting list of five hundred. The school board continuously drafted expansion plans to accommodate the backlog. Each year, enrollment dramatically increased. After we left China, the growth spurt continued. A sprawling, thirty-two-acre state-of-the-art campus was opened in 2002 in Beijing's Shunyi District. According to State Department statistics, at the beginning of the 2013–2014 school year, enrollment was 1,884. Just extraordinary.

Q: *Tell us about your home life in China. Were there many non-Diplomatic Service Bureau (DSB) domestics?*

AKAHLOUN: The practice of hiring them was becoming widespread. They were being employed by both diplomats and the business community. In other words, my situation was not unusual. The independent workers kept all the money they earned, while Diplomatic Service Bureau employees were obliged to pay some of their salary to the government. Before entering the housing compounds, all Chinese nationals needed to show DSB documentation to the guards posted outside the housing units.

Aiyi and I were cautious. We took necessary precautions, but the situation was volatile. Occasionally, she zipped past the guard on her own. Most of the time, I met her at the gate and led her inside without any complications. Periodically, however, the authorities clamped down and conducted aggressive identification checks. Then, it was potentially dangerous, because undocumented employees were hauled away and imprisoned. Their families also suffered harsh consequences.

Before Aiyi arrived in the morning, I usually looked out the kitchen window and counted the number of guards. If I spotted too many of them or anything suspicious, I walked to the corner and waved her away. She then circled the block until it was clear. If she noticed the Diplomatic Service Bureau's crackdown before I did, she phoned, "Bu shi, bu shi." That meant she could not enter the compound. It was a cat-and-mouse game. Living in a communist regime with strict government regulations, governing every aspect of life, was not painless. We both were nervous. Sometimes the surveillance lasted over a month. Most of the time, it was less. Whether she worked a complete week or not, and generally she did, I paid her a full salary. She was very loyal.

Q: You were without Chinese language training. How did you communicate?

AKAHLOUN: We communicated through our friend, Peter La Montagne, who spoke fluent Mandarin Chinese. Leila and Omar were studying the language and helped out as well. Every day, Aiyi and I would link arms and walk up four flights of stairs to the apartment. We counted the steps in Chinese and English. We laughed at each other's pronunciations, especially mine. Who knows what terrible things tumbled out of my mouth? When we tired of the numbers game, we moved on to other topics. Not much progress was made, but we sure had fun. Aiyi made friends with the maid across the hall who kept a watchful eye on us. One time I was ill, and she brought over some herb tea that helped considerably. I found the average Chinese to be friendly. In our neighborhood, they greeted us with a polite *ni hao* (hello). Family members, particularly the elderly and the children, were highly valued.

We were in China during a colossal period of transformation. The ancient and the new seemed to collide. Because of the country's giant leaps toward advancement, Beijing was swiftly losing its old world charm. Some of its rich heritage was being sacrificed. At the time, China was taking enormous steps to become a major international player.

In 1993, banners reading "China-the-Home-of-the-2000-Olympic Games" were hanging everywhere. That year it lost its bid, but the campaign continued and the effort eventually paid off. China hosted the 2008 Olympics, which were sensational.

While these Olympics were being held, Brian Williams, the anchor and managing editor of NBC *Nightly News*, featured Beijing's popular Family Li's Restaurant on one of his programs. This brought back special memories as we once dined there. The history behind the private restaurant is fascinating. The owner, Mr. Li Shan Ling, is a retired applied mathematics professor. His great-grandfather was a steward in charge of Life Affairs for the Imperial Court of the Qing Dynasty (1644–1911) and oversaw the running of the Imperial household and collected recipes from the palace chefs.

Mr. Li, apparently, became fond of cooking as a child, watching his father create dishes and studying his recipes. During the Cultural Revolution in the sixties, Professor Li was barred from working and began cooking for his family. Although the Red Guards destroyed the Imperial recipes, over time, he was able to recreate and record them. There are no signs posted at the entrance of this unassuming restaurant, and each meal is different. All of the relatives help plan the menu, shop for fresh ingredients at the market, and prepare the food served to about ten guests. It is a unique dining experience.

As for our Sanlitun neighborhood, at first it was very quiet. When the restaurants closed at 7:00 p.m. or earlier, the place was deserted and very dark. There was a cluster of diplomatic missions in the vicinity. Morocco, Mauritania, the Philippines, Germany, North Korea, and other countries were represented. Outside the embassies, the Chinese military guards stood at attention on top of white-and-red stripped boxes. Omar entertained them with his acrobatic pop-a-wheelie bicycle stunts. As a result, his bike sustained terrible beatings. It was repaired by a sympathetic elderly man at the street corner with an assortment of oddly shaped rusty tools. For twenty-five cents, the bike was fixed up as though it were brand-new. Because Omar endeared himself to the owner and his son, generally, the repairs were free.

At the public park, people practiced *taijiquan* (tai chi) and other traditional forms of exercise. Barbers, dressed in spotless white coats, cut their clients' hair, and shaved their beards in the open air. Business was booming. Toddlers wore traditional *kaidangku* (open-crotch or split pants). We saw children squatting and relieving themselves in public places. I understand now the tradition continues in the countryside. In cities, such as Beijing, Shanghai, or Guangzhou, disposable diapers are more popular.

A few blocks away, there was a grim-looking Friendship Store owned by the state, which originally catered to diplomats, the foreign business community, and tourists. When we arrived in 1993, the Foreign Exchange Certificate (FEC) was the only currency the *laowai* (foreigners) could legally use in China. The government sold FEC at roughly 20 percent more than the value of the local currency, Renminbi Yuan (RMB). Only designated restaurants and shops accepted our FECs. This discrimination against expatriats was frustrating. Street money changers were doing brisk business exchanging FECs for RMBs. Secret deals were done in dark alleys or behind closed curtains as both foreigners and Chinese nervously looked over their shoulders to see if the authorities were watching. They both risked prison time. Things started to get a bit out of hand, as a black market was sweeping the country. In 1994, the Chinese government began permitting foreigners to use local currency under limited conditions and finally phased out the certificates in 1995. The diplomatic community and all the expatriates rejoiced.

Every morning I heard a loud and proud rooster crowing in our backyard. At first, it woke me up before dawn. Soon, thankfully, it blended in with the other background noises from the open-air market across the street. The State Department's post report on China had recommended bringing a year's supply of canned goods. I was glad there was no time to heed the advice. A variety of cheap fresh vegetables were readily available. The post report could not keep pace with China's runaway development.

I loved our unconventional Sanlitun market. It was jam-packed with vibrant shoppers, bikes, three-wheeled carts, and mobs of happy children, wearing blue jogging outfits, yellow scarves, and matching baseball caps. They gleefully swarmed all around the cart selling deep-fried skewered frogs. My preferred street snack was the *jian bing*, a crepelike pancake stuffed with fried eggs, green onions, coriander, and chili sauce. Another favorite was the mouthwatering sweet potatoes that were roasted wintertime in an enormous metal drum. The process filled the cold and dry air with a pleasing aroma.

At the market, the vendors usually wore gray or blue Mao suits and caps. About a year or so later, they ditched their traditional clothes and switched to sport slacks, shirts, jackets, and leather shoes. The swift transformation was astounding. The merchants were generally pleasant to deal with, but they drove hard bargains. I took up the challenge and developed a strategy of my own.

Leila introduced me to a folk hero named Lei Feng, a soldier of the People's Liberation Army of China, who went around helping the poor and doing incredible deeds of good service. Every Chinese was flattered to be associated with such a selfless and modest person. When hassling with stubborn vendors, I smiled and repeatedly said, *Ni She Lei Feng* (loosely translated, you are a hero) to soften them up. The expression awakened their revolutionary spirit, and the prices were generally lowered. But I did not stop there. I learned how to count in Chinese and carried a purse-size scale with a hook attached to the end. I owned three of these prized possessions. One of our embassy translators gave me the first one—an antique—but it served the purpose. Before long, I upgraded. My star performer was a bright yellow one with a fancy calculator on the back. After negotiating the price, out came my instrument, and the vendors speedily dropped more fruits or vegetables into the bag. It was quite a source of entertainment.

I was fast becoming fond of the Chinese culture and the way of life. Initially, I rode the embassy shuttle to work. In less than six months, I purchased a Flying Pigeon, the Cadillac of Chinese bikes, sturdily built and easy to maneuver. Like the Chinese, I wore a white cotton mask to block out some of the pollution and rode my bicycle everywhere. I owned several of them because they quickly turned gray. Going to work, I rode through the neighborhood *hutong* and saw early risers going to the communal showers and brushing their teeth at the public fountain.

In the afternoon, the courtyard filled up with children and the elderly who sat under trees, playing mahjong or watching their caged songbirds. Women washed clothes and hung them out to dry. During winter, piles of cabbage and compressed coal used for heating and cooking were stacked against the walls. These smoky coal fires heavily contributed to China's pollution.

During the course of our tour in China, several thousand hutongs were flattened. Even the protected ones are being bulldozed and replaced by multistory, apartment, and commercial centers. An undisclosed number of them were destroyed to make room for the 2008 Olympics. Chinese authorities claim they are overcrowded, unsanitary, and pose a fire hazard. Many houses lack plumbing and have no way of putting out fires, but the reality is they were occupying prime urban real estate. Meanwhile, the demolition continues and some of China's legacy is being lost. Sadly, treasured memories of an older generation are vanishing.

Q: *All for the sake of modernization. During your assignment, you witnessed this expansion. Can you elaborate on this?*

AKAHLOUN: As I keep emphasizing, the high-speed growth was phenomenal. The average Beijing household income doubled between 1993 and 1995. When we arrived, China had roughly 1.2 billion people. Ten million of them were in Beijing. As of early 2014, the country's population had increased to approximately 1.39 billion. This level of growth is staggering.

The Chinese loved the U.S. fast-food culture. In April 1992, the largest McDonald's in the world opened on the southern end of Wangfujing near Tiananmen Square. We ate there frequently; its size overwhelmed us. The restaurant had seven hundred seats and twenty-nine cashiers and reportedly served forty thousand customers on its first day of business. By summer of 1994, it was a landmark. Despite having a twenty-year lease with the Beijing municipality, the building was torn down after two years to make way for a $1.5 billion shopping housing and office complex.

China's push for a socialist market economy had some disadvantages. My friends and I frequently visited Beijing's notorious Panjiayuan dirt market, a huge area for selling and collecting Chinese handicrafts and antiques. It was enormous and delightfully chaotic. It reminded me more of a festival than a flea market. Sunday morning we woke up at 4:00 a.m. to get there before the bustling crowds arrived. The vendors unceremoniously spread out their wares on the bare ground or on threadbare blankets. Items including paintings, jewelry, ceramics, teapots, ethnic clothing, and paper lanterns were sold. Ming- and Qing-style furniture, old pipes, and opium scales and relics from the Great Cultural Revolution were also displayed. All kinds of trinkets or treasures could be bought there. You had to be especially alert when buying antiques. Some of them were deliberately dented or painted to resemble originals. Even the dealers were fooled.

I purchased porcelain ginger jars and several Laughing Buddha statues for my collection. When bargaining, I first decided if I really wanted the item. If so, how much was I willing to pay? I usually offered 25 to 50 percent of the amount asked and then started haggling over the price. Sometimes the strategy worked. Other times, it didn't. In this case, I was not afraid to walk away. After the market was displaced, the earthy atmosphere vanished.

The same thing happened at Hong Qiao near the northern gate of the Temple of Heaven, which was a rustic bazaar with nearly fifty tiny shops. Once again, everything conceivable was sold. It had a tin roof, a dirt floor, and plenty of dust. No heat. Throngs of people elbowed their way through the narrow circular passageway. It was enchanting. Then, in 1995, all the merchants were forced into a large building with several floors and stalls. The basement contained a fish market, and the upper section was reserved for antiques and a pearl market. This was primarily the Chinese government's way of imposing taxes to sustain the economic boom. However, the move and subsequent events turned out to be momentous.

One of my responsibilities was scheduling shopping excursions for members of congressional delegations (CODELs) and other high-profile visitors who wanted to purchase quality Chinese goods, particularly jewelry. Marion Hird knew a "pearl lady," who was selling superior earrings, necklaces, and other merchandise at reasonable prices. Off we went to Hong Qiao to see her and arrange for private showings. The rest is history. Visitors raved about their exquisite purchases, and the word spread. Thereafter, I became the vendor's point of contact and set up appointments for official embassy parties, including President Clinton's entourage in 1998.

Q: Let's switch gears and discuss your professional life. What was the office setup?

AKAHLOUN: In the personnel section, there were two officers (my supervisor and I) and three part-time intermittent or temporary (PIT) personnel assistants who were American spouses. There were also two Chinese nationals. The administrative section consisted of two Foreign Service officers, an American secretary and two Chinese translators/ interpreters. We supported four consulates (Guangzhou, Shanghai,

ELEANOR LOPES AKAHLOUN

Chengdu, and Shenyang), the Embassy Ulaanbaatar in Mongolia, and eleven agencies in Beijing. By 1997, China wide there was some three hundred Americans and 550 Chinese employees. As the Deputy Personnel Officer, I supervised one American PIT and our two Chinese employees. I was the point person in our everyday dealings with the Diplomatic Service Bureau (DSB).

I screened, hired, and trained Chinese personnel, helped renew labor contract agreements, and monitored Chinese compliance. Managing the American and Chinese incentive awards program for our posts was also part of my responsibilities. Every year I revised my job description to reflect the growing complexity of the work and to incorporate steps that would lead to the mission's long-term objective of converting Chinese employees to Foreign Service Nationals.

Prior to my 1993 arrival, the embassy routinely accepted the Diplomatic Service Bureau's candidates even though more desirable ones were locally available. The Chinese government lacked a large pool of professional, English-speaking candidates because Chinese college graduates preferred to work in the private sector for higher salaries. The principle of the public sector competing with its own market economy was a totally new concept for China. Some frustrated U.S. officials were sidestepping the bureau and finding their own applicants. This created pandemonium. My office began implementing tougher screening measures and pressed for more qualified candidates. The less skilled ones were rejected. Another big complaint was the alarming turnover rate of employees. Oftentimes, they were pulled after being fully trained by us and sent abroad to work at Chinese diplomatic missions overseas. As a result, our office operated in a constant crisis/training mode.

Q: The Chinese wanted to select people, both in the chancery and domestically who worked for the Americans. Was there concern about the loyalty of these individuals? Presumably, the foreign employees were overtly reporting to their government on what was going on inside. How did you handle this?

AKAHLOUN: We assumed the Chinese employees were obliged to report to their government on U.S. Embassy activities and exercised extreme caution. For instance, two nationals worked for me and whenever I gave one of them a personal gift it was done secretly and very discretely. I wrote a note. We could not speak openly because the walls had ears. The Chinese held in-house Saturday training for the employees and charged the U.S. government overtime for these special sessions. This practice was later discontinued when we negotiated the 1996 DSB labor service contract.

We kept classified information in storage containers located behind a cipher-locked door, leading to the offices of my supervisor and the rest of the American administrative team. The bulk of the sensitive documents and equipment were safeguarded at San-Ban, the main chancery. The administrative offices at our Ar-Ban complex posed less of a threat. Nevertheless, Chinese nationals were escorted back into the section where our safes were located. My office was outside this restricted area, but I had several bar-lock cabinets of my own. My Chinese personnel assistants were opposite me and shared a room with two or three other DSB employees. Outside my window, there was a great view of the popular Silk Alley market. People, taxies, and pedicabs clogged the narrow entrance way. The area was full of intrigue.

We had to shield our Chinese employees to retain them and keep them functioning in a constructive manner. If they knew too much, it would be an ethical dilemma. It was problematic, but we did our best not to become too paranoid. We were friendly and encouraging yet vigilant. Our antennas were always up so we were minutely and intimately aware of our surroundings. Because of exposure to various cultures, Foreign Service personnel operate with a sixth sense, so perhaps finding a balance was less complicated than it sounds. Yet it was not easy. Let's just say, we were contending with a dysfunctional environment.

China's "propaganda machine" worked flawlessly. The Diplomatic Service Bureau sponsored various events for foreign diplomats and their families. We were taken on cultural outings to see ancient shrines and temples and invited to elaborate banquets. At the events, there were "lucky draws." It didn't take much luck to win; everyone went home with a prize. One time the Chinese invited the diplomatic community to a Karaoke night. There were plenty of refreshments, prizes, and games. Omar, age ten, entered a sack race with the U.S. Embassy interpreter, Mr. Zhang, who was at least forty-five. As Omar neared the finish line, Mr. Zhang strove to overtake him and embarrassingly fell flat on his face. In China, you never ridiculed anyone when mistakes were made. So I congratulated him on his fine accomplishment of nearly winning the race. The gatherings were useful in raising my cultural awareness and helping me better understand my Chinese government contacts.

Although there was no time to take Chinese lessons either in Washington or in Beijing, somehow things worked out. My supervisor spoke the language, and the embassy's Chinese interpreters were proficient in English. My DSB counterpart was also fluent in English, and the director, Mr. Wang, and I conversed in rusty French. Our personalities meshed, but he clashed with my boss. Some of the bickering involved Chinese grade levels, salaries, and length of training periods.

On one occasion we hired an individual during my supervisor's absence, and when she returned, she was livid. The Diplomatic Service Bureau had proposed several applicants to fill my personnel assistant position, which was vacant at that time for three months. At last, a perfect candidate surfaced, but contrary to the wishes of my boss, the DSB asked for an abbreviated training period at a grade eight, step-three level. We were given one last chance to hire the individual. I consulted with the administrative counselor, who decided to bring her on board. The next day, I received an inflammatory message from my supervisor. "DSB took you for a ride . . . she better be good." A few minutes later, she barged into my office and said, "Okay, Penny, we are hiring her, but you will have three months to fully train her. If she doesn't meet the standards, she's out the door."

Now the excitement began. My new Chinese assistant and I had the herculean task of studying two voluminous Foreign Service Institute Position Classification Management manuals within an absurd time frame. The task was important because it laid the foundation for revamping the way Chinese employees were to be contracted by the U.S. government. I speak more about this topic later. For the moment, I drew up a lesson plan and gave her daily assignments. Most mornings we devoted one or two hours reviewing the evening's homework. She was bright and enthusiastic and read each lesson three times—first to get the overall view, second for context, and third to highlight relevant points. We never discussed details, but the personnel assistant sensed the urgency of her becoming a classification expert overnight. Around 2002, we accidentally met at the Foggy Bottom metro station in Washington, D.C. She had just finished formal training at the Foreign Service Institute (FSI) and received a 98 percent—the highest grade earned by any Foreign Service National. The Chinese employees at the

U.S. Embassy and I developed mutual respect for one another, and we worked well together.

Part of my job was managing the American Employees' Evaluation Reports (EER) program for Beijing. One memorable dilemma involved a Foreign Service officer's performance evaluation that appeared to be biased. Because I feared it would adversely impact on his career and the officer might be sent home prematurely, I spoke with his superiors. One of them was the Deputy Chief of Mission whose decision making was seldom questioned. Ultimately, the report was forwarded to Washington without being modified. However, I was able to facilitate a transfer to another section, and the employee and his family happily completed their Beijing tour.

Q: Were you involved in many of the high profile visits to China?

AKAHLOUN: Over time, I became increasingly occupied with these VIP trips. China was being flooded with senior executives from the banking and business communities and key U.S. government policymakers. For the latter group, we labored around the clock. Our visitors required hotels, transportation, press arrangements and much more. They received the full treatment. For example, in March 1997, Vice President Al Gore overlapped with U.S. House Speaker Newt Gingrich and then Congressman Bill Shuster arrived—three high level visits in the space of two weeks. At the time, at least 20 percent of Congress had visited China. One objective of the visits was to promote trade between the two countries. The U.S. was trying to influence the Chinese to open up more markets for American goods and services.

During a 1994 Warren Christopher visit, I was among the Americans on the tarmac at the airport coordinating his departure. While waiting for his motorcade to arrive, I was invited on board the secretary's jet— the refurbished Air Force One plane formerly used by President John F. Kennedy. That was a special treat. That same year, Bill Clinton and Al Gore introduced our federal agencies to the Internet. In October 1994, I sent my first email at age fifty-one. For me, this was a major breakthrough.

During President Clinton's 1998 visit, he stayed at Beijing's historic Diaoyutai State Guest House, a complex of houses and gardens reserved for visiting foreign dignitaries and provincial government officials. I was detailed to the presidential motorcade, ensuring cars and people passed security checkpoints and arrived at their designated villas. I also organized the bazaar, where Clinton and his entourage shopped. When he entered the room, he asked, "Is this the staff office?" I replied, "Yes, Mr. President. Welcome to China. The embassy has been working very hard on your visit." He smiled, shook my hand, and thanked us. At one point, Chelsea Clinton approached me and briefly chatted. She was poised, friendly, and sincere. The Clintons seemed to have done a fine job raising her.

The next day at a "meet and greet" function for families, I introduced Omar by saying, "Mr. President, I met you at Diaoyutai. This is my son." He smiled and gave Omar a vigorous handshake. There was also an opportunity to attend the official welcome ceremony at Tiananmen Square where President Jiang Zemin and Clinton reviewed the troops. There was a huge fanfare. The nine-day, five-city extravaganza included stops in Xian, Beijing, Shanghai, Guilin, and Hong Kong. In Beijing alone, we set up at least seven control rooms for the president and his massive entourage.

Q: Your assignment in Beijing was longer than average. What motivated you to stay?

AKAHLOUN: My initial two-year assignment was extended to five years, which is unusual in the Foreign Service. Despite many difficulties, I remained in China from 1993 to 1998. I did so primarily because the work was satisfying, and I wanted to give Leila and Omar a sense of relative stability. Another reason was to forge ahead with Washington's goal of converting Chinese employees to Foreign Service National status. Moreover, Americans were earning a 10 percent hardship differential over their base salary to compensate for harsh living conditions, such as being under constant surveillance and breathing contaminated air.

To elaborate a bit more on the health issue, the embassy's medical unit, capably run by Dr. Tom Yun, watched over our well-being. Some emergency medical care was also available at the International Asia Emergency Assistance Clinic that treated expatriates. However, given the general lack of quality care at the time, life-threatening cases or those involving urgent attention required a medical evacuation to Singapore or Hong Kong.

To summarize, Beijing was definitely challenging. In order to survive, it was necessary to be adept at bridging cultural divides. We were continuously bombarded by diverse scenarios and coping with them required deep commitment and a tremendous sense of humor. Some days were emotionally and physically draining, but I relished the challenges and welcomed the opportunity to make a difference in Sino-U.S. relations in a small way.

Q: You obviously enjoyed living in China. Apparently, your decision to take the assignment was a good one. When did you send Leila to Washington for college? How intensive was the admissions process?

AKAHLOUN: She left in 1995. "Operation Leila Goes to College" was a full-time endeavor during her junior and senior years in high school. I was on a mission and spared no effort to reach the finish line. At one point, I spoke to former Massachusetts Senator John Kerry (now U.S. Secretary of State) who was visiting China. Since his child was attending college, he was aware of the financial burden imposed on parents. He was very kind and sympathetic and offered positive feedback. Ultimately, Leila received some private scholarships and applied for federal loans. Eventually, she opted to attend Georgetown University in Washington, D.C.

Leila and twenty-five other seniors graduated from the International School of Beijing that summer. Marion Hird, Becky Yun, and I elaborately decorated the stage of the Kempinski Hotel where the commencement was held. Days later, she departed China for Uruguay via Tokyo, New York, and Brazil. An intimidating trip for a youngster of seventeen, but when we left Uruguay, I promised she would return for her former classmates' graduation.

Before she went off to college, we went sightseeing as much as possible. One event is worth sharing. Most of our trips went according to plan, except for the very first one. That was sheer madness. Over the Christmas break, we were traveling to Guangzhou and Hong Kong. We departed on December 27, 1993, and returned January 4 of the following year. En route to the Beijing International Airport, I discovered a dreadful mistake. I foolishly took Ahmed's passport instead of mine. It was too late to turn back—we would miss our flight. So we went forward.

At the airport, we amazingly passed through four checkpoints, boarded the plane, and arrived in Guangzhou three hours later. The city was muggy, congested, and severely polluted. We shed our bulky winter coats, haggled with the cab driver, and rushed to the American Consulate at the Pearl River Delta. Because of the horrendous traffic jams, we arrived late. I left Leila and Omar at our hotel room under the care of the Community Liaison Officer (CLO) and spoke with a consular officer tasked with assisting Americans in China. He was not too excited to see me and said it was impossible to obtain a new passport before closing time as the cashier had already left. Besides, passport pictures were needed. All valid arguments, but I persisted. He finally checked with his supervisor who agreed to issue the document.

The embassy was closing in thirty minutes, but the photo shops were already shut down for the evening. Finally, one accommodated me and reopened. That was an expensive proposition. I returned and waved the pictures in the consular officer's face. He issued the passport but reminded me that a Chinese visa was necessary before boarding tomorrow's 10:00 a.m. train to Hong Kong. That evening we put our worries aside and enjoyed a delicious buffet dinner at the White Swan Hotel's lavish courtyard restaurant. The view was marvelous—a four-story waterfall, flowing from a colorfully lit pagoda. There were lots of tropical flowers and plants and brightly lit bridges that crisscrossed over pools of crystal clear water filled with gold fish. The twenty-nine-story hotel was pure opulence.

The next morning we boarded the hotel shuttle to the train station. All went well until we reached the fourth checkpoint. Immigration authorities motioned us aside. We waited forty-five minutes not knowing our fate. Then a polite English-speaking official appeared and said I could not leave Guangzhou without a Chinese visa, but Leila and Omar were able to travel. The train was leaving in five minutes, which necessitated a split-second decision. What a dilemma.

The children were anxiously looking forward to their Christmas vacation, and I hated to disappoint them. "Leila, honey, what should I do? Can you handle this?" Her eyes sparkled, and she instantly said, "We can do it, Mom." Omar agreed. I trusted their judgment. Hong Kong and U.S. dollars, passports, luggage, and contact information were hurriedly exchanged with instructions to take a cab directly to our booked hotel. The U.S. Consulate's Hong Kong address was written in

Chinese for the taxi driver. We hugged and kissed one another amidst assurances that Mom would join them shortly.

Despite the heroic efforts of the consulate general's Chinese administrative assistant to help me obtain a visa, we received the run around. Guangzhou's Foreign Affairs Office (FAO) referred us to the Bureau of Security, which sent us back to FAO. We were going no place fast. I requested Beijing to overnight express my diplomatic passport. Meanwhile, I phoned the children who had been in contact with the Pizarro's, our friends from Uruguay now living in Hong Kong. I was exceptionally proud of Leila and Omar. We had been in China four months, and there they were handling the passing of their father with fortitude and overcoming the many hurdles of living in Beijing with admirable determination and maturity.

After two sleepless nights, my passport arrived. The clock was ticking. It was now 4:00 p.m. on December 30, and there was still one major obstacle. During the holiday season, all methods of transportation were booked solid. I sought advice from the administrative officer. As luck would have it, his colleague was planning to take an overnight ferry to Hong Kong at 9:00 p.m. that evening. The next thing I knew I was in a taxi with the officer and her two friends, heading for the pier. We shared a crowded lower-deck berth with Chinese passengers, which turned out to be quite an unforgettable experience.

We docked at Kowloon at 6:00 a.m. Custom formalities were quick and efficient. I hopped on the Star Ferry and soon reached the Hong Kong side. Upon arriving at the hotel, I was shocked to learn that my babies had spent three nights in a red light district! No one warned me. The consulate assured me the area was safe and popular with visitors. I wonder who gave them this recommendation. My children earn high marks for coping with the unconventional experiences I have afforded them.

Thanks to the Pizarro family, we saw a great deal of Hong Kong, which sparkled over the Christmas holidays. New Year's Eve we feasted at an all-you-can-eat Mongolian restaurant then crossed Victoria Harbor on the Star Ferry, which cost practically nothing. It was only a ten-minute ride from Hong Kong Island to Kowloon, but the view was utterly spectacular. Dozens of skyscrapers were lit up. The exteriors of the towering structures were decorated with brilliant lights, some of which changed colors every few seconds. A jolly Santa Claus, dashing reindeers, greeting cards, enormous Christmas trees, twinkling snowflakes, and other motifs illuminated the skyline. The reflection of countless lights danced on the water. It was dazzling.

We returned to Guangzhou on Sunday, January 2, 1994. The train was clean and comfortable. White lace curtains covered the windows. During the two-hour journey, I struck up a conversation with a friendly Chinese Malaysian businessman. After noticing my rosary, he quietly informed me that he was a third-generation Catholic. We bonded over our shared religious beliefs. Upon arriving, his chauffeur drove us to our hotel. We rode in style—a big shiny, black Mercedes. Our journey home was almost as eventful as the one to Hong Kong.

Q: I think this has the making of another Akahloun adventure.

AKAHLOUN: Well, Embassy Beijing was having trouble with its VS-100 computers, and I fool heartedly volunteered to carry back one hundred pounds of sensitive equipment that had to be in sight at all times. A driver, systems analyst, interpreter, two kids, and I escorted our excess baggage to the airport. There we were told that the heavy pouch could only accompany us on board the aircraft if we purchased a ticket for it. That was hurdle number one. What a stir. Meanwhile, a thick fog rolled in, and all air traffic was suspended. After a seven-hour delay, our flight departure was announced. Since the embassy staff had long departed, we were essentially on our own and at the mercy of the airlines. After some arm-wrestling, the ground crew carried the computer hardware into the cabin for us.

We landed in Beijing at 9:00 p.m., and the pouch was off-loaded and placed on a dolly. Now, at least, it could be pushed. There was, however, a slight complication. There were no elevators to be found. I told Leila and Omar to go ahead and wait for me at the baggage claim section while I walked down a long ramp that mysteriously led me to the departure lounge. I was completely turned around. Fortunately, there was a diplomatic assistance counter nearby. I frantically showed an agent a picture of Leila and Omar and asked him to search for my lost children. After an agonizing twenty minutes, he returned and said he was unable to locate them. Sensing my desperation, he escorted me to the arrival section of the airport. Outside in the parking lot, I spotted a waiting embassy van. After hastily leaving the pouch with the driver, I began combing every inch of the terminal for my missing babies. What a tremendous relief to find Leila and Omar. Happily, the nightmare was over.

The next excursions were far less stressful. In March, we visited the Great Wall of Jinshanling (Golden Mountain). Leila and I were absolutely thrilled. We counted to three and touched the wall simultaneously. Actually, there are many parts to the Great Wall. It is a succession of fortifications that wriggle their way, like a gigantic dragon, along mountain ridges and passes. The wall was built over two thousand years ago to defend the Middle Kingdom from Mongol invaders on horseback. The exact length is unknown because portions of the wall have almost disappeared due to natural and human destruction. The four sections we visited were an incredible sight to behold.

The following month, April 1994, we went on an adventure of a lifetime. We journeyed to Mongolia, the land of Genghis Khan who was the great ruler of the Mongol Empire. His armies occupied enormous territory from Eastern Europe (Balkans) to the Pacific coast and from Siberia to the Arabian and South China Sea. We departed Beijing on the Trans-Siberian Railway and headed north for Ulaanbaatar, the capital of Mongolia. A colleague and I acted as nonprofessional couriers, delivering diplomatic pouches, personal mail, and food supplies to our embassy in Ulaanbaatar. We packed enough rations for us and our families for the four-day trip. I never envisioned myself journeying to the exotic Far East sitting on a legendary train bound for Siberia with a view from the window of nomads herding two-humped camels on the sands of the vast Gobi desert. Wow!

The long train ride, however, required a certain degree of patience and flexibility. Our soft-sleepers were misrepresented. There was nothing feathery about them. The train was devoid of heat. We were all bundled up. We also kept our weary eyes on the unsavory passengers boarding the train at various intervals. The toilets left much to be desired, and the stench took our breath away. As the train approached a scheduled stop, they were closed. As a substitute, we placed a large coffee container in the middle of our cabin floor. In retrospect, I am not sure this was a wise idea. Omar accidentally kicked the can over and its contents—urine, tissue paper, and muck—spilled everywhere. I hugged him and cleaned up the mess. There's never a dull moment traveling with children.

We stopped at the Chinese border town of Erlian where the train's bogies (wheels) were exchanged. Mongolian trains run on a Russian track gauge that is slightly wider than the standard one used in China. The others got off and stretched their legs, but I was curious and stayed behind. The train was slowly backed into a gigantic shed. Painstakingly, each wagon was hoisted several stories high in the air where its wheels were ceremoniously switched. The entire process, coupled with passport and customs formalities, took eight hours. What a fantastic experience.

Thirty-seven hours later, we reached Ulaanbaatar. The capital was sparsely settled, cold, and extremely poor. Soviet influence was quite evident, as Lenin statues were prominently displayed. Some people were driving old 1960 Russian model cars. The Mongolians were pleasant. The nomads on the outskirts of town lived in white tents called yurts (gers). We went inside one owned by an embassy employee's relative who offered us sweets and a traditional drink made with tea, milk, and salt. It was really more of a soup but rather tasty.

Leila and Omar and the three other children with us were excited to ride Mongol horses that have a stocky build with relatively short legs and a large head. They quickly mounted them, galloped away toward the mountains, and rapidly disappeared over the horizon. I held my breath and prayed. A disquieting hour passed before they resurfaced. Omar remarked, "I had a hard time protecting my 'family jewels,' but it was fun." We flew home, somewhat apprehensively, on an outdated Russian plane.

Q: Previously you mentioned taking the children to Morocco. Did that trip materialize?

AKAHLOUN: Nineteen-ninety-four was a big year for Akahloun adventures. We were constantly on the move. In June, we went on a month's Rest and Recuperation (R&R) vacation to Morocco. The children were initially reluctant to go but warmed up to the idea after learning about the stopover in Paris. The ten-hour flight was smooth, but our hostel near the Arc de Triumph fell short of expectations. Space between the foot of the bed and the bathroom door was, at best, five inches. No shower curtain and no television. Leila and Omar revolted. The next morning, they located a clean, inexpensive hotel in the same area, where we made reservations for our return trip.

Everyone—Momma Habiba and Momma Aini, Uncle Jamal, Aunt Souad, Uncle Abderrahman, Nadia, Nouza, Mounia, Nawfal, Amin,

Fahd, Hind, Hannah, Houda, and Adil—embraced us. The entire family was wonderful and showered us with presents and scrumptious meals. Despite a language barrier, all the children got along exceptionally well and enjoyed playing games together. It was as though they grew up next door to each other.

Leila, Omar and I also visited Casablanca, Tangier, and Marrakech. They were fascinated with the medina and captivated by the snake charmers at the Djemaa El Fna Square in Marrakech. We took pictures of the creatures dangling from their necks. The Great Mosque of Hassan II in Casablanca was also a favorite spot of ours. Everyone was overjoyed that we remembered them. But how could they be forgotten? They were warm, hospitable, caring, and generous people. As a result, my children were able to better identify with their culture and appreciate its significance.

The end of 1994, we flew to Australia and celebrated Christmas and the New Year. From Sydney Harbor, known for its beauty, we had fantastic views of the famous Opera House and the Harbor Bridge. It was an ideal location to watch the fireworks that magnificently illuminated the city. We saw adorable koala bears and kangaroos hopping on their hind legs carrying their young in a pouch. Omar's best memory was a scenic national park tour, which surprisingly ended up at a topless beach. Leila and I kept diverting his attention to no avail. Incidentally, during the trip, I redeemed myself from our dodgy hotel and cramped Paris quarters. We were accommodated at a four-star hotel. We loved every minute of our vacation.

Q: How was Omar faring in China?

AKAHLOUN: That is a good question. Although considerable time was invested in Leila, her brother was not neglected. Omar displayed typical age ten behavior—full of energy, curiosity, and mischief. I think boys generally mature intellectually and emotionally at a different pace than girls. They are not less intelligent, but sometimes they require more time to catch up. During this phase, school can be somewhat tough for them. In Uruguay, he received his first homework assignment in the third grade and now was thrust into a demanding academic environment. His teachers and I became best friends. Omar has many attributes. He is very enterprising. Once he set up a lemonade stand on our street corner. His biggest client was the underground priest living in the compound, but curious Chinese customers also stopped by. He showed great promise, and I was determined to cultivate his hidden talents.

Omar's buddy lived downstairs on the first floor. His mother was a diplomat with the Embassy of Botswana. Sometime in 1994, his father was tragically killed in an automobile accident. Arthur and Omar spent significant time playing outdoor games and visiting the market. They were constantly on the go. Every time Omar entered the house, I would give him a kiss on the cheek. But he was growing up and becoming more independent. One day he half-jokingly said, "You know, Mom, it's a good thing you don't have ten kids because your lips would fall off."

My dear son loved playing pranks and buying firecrackers, water guns, and balloons at the market. One favorite game was throwing water-filled balloons from the balcony at the people walking on the sidewalks or riding their bikes. He and Arthur would launch their missiles and then duck. Once, he was spotted, and an enraged pedestrian chased and cornered him upstairs. Mercifully, he was not harmed. His guardian angel was looking after him that day because I was at work. Then there was the broken-window affair. He used to bounce his basketball against the wall, but once he missed the target and the ball went sailing through the entrance, shattering the glass window. Thank God the embassy interpreter, Mr. Zhang, and I liked each other. He was gifted at making problems disappear.

Q: Do you think Omar was missing his sister once she left for college?

AKAHLOUN: Absolutely. Even though there was nearly a six-year age difference between them, their relationship was a close one. Leila's departure was also traumatic for me. In August 1995, Deng Xiaoping, the architect of modern China, turned ninety. Then on October 1, the People's Republic of China celebrated its forty-sixth anniversary with a series of impressive National Day events. None of this fazed me—I missed my daughter. Finally, Marion Hird, a great source of support and comfort, convinced me it was time to stop mourning and face reality—our girls were all grown up and faring rather nicely without us. Nearly six months after Leila and Jennifer left for college, her driver took us to the Simatai Great Wall outside of Beijing. En route we witnessed a special Chinese harvest. An entire countryside village was busily clearing massive fields of cabbage heads and transporting them with donkeys, carts, and horses to neighboring storage sites. The activity blocked the road for some time, but we amused ourselves by trading stories. We giggled like little school girls. Marion's cheerfulness always added spicy flavoring to our outings.

Q: *Tell me more about China's transfiguration.*

AKAHLOUN: When we arrived in 1993, the women's outfits left something to be desired. By western standards, they were poorly coordinated, especially with the outlandish hats selected. Truth be told, I wore my share of these over-the-top creations to the office. A year later, things drastically changed. The women dressed more fashionably, men shed their Mao jackets, at least, in urban areas, and construction cranes covered the sky. At the same time, Jenny's opened up in our neighborhood. It was a new concept—a convenience store similar to our Seven-Eleven. The shop catered to Chinese and foreigners and sold fresh fruit, vegetables, and canned goods at fixed prices. It was enormously popular. Soon other types of businesses emerged. We still had the market and the old man and his son fixing bikes outside the hutong, but the area was transforming overnight. After a number of drinking establishments opened, Sanlitun Lu was renamed Bar Street. This once desolate street after seven in the evening was now alive and bustling with activity until the wee hours of the morning. The makeover was substantial in other arenas as well. For instance, Russian and East German coaches polished the skills of Chinese gymnasts and ice skaters. Professional U.S. basketball players entered the country and taught the Chinese how to become better at the game. It was mind-boggling.

Q: *I am curious about what you think of the 1974 one-child-per-family policy? Was it effective?*

AKAHLOUN: It succeeded in controlling the population growth, but created social problems. Enforcement in urban areas was rigid. Females at our embassy were collected and driven in a van to a clinic for a monthly examination. Implementation elsewhere varied. Forced

ELEANOR LOPES AKAHLOUN

abortions and female infanticide were frequent. Sometimes family planning officials confiscated babies against parents' wishes and placed them into orphanages. Boys were preferred and outnumbered girls. These overindulged boys turned into "little emperors." Recently, I read an article about wealthy couples turning to fertility medicines to get around the law. Apparently, there is no penalty for multiple births as long as it is the first pregnancy. China is now easing its one-child policy.

Q: *What are some other reflections?*

AKAHLOUN: My position required me to travel to U.S. consulates in other parts of China. In the spring of 1996, I went on a temporary assignment to Chengdu, Guangzhou, and Shanghai. I audited positions, held supervisory training sessions, and reviewed labor service contracts. Chengdu, the capital of Sichuan Province, was a real eye-opener. It is the breadbasket of China and the home of the giant panda bears. At the Wolong National Natural Reserve, I watched several of them eating bamboo, climbing trees, wrestling, and playing on the slide. It was the cutest thing. The *Qing Shi Chao* wholesale market was heaven for farmers. I saw mounds of string beans being shoveled into farmers' grain bags and drums of night soil being poured into buckets, loaded onto carts, and then wheeled away. The smell was potent.

In the fall, I visited Shenyang, a gray industrial city for consultations. Here I discovered a statute of Chairman Mao Zedong standing tall and majestic at Zhongshan Square. At the base, there were a collection of heroes—students, peasants, and soldiers—waving copies of Mao's *Little Red Book*. Teenagers wearing baggy pants and Chicago Bulls baseball caps turned backward were skateboarding around the statue. The elders in traditional Mao suits seemed oblivious to their surroundings. What an amazing contrast. Guangzhou's main market sold ants, scorpions, dogs, cats, and other delicacies. Indeed, Chinese chefs are imaginative. China was full of surprises. The country's intrigue and mysticism greatly influenced my decision to extend.

Summer of 1996 Leila returned from her first year at Georgetown and worked as a consular assistant at the embassy. After her departure, it was time to move forward with my next project—"Operation Omar Achieves." His grades were slipping, so I swung into action. Omar was approaching his teenage years, and I felt more supervision and guidance was in order. Ahmed had been the disciplinarian in the family. Now it was my responsibility to make sure Omar was on track.

I decided to adjust my office hours to be more physically present and vigilant, and the administrative counselor agreed to my request to work a flextime schedule from 7:30 a.m. to 4:30 p.m. Television viewing was restricted. Motivational notes were taped to his desk and the walls of his room. He was swimming in them. Because of the demands of the office, I was not always at home when he arrived from school. But I stuck to the arrangement as much as possible, and his grades improved. Meanwhile, at the office, we were preparing for upcoming Chinese labor contract discussions.

Q: Okay, let's discuss these negotiations of 1996.

AKAHLOUN: Conversations began the nineteenth of September and lasted nearly four months. The Diplomatic Service Bureau (DSB) felt the salaries we paid the Chinese employees were too low and jeopardized our chances of obtaining prime candidates. DSB proposed a service charge increase of 17.3 percent in alignment with Beijing's Price Index of Benefits. We disagreed and heated debates ensued. There was sparse love between my boss and Mr. Wang, the manager. Fundamentally, the disagreements between them stemmed from personal and ideological differences. Several topics were at issue, including the government's pocketing 50 percent of the employees' salaries, excessive embassy transfers, and mandatory Saturday debriefings. After the fourth session, I went on home leave for Christmas, and the talks continued in my absence.

Leila joined us and flew from Washington to Onset, and we had a marvelous time until my mom suffered a mild stroke. She was hospitalized but released the following day. Thankfully, she snapped back quickly. In Washington, D.C., we attended Leila's Georgetown gospel choir concert and took in a Hoya's basketball game.

When I returned to Beijing, all parties were consumed and receptive to wrapping up contract negotiations. We agreed on a 19-percent service charge over two years. The clothing, meal, and transportation allowances were to be paid directly to the employees. This applied to bonuses and awards as well. The signed contract was worth over one million dollars.

Three days later, another crisis arose. This time it involved my indispensible personnel assistant. For two years, I relied heavily on her services. She closely monitored the monthly DSB payroll and identified meal, clothing, and overtime discrepancies. More important, she was able to collect all the overpayments. She also assisted with the awards program and learned to classify positions. Because of poor vision, she wore thick eyeglasses. One day she was photographed for a new embassy badge and the camera flash affected her eyesight. She was then moved from a dimly lit workspace to a lighter corner of the room. After a few months, her vision deteriorated. Regrettably, she stopped working altogether. The bureau was not providing her any financial assistance, and the U.S. government could not technically intervene, so I paid her medical bill, which amounted to $350. I tried to help as much as possible, but it was one of those painfully out-of-control situations. And, believe me, there were a surplus of them.

A short time later, in February 1997, a political storm of epic proportions landed in our backyard. Hwang Jang-yop, a high-ranking North Korean official, and his aide, Kim Dok-hong, defected. They walked into the consular section of the South Korean Embassy, located one block away from our housing compound, and sought political asylum. The incident immediately captured global attention. Beijing police sealed off the area, and our neighborhood effectively became an armed camp. Roadblocks were installed. Spike barrier strips were placed across the roads leading to the South Korean Embassy. Military tanks surrounded the place. Buses filled with soldiers in riot gear stood by ready for action. It was a powerful display of force by the Chinese government.

Unbelievably, Omar penetrated the barricades. The soldiers allowed him to play street hockey with his friend, the German Ambassador's son. Sometimes their pucks landed under the tanks, but they retrieved them without difficulty. Sundays we attended mass at the Chilean Embassy, next to the South Korean Embassy. Because Omar spoke Chinese, we easily passed through the checkpoints. Along the way, soldiers smiled and waved at him from inside their army tanks. It was an uneasy situation for me, but not for Mr. Akahloun. He was in full command and relishing every moment. After thirty-four days, the Chinese authorities permitted Hwang Jang-yop and his assistant to depart for the Philippines. Many weeks later they made their way to South Korea.

After the turmoil, I focused on keeping Omar constructively occupied during his summer school recess. The American Employees' Association (AEA), our embassy's mini commissary, was looking for volunteers for their 1997 Camp Adventure program. It was a nonpaying forty-hour job assisting professional counselors. At fourteen, Omar was two years shy of the age requirement, but I convinced the manager, Maureen Walsh, he was mature for his age. She went along with the program. Now I had the chore of persuading Omar. Although he thought I had lost my mind, he reluctantly committed to a one-week trial period. After that, he ended up loving the job.

Out of five volunteers, Omar was the youngest and the only one to last the entire summer. He became a role model for the fifty campers. Ms. Walsh was so impressed with his diligence that she sent him an official letter, which in part stated he was "responsible and punctual . . . cheerfully carried out his tasks . . . possessed an infectious can-do attitude." AEA was so pleased with him that he was given a check for $125.

Late August, we received upsetting news. My mom was suspected of having cancer and was scheduled for exploratory surgery. Arrangements were hastily made for Omar to board with Irwin and Mary Stein, two of ISB'S most dedicated schoolteachers, and I jumped on the next plane home. My mother was emotionally strong and continued her normal community service activities. The September 15, 1997, exploratory operation went reasonably well, but pockets of the tumor remained. The final diagnosis was ovarian cancer and coronary artery disease. She underwent radiation therapy and confronted her pain and suffering with exceptional strength, courage, and faith. This comforted me. Two weeks after the surgery, I returned to China. Omar was delighted to be released from his all-work-no-play environment.

During the summer of 1997, the embassy was operating with a skeleton staff because of personnel shortages and turnovers. My workload had increased by 40 percent, and I was pretty much burnt-out but still committed to the goal of converting Chinese employees to Foreign Service Nationals. The saga never seemed to end. I sent a message to post management and Department officials requesting urgent help for the conversion project and then followed-up with a detailed plan of action. Five hundred fifty-five China-wide jobs needed to be classified. For now, we would focus on Beijing's 238 positions. Personnel Officer Lou Hebert was dispatched from Washington to assist with the project. He arrived in January 1998 and remained at post for six weeks.

Literally we were starting from scratch, as none of the sketchy descriptions on file conformed to the State Department's system. Maureen Lyon, an American personnel specialist, my two assistants, and I classified the less complicated positions and reserved the more involved ones for Lou. Only six months was left before my stateside transfer, so we worked feverishly to finish all the Beijing actions. Lou Hebert provided superb advice and assistance. After my departure, he kept me updated. Following several trips to China, he completed the remaining classification actions for the constituent posts. According to him, after lengthy and intensive rounds of negotiations with the Chinese government, the DSB employees eventually began receiving individual pay slips from our regional finance center in Bangkok. At that point, they were officially considered Foreign Service Nationals (FSNs). It was a victory for the Chinese employees, and I was more than pleased for them.

Q: *That was a major feat. China has advanced much quicker than anyone guessed. Somebody early on was smart enough to see where the country was going.*

AKAHLOUN: I believe one individual was President George H. W. Bush Sr., who in 1973 represented our interests as head of the U.S. Liaison Office in Beijing. Although Bush lacked the rank of ambassador, he unofficially acted as one during the approximately fourteen months he served in mainland China. He advocated a policy of first strengthening economic and diplomatic relations and later dealing with political issues. President Bush's efforts were largely considered beneficial for U.S.–Chinese relations.

In December 1978, about three years after Bush's departure, the U.S. severed diplomatic relations with the Republic of China (ROC). One month later, we recognized The People's Republic of China as the sole legitimate government of China and our mission in Taipei was closed. Soon afterward, the American Institute in Taiwan (AIT) was established, and the director of the office became an unofficial U.S.

representative, or *de facto* ambassador, to Taiwan. Beijing's U.S. Liaison Office was upgraded to an embassy in March 1979.

Q: At this stage, are there other thoughts you want to share?

AKAHLOUN: China was frustrating at times but exciting. During my tour, I worked with three administrative counselors, two senior personnel officers, and fifteen family members. Throughout the hectic assignment, I was surprised at the inner strength and coping skills of Leila and Omar. They inspired me with their courage and resiliency. They showed maturity beyond their age and weathered the ups and downs beautifully. I drew joy and strength from them. When our tour ended, Leila was on the dean's list at the Georgetown School of Foreign Service, and Omar made the honor roll at the International School of Beijing. This was enormously gratifying.

There were many electrifying trips, some of which were already described. Four more come to mind: Xian—the ancient capital of China, the start of the Silk Road, and home of the Qin Dynasty Terra Cotta Warriors and Horses; Datong—UNESCO World Heritage site of the Yungang Grottoes that contain magnificent Chinese Buddhist temple cave art; Longqing Gorge—famous for its winter ice-lantern festival and massive illuminated blocks of ice sculptured into animals and figures, and Chengde—known for its complex of imperial palaces used by Qing Dynasty emperors as their summer mountain resort. China is a paradise for those afflicted with a serious case of wanderlust.

I began packing out the first week of June 1998. On a 10-point scale of miserable transfers, this one ranked among the highest. It was agonizing. The first day I was supervising five Chinese men, wrapping, packing, and loading household effects into containers; an embassy plumber, repairing a bathroom faucet, and a carpenter, replacing a broken kitchen cabinet door. Two Diplomatic Service Bureau workers painting the hallways, splattered more paint on the floor than on the walls. We were dodging puddles of paint, and I wore a face mask to block out the overpowering fumes. On the second day, a young Chinese shipping supervisor helped me with a script for an awards ceremony being held the following day at the embassy. Because the entire staff was consumed with preparations for President Clinton's upcoming visit, there was not enough time for me to rehearse my speech. Fifteen minutes before the ceremony, the unthinkable occurred. Omar injured his ankle playing basketball at the Marine House.

At the time, it didn't look serious, so the awards ceremony went forward. One hundred and thirteen certificates were presented. By nightfall, however, the ankle swelled up and became very painful. Home treatment was not working. Bright and early the next morning, we went to the Asia Emergency Assistance Clinic for X-rays. It turned out he had a moderate sprain, which did not require surgery. To immobilize the ankle, he wore a cast that was removed a few days later due to an allergic reaction. Poor thing, he was relegated to hobbling around the house with crutches. Just when I thought nothing else could possibly go wrong, it did.

Two weeks after Omar's accident and four days prior to Clinton's arrival an electrical fire broke out in a room adjacent to my office. Thanks to the quick intervention of the U.S. Marine Guards, my area was spared. No one was injured because it happened on a Sunday, but the thought of our passports being torched was alarming. It seemed the deck was stacked against an orderly departure.

Q: When did you actually leave Beijing?

AKAHLOUN: The date was July 2, 1998. Shortly before this we saw a spectacular sunrise, which was a nice farewell. Rarely did Beijing's sky transform itself so brilliantly. The city was habitually covered in smog, which some days hardly allowed us to see much of our surroundings. The Chinese employees' reaction overwhelmed me. I went office-to-office, personally thanking everyone. Mr. Zhang walked me back to my room, smiling and shaking my hand the entire time. I thought it was going to fall off. Others took photographs. It was very touching. The next morning my personnel assistants unexpectedly greeted us with a big bouquet of gorgeous yellow roses. They were there to escort Omar and me to the airport. Aiyi was also present. When I hugged her, our tears flowed. She was considered part of the family.

Today's China still fascinates me. Since our posting in 1993, it has experienced a period of extraordinary growth. It has emerged as an economic and political powerhouse and has made significant inroads into the field of science and technology and in other areas. China's interests now span the globe, and its cooperation is vital in addressing many international conflicts. A new state-of-the-art U.S. Embassy in Beijing with space for nearly one thousand employees was dedicated on August 8, 2008. The event was synchronized with the start of Beijing's 2008 Summer Olympics. President Bush senior returned for the ribbon-cutting ceremony of the sleek $434 million, ten-acre compound. It is hard for me to wrap my head around these radical changes.

China is culturally and geographically diverse. It is unwise to assume the whole country is the same and that personal impressions of a few are true of all the people. From my experience, I would generally characterize the average Chinese as friendly and family oriented. Yet, I also saw the other side of China—the graft and corruption, abuse of power, and wealth and human rights violations. I once heard former Ambassador Roy Stapleton being interviewed on a television program. He believed to reduce mutual suspicion the U.S. and China needed to adopt policies that ensured a sensible, stable, and cooperative relationship rather than one dictated by competitiveness. All very true, but this is easier said than done. Foreign relations between the two global powers have always been a work in progress.

As for my next posting, I weighed various options but decided on Caracas, Venezuela. Although the post was internally dysfunctional from the Department's perspective, there were reputable high schools for Omar, and it was reasonably close to the U.S. This meant I could easily visit my parents and monitor their health. It was important to be as close as possible to them—a quick plane ride away in case I was physically needed. Caracas was also a stretch assignment with potential for promotion. I crossed my fingers and hoped for a positive outcome.

ELEANOR LOPES AKAHLOUN

Welcome to Sanlitun 2-1, our home from 1993 to 1998, Beijing, China.

Surveillance cameras and floodlights were mounted on top of the gate guards' quarters. Identification papers of Chinese citizens wishing to enter the housing unit were carefully examined.

The sidewalk repair shop where Omar's bike underwent repeated surgery.

Leila eating glazed haw berries in front of the Moroccan
Embassy across the street from our compound, 1993.

Standing in Tiananmen Square, the heart of Beijing, China, 1993.

My favorite Sanlitun market vendor holding her young child.

Customers flocking to a food cart to buy a Jing Bing,
a crepe-like food filled with egg, crispy fried dough,
green onions, cilantro, and a savory spicy sauce.

I relished munching on them. They were simply delicious.

Never went shopping without my scale. Interesting things happened
when I weighed the vegetables being sold to me by the vendors.

A Peoples' Republic of China guard stands at attention
in front of the American Embassy in Beijing.

Beijing's outdoor barber shops were cheap and plentiful.

Sanlitun streets leading to the South Korean Embassy, where two North Korean defectors sought asylum in February 1994, were barricaded. We were allowed to enter the "hot zone" to attend church services. Along the way, we encountered bus loads of riot police and military tanks.

Omar hitching a ride to town on the back of a stranger's
animal, Ulaanbaatar, Mongolia, April 1994.

A hospitable Mongolian couple next to their
countryside yurt outside Ulaanbaatar.

A friendly Sanlitun water-gun fight between Leila and
Omar during his 11th birthday party, June 1994.

Introducing tacos to Uncle Abderrahman, Mounia,
Amin, and Nawfal in Rabat-Sale, Morocco, on July 18,
1994. Who would have imagined? They loved it.

Teeth, teeth, and more teeth. Leila and Omar inspect the merchandise on display, Jema El Fna Square, Marrakesh, Morocco, July 1994.

At the same square, Leila and Omar with snakes around their necks.

In 1994, enjoying Thanksgiving Day with Marion, Bill, and Jennifer Hird.

Amy Hird, next to me wearing a headscarf, was away at college and joined us for the Christmas holiday season at our Sanlitun apartment, 1994.

On home leave in 1995. Omar and his grandfather counting
their treasure trove of pennies in Onset, Massachusetts.

My mother at a large reception she organized in Onset
for Leila's 1995 high school graduation.

An unforgettable excursion to the Simatai Great Wall, 1995.

Cooking and washing clothes in a public courtyard. Shortly after venturing inside this Beijing hutong in 1996, it was demolished.

Leila, Wayne, and Lee in 1996. Christmas in Onset was full of joy and laughter. My parents elaborately decorated the house and filled it with an abundance of love.

Mom and my godchild Champ handing out Christmas presents.

Nephew Beanie with Leila and Omar in Onset, 1996.

Outside Beijing at the Taihen Farm Village, a proud grandfather waiting patiently with a shovel to clean up after his squatting grandson.

President Bill Clinton and Chinese President Jiang Zemin reviewing troops upon arriving at the Great Hall of the People on July 27, 1998.

With Chelsea Clinton at the Diaoyutai State Guest House, Beijing, 1998. President Clinton converses with a vendor behind us.

Sitting in the American Embassy garden preparing for a China-wide awards program, Beijing, June 12, 1998.

Delivering opening remarks at the ceremony,
where 113 certificates were presented.

A 1998 family reunion in Onset. (Front row, left to right) James Pina Jr., my nephew's son, my mother and father, my aunt Katherine Fernandes, Bronson Lopes and his mother, Marianne Lopes. (Back row) Wayne Rodriguez, my niece's son, Aleita Rodriguez, my niece, Robert Pina and James Pina, my nephews, Leila, and Lawrence Lopes, another nephew.

CHAPTER FOURTEEN

You Can Never Go Home Again

WASHINGTON, D.C., AND HOME LEAVE, 1998

After five years, parting company with China was traumatic. Returning to the U.S. after such a lengthy stay abroad, was an unsettling experience. More than ever I realized "what once was" can never be revisited. Like it or not, change is inevitable.

Q: How challenging was the reentry?

AKAHLOUN: Reentry is not as simple as it is made out to be. Oftentimes, we assume we can pick up where we left off. Occasionally we do, but sometimes the process is more complicated. Returning home can be more stressful than going abroad. Overseas we realize life will be different, so we prepare ourselves for surprises. Once we arrive home and find our old routine or familiar patterns missing, the situation can be shocking, confusing, and lonely.

After China, I experienced mixed emotions—excitement, sadness, and fear. The reentry was harder than previous ones because of the period of time I had spent outside of America and the profound difference between the two societies. Back home, I no longer instinctively knew the right thing to do in every social setting. At times, I behaved awkwardly. Frequently, I jumped queues in stores and afterward apologized to irritated customers and cashiers. A person waiting their turn in line to be served was an alien concept to me; I had grown accustomed to another lifestyle. In many aspects, I was discovering my culture for the first time.

My memories, especially those of family members, were frozen in time. I realized my loved ones did not stay the same while I was gone. My niece and nephews were grown-ups, and my parents had aged considerably. My mom underwent an exploratory operation for cancer in September 1997, and my father had knee surgery for a second time a few months later. Although still independent, they began curtailing many of their vigorous activities. Seeing my mother and father so physically weak and delicate was heartbreaking. I was grateful for all the unselfish sacrifices they made on my behalf.

Regrettably, being abroad for decades strained my relationship with my sister. One of the most difficult part of life in the Foreign Service is being separated from those you love and missing significant milestones—birthdays, graduations, weddings, funerals, and reunions. Long-distance relationships can be challenging to maintain. Disagreements not addressed face-to-face can fester over time. Living abroad has considerable upsides, but it also has its unavoidable downsides as well.

Life is a series of adjustments—some pleasant and others distressing. We all encounter changes and cycles like Mother Nature's seasons and tide. Each of us experience joyful moments mixed with those causing great agony. How we cope can either strengthen or defeat us. I kept reminding myself that what I was experiencing was normal and part of an ongoing readjustment process. The same set of instincts, skills, and strategies used to adapt to my foreign assignments was to be applied to these circumstances. Although I treated my own culture as if it were unfamiliar, I trusted that everything would eventually fall into place.

Concerning my mother and father, regardless of the emotional turmoil, it was necessary to accept their stage of life as being inescapable. There are no absolute assurances as to the length of our lives. Inevitably, time runs out. There are beginnings and endings in life. This wasn't the first time I was coping with an agonizing situation. Overcoming obstacles was not new to me, and I found the best way through them was to be realistic. Come what may, my dear parents would always be warmly tucked away in my heart.

CHAPTER FIFTEEN

NATURAL DISASTERS
AND HUGO CHAVEZ

VENEZUELA, 1998–2001

Although surrounded by extraordinary natural beauty, life in Venezuela was not a fairy tale existence. We survived mudslides, floods, burglaries, and the antics of an unpredictable leader.

Q: Caracas is a notoriously dangerous city. Did you feel secure there?

AKAHLOUN: It was not the safest place. In fact, at the time, Caracas was one of the world's top crime capitals. Purse snatching, pickpockets, muggings, armed robberies, and kidnappings were widespread. Carjacking victims were usually led to ATM machines at gun point and forced to make bank withdrawals. Sometimes they were killed. Cash in hand, the criminals sped away. At night, drivers did not stop for red lights. Everyone knew someone who was victimized. The embassy staff was frequently targeted.

We lived in a large modern apartment complex, just a five-minute walk from work. The structure was constructed on the side of a cliff but solidly built and heavily guarded and patrolled. We had a fistful of keys and finding the correct one to open and lock the doors was time-consuming and nerve-racking. With the amount of security measures in place, the compound seemed impenetrable. In spite of this, one morning about three weeks after our arrival, we heard someone screaming, "*Ladron, ladron* (thief, thief)!" It was 3:30 a.m. I thought it was a dream, but then I heard, "Pow, pow, pow!" And another "Pow, pow!" I ran to Omar's room and woke him up. We returned to my bedroom, bolted the door, and peeked through the shutters. A Venezuelan neighbor was standing outside his balcony, waving a gun. The thief escaped.

Later, we discovered the robber cleverly scaled our side of the building with mountain-climbing gear. He entered several apartments, including the one above us where $200 dollars was stolen. We narrowly missed being burglarized as our broken balcony door was repaired the previous afternoon. We joked and called the intruder "spider man," but the incident was disturbing.

The compound's sophisticated alarm system did not prevent hijackers from entering the garage. Once inside, they jumped into people's vehicles, opened the gate, and drove away to the nearest bank. This happened at least twice during my assignment. Carjacking was a problem by day and night. That was one reason I decided against bringing a car to Caracas. Incidents such as these, plus high unemployment (about 40 percent), rampant inflation, corruption, overcrowding, and a crumbling infrastructure, discouraged most Americans from venturing too far from the relative safety of their homes. The ambience cultivated fear and produced low morale within the embassy community.

Q: What time frame was this?

AKAHLOUN: We arrived in Caracas in 1998 and served there until 2001. There were two excellent high schools available. We selected the smaller school, Colegio Internacional de Caracas (CIC), because the atmosphere was friendlier and more diverse. In addition, CIC had strong athletic and community outreach programs. It was located on a hill, surrounded by barrios (shantytowns), and commanded a sweeping view of the El Avila Mountains.

As for the U.S. Embassy, it occupied a twenty-seven-acre mountainside site in the Colinas de Valle Arriba area, overlooking Las Mercedes and the rest of the valley. It was a striking five-story red granite building. Contrary to China, all agencies were housed within the embassy. The view from my office was spectacular, but there was an administrative notice that frightened me. A rattlesnake had been killed at the rear of the compound on a path I generally walked. We were also reminded to watch out for spiders, warned that scorpions were prevalent during the rainy season, and urged to be on the lookout for three stray dogs, suspected of living on the fringes of the embassy grounds. Later, I encountered something that helped offset the embassy's threatening circular.

Early one morning en route to the office a breathtaking sight greeted me—a family of ten beautiful blue and gold macaw parrots flying overhead. The colorful birds sat on top of the trees and perched on the power lines that surrounded me. They visited long enough for me to marvel at their beauty and listen to their loud chatter. After a while, they flew away toward the mountains. I was glad to see them in the wild instead of in captivity.

Q: Quite unusual. What other first impressions come to mind?

AKAHLOUN: The people were an attractive mix of Caucasian, African, and indigenous Indian groups. Lush tropical flowers and palm trees were in abundance. The vivid blue sky was amazing—radiant sunshine and soft, white clouds. From my balcony, there was a cool refreshing breeze. The wind gently swept across the sky and kept rearranging the clouds into different shapes and sizes. Sunrises and sunsets were exceptional. And the climate was ideal. Down in the narrow valley was a cluster of tall multistory buildings and beyond that was the picturesque El Avila Mountains. Clouds often covered its peak, which was approximately 7,200 feet high. Malaria and dengue fever were common. Aside from this, there was some concern about natural disasters and our personal safety. Venezuela is located in an active earthquake zone and is prone to hurricanes, flooding, and landslides during the May-to-December rainy season.

Q: In terms of size, how did Embassy Caracas compare to the mission in China?

AKAHLOUN: In Beijing and the constituent posts, there were over 300 Americans and about 550 Chinese employees. Caracas had approximately 170 Americans and 175 Foreign Service Nationals. It was a much smaller operation but one in crisis. I was the only personnel officer. The Department of State has since adopted new terminology.

ELEANOR LOPES AKAHLOUN

Personnel officers are now considered human resources officers, and Foreign Service Nationals are presently referred to as Locally Employed Staff (LES).

Many factors contributed to the existing chaos. The Venezuelans were friendly and fun-loving but somewhat contentious workers. The Americans were accomplished, dedicated servants who sometimes overlooked their supervisory responsibilities. It was a case of mismanagement and retention problems. Historically, the embassy sustained heavy personnel losses. By June 1997, the recruitment situation reached a boiling point. There were also economic and political issues, high inflation, and an influx of multinational oil companies that were providing generous salaries and benefits. Our senior employees were being hired by these companies and doubling their wages.

My office mirrored the fluctuation in staffing endemic to the entire embassy. Four out of the five employees were new. Eighty percent of the staff had turned over in a relatively short period of time. Angel Garcia replaced the former senior personnel specialist who had been employed by the U.S. government for over twenty years. Angel was doing excellent work but was on the job only four months prior to my arrival. One personnel clerk started working two weeks earlier while another one was leaving in a matter of days.

I thought I had prepared myself adequately by reading several briefing papers and consulting with various officials from the State Department and other foreign affairs agencies. In addition, I spoke with various contacts at our neighboring embassies. Circumstances were worse than anticipated. To illustrate, there were a number of American family members and Personal Service Contract employees (PSCs) hired without proper paperwork or authorization. The staffing pattern for the Americans and the local employees had to be reconstructed. The files were incomplete, and there was no institutional memory to rely on.

Q: A pretty broken operation. What action did you take?

AKAHLOUN: I devised a multifaceted recovery plan that entailed various in-house training sessions for all local employees and their American supervisors. It was a holistic approach to stabilize the embassy and one endorsed by the ambassador and Washington. The first order of business was restructuring my office. Personal goals were set up.

We all submitted daily reports on our day's activities and gathered weekly to measure progress. We linked our office goals to the mission's objectives. High on the agenda was increasing the wages of our Foreign Service Nationals. We collected salary and benefit information from our competitors and bombarded Washington with compensation surveys until we received an encouraging 13 percent, across-the-board, salary increase. At the same time, Washington announced I was promoted, which was a pleasant surprise.

Leadership workshops were conducted over the course of one year. Interpersonal and listening skills, supervisory skills, time management, job stress, and other subjects were covered. Position classification management was also highlighted. Virtually, a miniature Foreign Service Institute (FSI) training program was set up. The project would not have succeeded without the invaluable contribution from Guatemala's Personnel Specialist Aida Castellanos. Both of us were passionate about encouraging, empowering, and motivating people to fulfill their dreams and claim what life had to offer.

Conflict resolution was an enormous part of my job. Over three-quarters of the local employees, in addition to many Americans, passed through my door seeking counseling. Some of them merely chatted about career-enhancing, training opportunities. Other cases were more complex. To give you an example, one individual's superior performance began to decline. The supervisor complained about the employee's poor quality of work and his frequent absences. Finally, he divulged that he was suffering from HIV/AIDS and withheld the information for fear of losing his job and being ostracized by his colleagues. Over the course of time, the situation markedly improved. A fair amount of the Venezuelans in the embassy were also dismissed for malfeasance. After a year, thanks to a team of dedicated individuals, the state of affairs began reversing itself. Foreign Service National salaries rose, the turnover decreased, awards policies were enacted, family member employment increased, and embassy morale improved.

Q: *Hugo Chavez became President of Venezuela in 1998. Were you present during the election?*

AKAHLOUN: Yes, I was there at the time. Chavez was a charismatic leader with a feisty nature. Following a failed coup d'état in February

1992, he was subsequently jailed and pardoned two years later. After being released, he decided the best way to gain power was through politics. He proved himself a political survivor and sometime later was elected president. Chavez won the election in December 1998 based on a platform of helping the poor. He promised to use oil revenues to end poverty. He also campaigned for constitutional reform and used considerable anti-U.S. rhetoric. The elections were volatile. One evening we went to dinner with friends and along the way we witnessed a gun battle at one of the nightclubs. We fled and subsequently avoided going downtown because of the numerous demonstrations and the potential for violence.

Q: Diplomatic relations between Chavez and the U.S. government turned bitter. Was it this way at the beginning?

AKAHLOUN: It was always complicated. When the theatrical leader took office in 1999, he began putting into action many social reforms, implemented a new Venezuelan Constitution that enabled him to perform functions normally reserved to the Venezuelan Congress and nationalized several key industries. His government was accused of being corrupt by multiple sources in various ways. The relationship between Cuba and Venezuela was close. Fidel Castro was his ally, and Hugo Chavez considered him a mentor. Despite the strains, economic self-interest prevented a complete rupture between the U.S. and Venezuela. We remained an important trading partner, buying about 40 percent of the country's oil exports, throughout the presidency of Chavez, who died in March 2013 after a long bout with cancer. Hugo Chavez was a highly controversial and divisive figure both at home and abroad.

Q: Do you remember other events that produced turmoil?

AKAHLOUN: The Venezuelan floods and mudslides of 1999. This was catastrophic. In the Vargas State of Venezuela, torrential rains and flash floods over several days and nights in December killed tens of thousands of people, destroyed their homes, and eventually collapsed the state's infrastructure. Relief workers reported that one neighborhood, *Los Corales*, was buried under nearly ten feet of mud and that some other towns entirely disappeared.

The heavy rains also struck metropolitan Caracas with a vengeance. By December 15, the continuous downpour led to incredible flooding and mudslides. In an instant, thousands of people and their homes were swept up and buried. Waste piled up at the bottom of the El Avila, where it surrounded high-rise apartment buildings. Many people were stuck on rooftops for days because they were trapped. Those impoverished suffered the greatest losses. The majority of them lived in illegal and unsafe shantytowns on the sides of the hills and mountains near the city. The creeks swelled and debris flowed down the mountainside at over thirty-five miles an hour, leaving a wide path of destruction and countless Venezuelans homeless. Some of this was being televised; Omar and I watched in utter amazement.

President Chavez called in the military to evacuate an estimated 190,000 people and to restore civil order. Looting was rampant. The U.S. participated in search and rescue operations and flew in Hazmat teams to clean up hazardous waste spills. The American and Venezuelan Red Cross set up outposts, where victims received food, portable water, and medical care. The final death toll was roughly calculated at ten thousand to thirty thousand people. The actual count was nearly impossible to determine because of the country's incomplete census records. In reality, the figure was probably much higher.

On the U.S. home front, things were also in a state of pandemonium. Ten days prior to the disaster in Caracas, my mother underwent colostomy surgery because of a bowel blockage. The following week my father suffered a stroke, paralyzing him on his left side and leaving him incapable of eating or drinking. They were both at Toby Hospital in Wareham, Massachusetts, and I desperately wanted to be with them. Omar and I had planned a trip home for the Christmas holidays. By now, this seemed doubtful. The disaster crippled the airport, and all flights were suspended. There I was a continent away brokenhearted and despondent at the thought of not being able to see or help my parents.

Only one highway led to the airport, and no one knew if the road, bridges, and tunnels were intact. After a day and a half, a U.S. C-103 military transport plane flew in rations for fifty-eight trapped American tourists who were without food and water in sweltering heat. It was now December 17, 1999. Early the next morning, my boss, Rob Weisberg, dashed into the office and announced there was a stranded commercial plane flying the tourists to Miami in the evening. A few open seats were available. "Do you and Omar want to go? You have ten seconds to decide." Two Embassy vans and their passengers were soon to embark on a perilous mission. Once the expedition began, there was no turning back. The odds of reaching the airport were less than 50 percent.

I knew if we failed to leave the country that very moment, we would be marooned for months. I urgently needed to be with my parents. I was also thinking of Leila. If anything happened to Omar and me, she would be left alone. But a silent voice cried out, "Do it, Penny!" The vehicles were leaving in thirty minutes. I ran home and broke the news to Omar, who was ecstatic. I threw a few clothes into our suitcases and reached for the passports. Mine was in its proper place, but Omar's was missing. I was in a state of panic but retraced my steps and tracked it down. We sprinted down the hill. Our convoy was the embassy's first attempt to reach the airport over compromised mountainous roads. At best, it was a risky proposition.

The General Services Officer, a former Army Green Beret, drove the lead van, and we followed in a second car driven by a Foreign Service National. We moved at a snail's pace. Since there was only one lane, we stopped several times, allowing Venezuelan army trucks to pass. We zigzagged along what once resembled a road, dodging boulders, uprooted trees, and other debris left behind by the water and mud. A crucial tunnel was almost blocked. Luckily, we squeezed through it. We crossed rubble-filled bridges, some of which had chunks of missing concrete slabs dangerously exposing the ravine below. I held my breath and prayed. Our intrepid leaders did a remarkable job.

The landscape looked war-torn, and we saw homeless people, without shoes, walking aimlessly along the roadside. They had vacant stares and clutched one or two plastic bags, containing all their worldly possessions. Omar was calm, reflective, and managed to keep a sense of humor. For a fifteen-year-old, he coped very well. There were two petrified Washington TDY visitors riding with us. I must admit the ordeal was unnerving for everyone. At last, we reached the airport, which was being used as a refugee center. The toilets made China's countryside outhouses look good by comparison. We had to wade through puddles of excrement. It was just awful; we felt extremely blessed and lucky to be leaving the country.

Q: How was the government managing this?

AKAHLOUN: The Venezuelan government was making an effort to handle the crisis, but it was overwhelmed. Reaching our destination was only half of the battle. Some 70 percent of the airport personnel were affected by the disaster, and all operations were suspended. Lack of electricity also contributed to the disruption. In the absence of a ground crew, the military assumed charge. We relied on them for fuel and flight clearance, but they were not very "customer friendly." At plane side, it felt strange lugging our heavy suitcases up the steps and placing them inside the cabin. We secured them as best possible. Finally, around 9:00 p.m. that evening, in virtual darkness, the aircraft took off. We arrived in Miami at an absurd hour, exhausted, and without prearranged hotel reservations. It was very chaotic. Eventually we reached Massachusetts and saw my parents.

My father remained paralyzed but coherent most of the time. During my visit home, we transferred him from the hospital to a nursing home. He never regained his health and was tube-fed the rest of his life—four years, eight months. It was heart wrenching to see him in that condition. Despite the trauma, he always smiled and said, "Things could be worse." Sadly, my mother's health deteriorated, and she passed away the ninth of January 1999. They were individuals of great integrity and endurance and terrific role models. Clearly, we had made a wise decision departing Venezuela when the opportunity presented itself.

A month later we returned. The normal forty-minute drive from the airport to our home in Caracas took over three hours. But the Venezuelan National Disaster Committee, together with a strong international presence, was making some progress. Tens of millions of dollars were poured into reconstruction projects.

Q: Were you able to resume your work where you left off?

AKAHLOUN: With an effort, business was back to normal. My team—Angel Garcia, Julio Ojeda, Maikol Genovese, Sandra Vega, and Alcira Bermudez—were given a group Superior Honor Award and cash for their outstanding performance before, during, and after the flood disaster. Later, Administrative Counselor Rob Weisberg, the Deputy Chief of Mission, and I received individual Superior Honor

Awards for our efforts. I was recognized primarily for initialing and implementing a mission-wide training and counseling plan that helped stabilize the workforce. My name was also forwarded to Washington for consideration of the Bureau's Personnel Officer of the Year award. Things progressed smoothly until midsummer when Mr. Weisberg was transferred to Indonesia as Deputy Chief of Mission.

The new administrative counselor was a former college professor who joined the Foreign Service late in her career. Prior to Venezuela, she served with the Office of Inspector General (OIG). Our post was due for an inspection, which the Department routinely conducted at all its embassies every few years. She had somewhat of an abrasive personality that eventually clashed with several members of her team. After the inspection, some of the results disappointed her. It might have been a coincidence, but later two key members of the embassy found themselves working elsewhere, and she marginalized me.

It was a one-step forward and two-steps-backward scenario. However, I refused to be demoralized. Instead, I compartmentalized as much as possible, worked harder, and focused on mission goals. Too much time and energy had been invested in the embassy's restoration plan for me to give up now. I remained optimistic, self-confident, and explored different avenues to continue improving the morale. To maintain my sanity, I took short breaks. One unforgettable Thanksgiving weekend Omar and I went to the island of Bonaire, considered a scuba diver's paradise, with a group of friends. The deep turquoise water was crystal clear, and the beautiful coral reefs were right at the water's edge. While Omar took his scuba-diving lesson, I was content snorkeling close to the beach. After this, he felt I was ready to graduate and encouraged me to join him and the others for some deep-water action.

Let me paint the picture for you. We are on this tourist boat a few miles from shore, though for me, it seemed like the middle of the ocean. Everyone entered the water, and then it was my turn. I hesitated, but Omar reassured me, "Come on, Mom, you can do it. Jump!" As I hit the water, I panicked and swam immediately toward the boulders lining the shore. He kept screaming for me to turn around, but I continued swimming and swimming. I was out of breath when I reached the rocks, which were slippery and awkward to walk on with rubber fins. Omar caught up to me. "Mom, what's wrong with you?" he asked. "I don't know. I was frightened," I said. (Somehow at the delicate age of fifty-seven, fear and related words were slowly crawling into my vocabulary.) My son took charge. "Mom, we've got to swim back to the boat. Take off your necklace and rings too so you don't attract sharks." Obviously, I was out of my element and not thinking very clearly. He put everything in his pocket and said, "Follow me." But swimming against the strong current was difficult, and the pathway was narrow and dangerous. Omar pointed to something swimming under me. It was a barracuda!

We were fortunate to explore the beautiful vacation destinations surrounding Caracas and to fly home as often as possible. We cherished each moment with my father and family. While in Onset, the end of 2000, Omar's health became a concern. He was tired and thirsty all the time. I thought he had mononucleosis. When we returned to Caracas, I suggested he see the doctor, but he refused. He was busy studying for final exams and practicing for the upcoming Caribbean Area Schools Sports Association (CAISSA) tournament in Santo Domingo in the Dominican Republic. By now, he was considered one of the team's most valuable players and had acquired several trophies. I decided not to push the issue.

One Sunday, in the middle of mass, he developed a severe headache and became dizzy. So we returned home. The following day, there was a school break. When I phoned him, he said, "Mom, I don't feel well. I just can't concentrate, and I'm not studying very much." That was it. I made a doctor's appointment on the spot. Soon we were in her office. After being examined, she said, "Omar has Juvenile Diabetes. His blood sugar level is 1100." He could have gone into a diabetic shock at any moment, as his test results were well over the normal 80 to 120 range. Nothing but the grace of God saved him. He was seventeen. Can you imagine? And naturally he was anxious because the basketball tournament was taking place in two or three weeks.

Omar was treated immediately, and I slept on a cot next to him. The next day, for the first time, he injected himself with insulin. He was given special glasses and told his blurred vision would clear up. When we returned home three days later, he said something that is indelibly engraved in my mind. I was in the kitchen very distraught and completely lost as to what to prepare him for lunch given his new dietary requirements. It was new territory for me, and I was panic-stricken. My eyes reflected my anxiety. He tenderly wrapped his arms around me and said, "Mom, don't worry, we'll get through this."

Q: A remarkable display of bravery.

AKAHLOUN: Omar is a very courageous person. I dropped by my office and spoke to my supervisor. I asked for a week's leave and inquired about the possibility of working flextime. In a forthright manner, she responded, "Well, Penny, I see no reason why you can't. Frankly, you are of no use to me now." She had a bewildering personality. While her remarks were insensitive, she was considerate enough to issue me cell phones so Omar and I could communicate at all times. He managed his condition well, but there were scary moments. Shortly after returning to school, the nurse phoned. His blood sugar level plunged to 48. The doctor promptly switched his insulin. I was constantly in touch with his friendly, reassuring physician, who was a lifesaver for both of us.

The last five months of the tour were frantic. Omar surprised me with twenty-five red roses on my birthday. Despite the challenges confronting him, on June 2, 2001, he graduated with honors and was accepted to George Mason University. I was overjoyed. The campus was approximately ten miles from our old home in Springfield, Virginia. At that point, I thought it was best to finish out my career at the State Department in Washington, D.C., to be near him. We said good-bye to Caracas on June 15, 2001.

In Rome, Italy, June 16, 2002, where Pope John
Paul II canonized Saint Pio of Pietrelcina.

Nelson Mandela at his 89th birthday celebration with Dr. Mamphela
Ramphele and Leila, Johannesburg, South Africa, December 2007.

Bidding the Foreign Service farewell after 43 years at an official
2008 retirement ceremony in the State Department's Dean
Acheson Auditorium, Washington, D.C., December 16.

Volunteering at President Barack Obama's campaign
headquarters in Springfield, Virginia, November 2008.

In October 2010, we are reunited with Momma Habiba Zefri
and my nephew Amin Loukili after a 16-year absence.

Leila and I sharing a delightful evening with Uncle
Jamal, Uncle Abderrahman, Mouina, my niece, and
Aya, her daughter, in Rabat, Morocco.

With James R. "Rudy" Carter on May 21, 2011, in front of the Graveyard of the Atlantic exhibit, U.S. Life Saving Station, Portsmouth Island, North Carolina. He is related to Henry Pigott, one of the last inhabitants of the island, and Joseph Abbot, a cook who prepared meals for my grandfather and the other stranded *Vera Cruz II* passengers.

We met these friendly people in Curral Grande on the Island of Fogo, Cape Verde. The women on the left had an uncanny resemblance to my grandmother.

Enjoying a refreshing breeze from the Atlantic
Ocean on Brava Island, Cape Verde, 2011.

Standing in a lagoon on July 31, 2011, at the Fajã de Água Bay,
where my grandfather's incredible 1903 voyage to America began.

Leila, Omar, and I jubilantly arriving at British Base A at Port Lockroy in Antarctica on January 5, 2014, and fulfilling our dream of walking on the earth's seventh continent.

Shoveling snow in Antarctica, the earth's southernmost region, 2014.

Here we are on board ship, January 10, 2014, celebrating
a successful expedition to the South Pole.

CHAPTER SIXTEEN

AN AIR OF GENUINE SATISFACTION

WASHINGTON, D.C.

The State Department, Board of Examiners of the Office of Recruitment, Examination, and Employment (HR/REE/BEX), 2001–2008

Following many years of living overseas, the move back to Washington, D.C., was a welcome change, and unexpectedly every bit as exciting as an overseas posting. After Omar entered George Mason University, I eagerly started working in my new office.

Q: How did you end up with the Board of Examiners (BEX)?

AKAHLOUN: Prior to Omar's diabetes, I was entertaining the thought of going out to Moscow as a supervisory human resources officer. After his diagnosis and my decision to be close to him, it was late in the bidding cycle, and most choice assignments were filled. I was offered a one-year FS-3 position with the Board of Examiners that was a "down stretch." This means the job was below my grade level and not career enhancing. However, the work of administering the Foreign Service oral examination to applicants sounded appealing and provided an opportunity to contribute to the Foreign Service in a unique way.

When Colin L. Powell became the sixty-fifth Secretary of State in January 2001, he advised the president and congress that the State Department needed more money, more people, better facilities, and improved management practices to carry out its mission. His Diplomatic

Readiness Initiative accelerated the process of recruiting the most diverse Foreign Service Officers in the Department's history. The program was a human resources strategy of getting the right people, in the right place, at the right time—and with the right skills. This diversity included more women and other minorities (gays and lesbians and those with physical disabilities). I was honored to join the office, particularly because I was only the second female Foreign Service Specialist selected for the Board of Examiners. The office had a reputation of being staffed with predominantly generalists.

My plan was to take three months' leave and then begin my tour with BEX. A time-out was necessary to recharge my batteries and restore my energy. Venezuela emotionally and physically consumed me, and I needed sufficient time to process Omar's situation, the loss of my mother, my father's stroke, and my decision to be assigned in Washington, D.C., and eventually retire there. The reentry was enormously draining.

My "to-do" list was daunting. George Mason University had scheduled several mandatory freshman workshops. Simultaneously, there were multiple medical appointments with State Department doctors and Omar's new endocrinologist. My social network, Momma Sharma, Miki Markoff, Bob and Lynette Asselin, Marion and Bill Hird, Beatrice Beyer Ancheta, and Mary Chin readily pitched in. They chauffeured us to medical appointments, the grocery store, our home in Springfield, and to university functions. Our friends also helped with house repairs and the unpacking. No chore was too small or burdensome for them. They were simply indispensable.

Three weeks later, Leila arrived. She graduated from Georgetown University the previous year and just completed an accelerated Master's Degree in International Relations at the University of Chicago. We flew to Massachusetts and had another enjoyable visit with my father, niece, and nephews. After tending to several financial matters, we returned to Washington and frantically shopped around for a new car. Three days remained of my so-called vacation.

Omar moved into the university's dorm, and two days later on August 26, I occupied our former house in Springfield. Over the course of several days, our personal and household effects from Caracas and various domestic and international storage facilities were delivered. The combined shipments, if imaginable, totaled 12,800 lbs. The amount of treasures one accumulates over the years is astounding. It was delightful getting reacquainted with my belongings, especially Ahmed's paintings.

A few days later, on Monday, September 10, 2001, I entered my new office and was ecstatic. No more grueling twelve-to-fourteen-hour workdays at the embassies and no more supervisory responsibilities. There was an informal, diverse, and friendly group of people working at the Board of Examiners. The atmosphere was less stratified than I earlier imagined. It pleased me to see a gender balance among the examiners and that all Foreign Service career tracks, also known as cones, were represented. There was a certain egalitarian cooperation regardless of an individual's rank or background. The examiners were committed and welcoming. I looked forward to my tenure there.

Q: Were you in the office on September 11—the day terror struck home?

AKAHLOUN: Oh gosh. Yes! September 11, 2001, tragically was unforgettable. I walked over to the Department of State's main building for a security briefing, which was necessary before we could log into the office's computer system. At 9:00 a.m. the class started. Moments later, an announcement came over the public address system for us to evacuate. Everyone thought it was another one of those ill-timed fire drills.

We stepped outside and spotted clouds of black smoke in the distance. We had no clue where it was coming from, but it seemed too close for comfort. I rushed back to Columbia Plaza and watched the television monitors, flashing the news. Two commercial planes had slammed into New York's World Trade Center, another one hit the Pentagon and a fourth one evidently crashed in a field near Shanksville, Pennsylvania, before reaching the alleged target of either the White House or the nation's Capitol building. Working at our overseas missions, we lived with the threat of a terrorist attack in the back of our mind, but in the U.S.—our safe haven—we were able to relax. Then a tragedy of this magnitude happens, and the ground is removed from beneath us. I no longer felt safe and protected in my own home, in my own country. It was terrifying.

Throngs of people descended on the Foggy Bottom Metro Station and assembled on the platform, which was so congested we could hardly breathe. We were told to turn off our cell phones for security reasons. In any case, because the circuits were overloaded, there was no service and no outside communication. I waited and waited for several hours for the Blue Line to take me home. When the train arrived, hundreds of people crammed inside. Once in Springfield, I drove straight to George Mason University to find Omar. Needless to say, he was relieved to see me and vice versa. That evening, I contacted Leila, busied myself with household chores, and prayed for the victims and their families. For the most part, I avoided watching television or listening to the radio. The news was too depressing. It was my second day at work. The rest of the week, our schedule was virtually uninterrupted. There were no candidates being examined, as we were preparing for a new assessment cycle that began in three weeks. But the U.S. government swung into action.

Following September 11, new and tightened security measures were instituted at airports and all public facilities, including the State Department, to help prevent another tragedy and to restore a feeling of safety among the people. About one week after "9/11," the first anthrax letters were mailed. They came in two waves. In November, a postal worker at the State Department's mail annex in Sterling, Virginia, opened a misrouted envelope intended for a U.S. Senator, and he contracted inhalation anthrax. The incident was frightening and disconcerting not only for everyone stateside but also for those working at our missions overseas.

Q: *Embassy visa and security policies were greatly affected. Tell us about the Foreign Service Oral Examination assessment process.*

AKAHLOUN: Exam day stressed out everyone. The applicants reported at one of two test sites around 7:00 a.m. They were given instructions, divided into two groups (usually six in each), and ushered into a briefing room. At 7:45 a.m. sharp, the lead examiner welcomed and congratulated them on being invited to the Oral Assessment Center. Next they moved to a group exercise room, sat at a round table, and reviewed their individual case studies.

At 8:45 a.m., four examiners filed into the room in a precise fashion. The entrance and seating arrangement was choreographed to provide the best view of the two individuals each assessor was grading. Candidates were given six minutes to make their presentations and twenty minutes to discuss the projects before reaching consensus. Meanwhile, we took notes and graded each performance against thirteen dimensions that measured certain factors, such as leadership, planning and organizing, analytical, interpersonal skills, and others.

During the first session, I tended to grade those with clearly demonstrable potential more generously. If they failed at the outset, recovery was nearly impossible. For the next segment, the structured interview, I tightened up. We talked about the individual's motivation to join the Foreign Service, focused on solving hypothetical situations found in embassy settings, and asked about the person's past work or school experiences.

Every day we examined different people. I found the work extremely enjoyable and gratifying, as it allowed us to positively influence the lives of future Foreign Service generalists and specialists. There was no downtime. Assessment days were tightly structured and very intensive. The most painful part of the day was informing applicants that they fell short of reaching the necessary two-point-five score to enter the Foreign Service. We broke the unhappy news as diplomatically as possible, but it was still disappointing for them. Regardless of how many times we delivered the results, it never got easier.

Incidentally, once I assessed with another Cape Verdean, Foreign Service Officer Anthony C. Fernandes. What a surprise. Ironically, his Onset relatives lived two blocks from my house. At the time, Tony was working on the Diplomatic Readiness Initiative (DRI) Task Force. Not only our office but the entire Bureau of Human Resources (HR) was mobilized and focused on efforts to encourage women and other minorities to take the Foreign Service examination. The diplomats-in-residence at various universities gave seminars; the recruitment branch held job fairs, and additional student interns were hired. In addition to our two Washington test centers, we opened several of them around the country.

Q: *It was an enormous effort. Some off-sites were held for two weeks and others four to six weeks. A few overlapped. What was your experience?*

AKAHLOUN: I was site coordinator six times and found managing the centers exciting. Traveling coast-to-coast to cities such as San Francisco, Seattle, Boston, Chicago, Miami, Ft. Lauderdale, Stamford, Dallas, Austin, and Phoenix acquainted me with America. I had been around the world but never fully explored our amazing country. I encountered some of the friendliest and nicest Americans ever. Once again, it gave me a chance to see that similarities in people are more visible than their differences. It was good to look at what unites us rather than what divides us.

Everyone in BEX had ancillary duties. Over the course of the assignment, I was a Personnel Assignment Officer, Special Accommodations Coordinator for candidates with disabilities, Mustang Program Coordinator and participated in our orientation/training sessions and other activities. Luckily, I received a promotion to FS-1 in 2004. Near the end of my tour, I served on the 2007 Selection Board for specialists. Another satisfying experience was giving a power point presentation on credit reports and personal finances to Civil Service employees. I worked with the Board of Examiners from 2001 to 2008, a total of seven years.

Q: Wow! There's a record. The Board of Examiners has a certain rhythm to it that doesn't fluctuate dramatically from one period to the next, but you managed to be innovative and resourceful and maintained your enthusiasm.

AKAHLOUN: I was passionate about my work, held on to my sense of humor, maintained a positive outlook, and continued to challenge and motivate myself. Many committed examiners, including Steve Leach, Rudy Watkins, Katherine Lee, Naim Ahmed, John Ohta, Howard Stedman, John Shippy, Fabio Saturni, Guyle Cavin, Adrienne Stefan, Philippe du Chateau, Dianne Andruch, Ann Syrett, Mark Woerner, and Marsha Von Durkheim, plus dedicated program assistants, led by Kelly Wright, unselfishly guided me. At the time, BEX had good leadership. Art Salvaterra was compassionate and humorous. Steve Nolan was also warmhearted and capable. Margaret Dean was kind and considerate and had exceptional organizational skills. All of them promoted hiring a diverse group of examiners in terms of profession, gender, and ethnicity. This played a crucial role in the recruitment process because more opportunities were given to a wider range of people.

I loved my job, liked the environment, believed in the goal of diversification, and tried to ensure that all promising candidates, including those of color, were given a chance to enhance the Foreign

Service and at the same time have a meaningful career for themselves. The strengths of some candidates with Foreign Service capability were not always captured by our criteria—the thirteen dimensions. The overall number of African Americans, Latinos, and other ethnic groups in the U.S. Foreign Service is disproportionately low.

In spite of the Department's outreach efforts, minorities are still underrepresented. I think early awareness and exposure to the State Department and educational opportunities are very beneficial. The pools and networks of identifying minorities also need to be expanded. In addition, more programs, such as the Thomas R. Pickering Foreign Affairs Fellowships, the Charles B. Rangel International Affairs Program, and the Serrano Scholars Program, should be established to ensure the wealth of experience that Americans of all backgrounds possess are adequately reflected in our diplomatic corps.

There have always been issues associated with diversity. From personal experience, I know the State Department has made great strides in opening its doors to the best talent available from all over America. Greater numbers of women, African Americans, and other minorities are being recruited and many of the earlier burdens confronting them— marginalization, limited advancement opportunities, and other injustices and indignities—have over time diminished. To have a smoothly run operation and to maintain a stable workforce, management must redouble its efforts to transform the system. There is no simple fix, but we must keep trying.

Q: What do you say to the argument that the Foreign Service is not a social or employment program? It can best function when it has specialized expertise.

AKAHLOUN: The Foreign Service should not be a social service agency, and it is not. I agree that specialized expertise, such as language skills, is essential. Our examination is very competitive, and our candidates are highly educated, talented, and motivated. We bring in the best-qualified people, regardless of background. In some countries the selection process is still tilted toward the wealthy—the elite. Many are sons of diplomats who study at the same universities. Our system is more open. The Department's in-take program aims to reflect a wide cross-section of our society. We also do an excellent job developing and mentoring our employees. I was hired as a secretary and eventually converted to officer status by taking advantage of the department's training programs. Emotional intelligence and social awareness can also be of significance.

The following cases might be rare but suggest an education can be obtained outside academic circles. Once I examined a young lady without a college degree who aced the exam. As a family member, working as an administrative assistant in Moscow, she acquired a wealth of knowledge. She had impressive people skills, technical skills, and demonstrated excellent common sense. All the examiners scored her exceptionally high, and she landed at the top of the register. In another case, a postman without a bachelor's degree passed the exam with flying colors. In the past, the Foreign Service had a reputation of being an elitist organization staffed predominantly with white, Anglo-Saxon Protestant generalists. Over time, our society has changed, and so has the State Department's culture.

Q: While posted in Washington, D.C., did you manage to still feed your love of travel?

AKAHLOUN: I was able to travel somewhat. As mentioned earlier, after suffering a massive stroke in late 1998, my father was confined to a nursing home, tube fed, and bedridden. He spoke some days more coherently than others. My mother passed away the previous year. My sister who lived in Massachusetts kept a close eye on the doctors and nurses and held them accountable. She and my niece, Aleita Rodriguez, and nephews, Wayne Rodriguez, Robert "Camp" Pina, Lawrence "Bennie" Lopes, and James "Scotty" Pina, were fantastic at supervising his care and uplifting him. It was very disheartening seeing my father so incapacitated.

I felt compelled to go on a pilgrimage in hopes that the power of prayer would see the family through our ordeal. Over the years, I maintained contact with our former friend from Montevideo, Father Joseph Marino (currently an archbishop), who had been reassigned to Rome. He invited me to Pope John Paul II's canonization of Padre Pio, a mystic Franciscan monk from southern Italy who was reported to suffer with Christ's bleeding crucifixion wounds (stigmata). Soon I was on my way to Rome.

There was a great deal of activity packed into my June 8-18, 2002, trip. I rented a Vatican City apartment, minutes away from Saint Peter's Basilica. The beauty and splendor inside and outside the Basilica defied imagination, and the Swiss Guards with their striking blue-and-gold uniforms and crimson-plumed helmets were magnificent. Father Marino arranged for me to attend the pope's general audience at Saint Peter's Square—sat in the third row and received Holy Communion. He escorted me into the Holy See's diplomatic reception rooms, and we rode in the pope's private elevator. I visited the Sistine Chapel, the Vatican Museum, the Basilica of Saint John Lateran, the catacombs and other sites. In addition, I went on a one-day excursion to Naples, the Island of Capri, and Sorrento. Funny thing, a few months earlier there was an eye-catching documentary on television, promoting tourism in Italy's dazzling Amalfi Coast. Incredibly, I was now in the exact spot. I had forgotten about the program until I arrived there. What a lovely surprise.

There was also a trip to Assisi. Saint Francis of Assisi is one of my patron saints, so it was especially moving to see his birthplace. Although I was constantly on the move, I spent considerable time meditating and praying for my father, my children, and family members spread out over Washington, D.C., Boston, California, New York, Paris, and Morocco. At the time, I felt truly blessed to be in Rome.

An estimated one million people from Italy and other countries converged on the city for the June 16, 2002, canonization. We coped with temperatures in excess of ninety-five degrees Fahrenheit. Those of us inside Saint Peter's square were given ice-cold bottles of water to prevent dehydration and were sprinkled with water from fire hydrants to avert sunstroke. It seemed as though we were baking in a hot oven, yet I was a happy camper. People packed the surrounding streets and watched the ceremony on giant screens. Once again, I had preferential seating and saw Pope John Paul II pass by in his mobile. I was only a few feet away from him. (Pope Paul was later elevated to sainthood; the historic event took place on April 27, 2014.)

After Padre Pio was proclaimed a saint, 12,237 colored balloons were released, one for each day since his September 23, 1968, death. We cheered wildly and waved white flags. My only regret was that the peaceful retreat ended far too soon. I flew from Italy directly to Massachusetts and stayed there two weeks. Then it was back to Washington. Life was uneventful for about eight months. On Wednesday, February 19, 2003, everything changed.

A snowstorm paralyzed greater Washington. Schools closed and so did the State Department. I took advantage by preparing for an upcoming San Francisco off-site. I briefly interrupted my packing to cook a Moroccan dish. The skin of the chicken felt strange, so I removed it and slightly nicked my thumb in the process. I washed my hands with soap and water and applied Neosporin. Later that evening, the thumb began throbbing. Yet there were no visible cuts. Two days later, my physician, Dr. Laraine T. Field, took a culture, and placed me on antibiotics. At that point, it was too late to find a substitute. I was taking medication, and everything appeared to be under control, so I flew to San Francisco. It was Sunday, the twenty-third of February 2003.

That Monday I reported for work with a bandaged thumb. I relied more on memory than written notes and entered my scores into the computer with my left hand. After receiving the lab results, Dr. Field prescribed *Cipro*, the potent drug used during the 2001 anthrax attacks. By the end of the week, my discolored thumb doubled in size and resulted in an emergency visit to the California Pacific Medical Center. When the doctor lanced it, I nearly fainted. The only thing that saved me was the thought of my father and how he had conquered so much pain and misery during his life and still said, "It could be worse." However, the situation deteriorated quickly. On Sunday, February 28, I couldn't bend my thumb and returned to the hospital. The physician referred me to the Buncke Clinic and strongly recommended I visit within twenty-four hours. My heart was pounding, and my knees were buckling. What a dreadful situation.

There were no openings at the clinic. After a desperate plea, I was told to come in at 11:00 a.m. The Davies Medical Center Clinic at 45 Castro Street turned out to be a renowned hand and microsurgery medical practice with some of the world's finest and brightest surgeons. The environment was not exactly morale boosting. Pictures of transposed body parts covered the walls. One in particular caught my eye—a toe transplanted on a hand to compensate for a missing thumb.

My first words to the physician were "Hello, I want to introduce you to my family." Pointing to a photograph, I said, "This is Leila and Omar. Please make certain I return home to them with my thumb intact." She smiled, removed the bandage, and quickly summoned Dr. Gregory Buncke, the head of the clinic. Commenting on the picture, he said, "This is a first in my career. You have lovely children." I tried to personalize things because I recognized that bonding with the doctor increases the odds of successful treatment. I wasn't taking any chances.

Dr. Buncke took an image (fluoroscopy) of my right thumb. Shaking his head, he said, "You have osteomyelitis, a bone infection." He consulted with Dr. Kevin Myers, and they decided to operate that afternoon at 2:00 p.m. My head was swirling with emotion. My purse containing cash, credit cards, jewelry, and other valuables was turned over to a security agent who had me sign a document exempting the hospital from any liability in case of theft. I just had to trust God.

My room overlooked Haight-Ashbury. In the far distance, I could see Nob Hill and my hotel, which raised my spirits. After surgery, my thumb was left open to drain and packed with gauze instead of being stitched up, and I was given a thumb/arm splint. It was surreal. The cards were stacked against me, but I was determined to reclaim my health. A favorite Bible verse encouraged me: "I can do all things in Christ who strengthens me" (Philippians 4:13).

The next morning, Dr. Myers said it was too soon to predict the future. He started me on a massive dose of antibiotics, which was administered intravenously. He also noticed a book on my bedside table. "Oh, you're reading Dr. Carson's book, *Think Big*," he said. "I met him while training at Columbia University's College of Physicians and Surgeons in New York. He gave an inspiring speech that helped me apply myself. He's very impressive." I liked young Dr. Myers and sensed I was in good hands.

Two days later my veins collapsed, and the doctors wanted to surgically implant a Peripherally Inserted Central Catheter into my left arm. I immediately consulted with my sister, whose medical expertise was extensive. Moreover, under duress she was unflappable; her good humor was contagious. She thought the plan was sound, so I went forward with the procedure.

The drama continued. An infectious disease specialist ordered more rounds of antibiotics to be given each day for six weeks. Saturday morning, I was discharged and placed under the care of a home nurse. Generous supplies of medicine and paraphernalia were delivered to my hotel room, which soon took on the appearance of a pharmacy. The nurse visited me and replaced the bag of antibiotics every twelve hours. I avoided strenuous work and could only lift objects weighing less than ten pounds. To avoid infection, my hands were kept dry. At night, I slept on my back with my arms propped up on pillows, so they were higher than my heart. The position was rather uncomfortable, but the thumb was mending.

Dr. Myers was shocked at the speed of my recuperation. Not me. Dr. Ben Carson wrote in *Thinking Big*, "Our attitude is a stronger indicator of our pending recovery than our physical status or prognosis." In addition to reading his book, I attended daily mass at a nearby chapel for spiritual renewal. Soon the doctor advised it was no longer necessary to soak the thumb three times a day or sleep with the splint. I began doing thumb-strengthening exercises, and a week later my medical team released me.

My colleague, Steve Eisenbaum, graciously volunteered to accompany me home. We left San Francisco on March 23, 2003. Dr. Field coordinated with the Virginia health provider and was standing by in case of emergency. All went as planned. The nurse, Barbara Burgeson, showed up at my home at 8:00 p.m. Ironically, she was a Jehovah Witness. As a child, she attended the same Kingdom Hall as Dr. Ben Carson. Treatment ended the fifth of April. The next day, on my sixtieth birthday, I returned to the office. At first, it was strange and cumbersome typing with my right hand, but gradually I picked up speed.

This might be a long-winded explanation of events, but it perfectly illustrates how something amazing happens when faith, love, and hope come together. We are all capable of doing far more than we realize. During tough times, we often discover the depths of our strength and realize that a higher power has enabled us to do what otherwise might seem impossible. At least, this was my experience. The next few years slipped by quickly, and without warning, I was no longer in the thick of the rat race punching the time clock.

PART THREE

CHAPTER SEVENTEEN

RETIREMENT: THE ALARM CLOCK
GOES OUT THE WINDOW

Washington, D.C., 2008

After a forty-three-year Foreign Service career, retirement brought along with it the luxury of doing everything I ever wanted and on my own timetable. No more deadlines. No more long commutes. These days, things easily go in one ear and out the other, and laughable senior moments are plentiful.

Q: You retired in 2008. Tell me more about your activities and interests. Are you enjoying the lifestyle?

AKAHLOUN: Retirement is a wonderful gift. It is a time for reflection, renewal, and revival. Life is as full as ever, and my sense of humor has never been sharper. At sixty-five, the Foreign Service's mandatory retirement age, I stopped working full time. Thank God, I am still alert, energetic, intellectually curious, and passionately pursing the projects I was unable to do while employed. At this juncture, the body slows up a bit, but the mind and soul expands. Growth is a lifelong process. I want to stretch my boundaries and develop into the best person I can be.

The Foreign Service Institute's March/April 2008 Retirement Planning Seminar and the Job Search Program was a joyful, satisfying experience that allowed me to draw up a roadmap for the future. It helped me focus and plan out the next crucial phase of my life, which included writing my memoir. Two weeks after leaving the State Department, I went on a retreat to St. Joseph's Oratory Shrine in Montreal and climbed the ninety-nine steps again. This time I cheated somewhat by using a pillow to cushion my knees. In May, my children surprised me with a marvelous retirement party at a downtown Moroccan restaurant. It was a special celebration with family and close friends. The gathering also gave me an opportunity to dwell on Leila and Omar's achievements.

Living overseas often gives young people a higher than average cultural understanding of the world. They are apt to be open and tolerant of diversity and able to comfortably mingle with various social groups. This is not to say that children raised abroad are superior to their peers or that they are exempt from life's pitfalls. This definitely is not the case. Their international exposure and experiences simply gives them a different perspective on life. Leila graduated from the University of Georgetown's School of Foreign Service in 1999 and received a Master of Arts in International Relations from the University of Chicago the following year. Omar obtained a Bachelor of Art's Degree in Anthropology in 2005 and a Master of Science in Conflict Analysis and Resolution in May 2008 from George Mason University. Both of them have a sense of service and are in rewarding professions that aim to accelerate social change. Having said this, let's continue with some of my other activities.

After becoming a Library of Congress researcher with a personal book shelf in an alcove of the magnificent Main Reading Room in the Thomas Jefferson Building, we started this delightful Association for Diplomatic Studies and Training (ADST) oral history project. Later, I studied family genealogy and traced my ancestor's history at the National Archives in Washington, D.C. The freedom to engage in these endeavors was not taken for granted. My mother shared stories about how she and other Cape Verdeans at Wareham High School in the thirties were excluded from their senior class trip to the nation's capital because the city was racially segregated, and this situation was to linger for some time. I also traveled to Johannesburg to visit Leila and celebrated my sixty-seventh birthday in Hawaii, vacationed in Miami with friends, and began practicing yoga—a magic pill for physical, emotional, and spiritual well-being. Yet, one of the most exhilarating and rewarding experiences was being a volunteer for Barack Obama's presidential election campaigns. Active State Department employees are not allowed to become politically active, but after retirement, the barriers to political involvement are lifted.

President Obama's 2008 campaign was built on the energy, enthusiasm, and ingenuity of thousands of grassroots supporters. One of our goals was to "turn Virginia blue," which meant convincing the political conservatives in the state to vote more along the lines of the Democratic Party. From sunrise to sunset, we made telephone calls, using various scripts that targeted specific categories of voters. We knocked on neighborhood doors, going block by block and person to person, to get people to vote. We did data entry work and performed other activities as well.

The teams of field organizers, many of them college students, were smart and committed. To give you some idea of their dedication, once I was canvassing the neighborhood with an individual who casually mentioned she and her colleague were recently out soliciting votes during a tornado watch. The storm hit, but they kept working as their office goal of knocking on one hundred thousand doors had not yet been reached. The volunteers came in all shapes, sizes, ages, and colors. The supporters were truly a rainbow coalition. Some were in wheelchairs. Others came from abroad. At the Springfield and Arlington campaign offices, I met foreigners—one Australian and a couple from Sweden—who specifically came to America to help out with the movement. There was such fervor. What an electrifying experience.

For me, it was necessary to become a volunteer because our country was in great turmoil. People had little faith in the current leadership. There was an economic crisis and a growing weariness of the Iraq War, which Obama had opposed. Americans were fed up with typical politicians and wanted someone new and different. Like many others, I thought Barack Obama was the best hope to bring about change. His keynote address at the 2004 Democratic National Convention in Boston was very impressive. His multicultural background was appealing, and he was able to move beyond racial politics and narrowly defined interest groups. He did not exude a sense of entitlement or resentment. This was refreshing. Obama was charming, clever, and compassionate. Equally important, he promoted bipartisan cooperation. His powerful message fired me up. He filled me with hope.

I also became involved in his 2012 reelection campaign, which was absolutely brilliant. President Obama built a campaign organization unlike any other in American history. It was people-oriented, data-driven, and led by talented neighborhood teams supported by field organizers who analyzed voters' attitudes and preferences. The campaign redefined how individuals used the Web, social media, and smart phones to participate in the political process. The organizers knew who we were and how to turn us into the type of person they wanted us to be. Technology was taken to a new level.

Once again, thousands of dedicated field staffers and volunteers made calls, using persuasion phone scripts and other guides. The detailed talking points helped ambivalent voters decide. We arranged rides to the polls. We canvassed and reminded people to vote. Social scientists believe people are more likely to do things when they have a strategy, so we asked what their plans were to vote on Election Day, November 6, 2012. In the end, on the strength of President Barack Obama's message, personality, and record, he was returned to office for a second term.

In his reelection speech, he told the nation, "We are not as divided as our politics suggests. We're not as cynical as the pundits believe. We are greater than the sum of our individual ambitions and we remain more than a collection of red states and blue states. We are, and forever will be, the United States of America." One day after his big victory, President Obama made a surprise stop at his headquarters in Chicago to address his campaign staff. He expressed his gratitude for their support and dedication to the reelection effort. It was an emotional thank-you that was later emailed to thousands of his supporters, including the volunteers who helped build his huge grassroots movement. I was enormously pleased to be able to contribute in a minor way in reelecting such a groundbreaking public figure to the highest office in our land. Retirement, indeed, gives us a chance to give back.

At any stage of life, and particularly during our golden years, we should give ourselves permission to laugh often, long, deep, and loud. The simple pleasures in life should be enjoyed and our passions explored. As we advance in years, it is also a moment to preserve our sense of youthfulness by eating a healthy diet, exercising, and meditating. When I think of age, I am reminded of a quote I once heard: "Youth is not a time of life—it is a state of mind. Nobody grows old merely by living a number of years. People grow old by losing their ideals..." Mark Twain sums it up best. "Age is an issue of mind over matter. If you don't mind, it doesn't matter."

CHAPTER EIGHTEEN

SUNSETS OVER THE GOLDEN DUNES OF THE SAHARA DESERT

MOROCCO

October 2– 23, 2010

Leaving the workforce, afforded me the time to travel for pleasure and to reconnect with some of my most favorite places and people on earth. The first stop was Morocco.

Q: When we last spoke, we discussed your assignment at the Board of Examiners (BEX) and your social and political retirement activities, including your involvement with Barack Obama's presidential campaigns. Now we are resuming our conversations with your 2010 visit to Morocco. Tell us about this journey.

AKAHLOUN: Much had transpired since my first trip to Morocco in 1968 when I worked at the U.S. Embassy. Momma Aini, Ahmed's second Mother, had passed away and was no longer with us. Momma Habiba, his biological Mom, was thankfully still alive and sweet and loving as ever. She was in her early or mid-eighties and realized her dream of going on a religious pilgrimage to Mecca. Ahmed's sister, Souad, a primary schoolteacher, had recovered from major heart surgery. Her husband, Abderrahman, a retired bank director, journeyed to Mecca as well. For Muslims, the Haj is the ultimate act of worship.

Mounia, my niece, obtained a Master's Degree in biology and had completed the coursework toward her doctorate. She interrupted her studies to marry Mohcine, a Moroccan military officer, and they now had an adorable toddler, Aya. (In April 2014, Alae was born and joined her sister.) Meanwhile, my nephew Nawfal completed postgraduate economic studies in Paris and married Saloua, a Moroccan classmate of his. They are now proud parents of Wahil, a son born last year. His younger brother Amin had grown into a tall handsome young man who had received his certificate in accounting and was studying for his baccalaureate, which he has since successfully completed.

Rabat now looked more prosperous. The downtown donkey carts seemed to be a thing of the past. Residential and shopping complexes had sprung up and others were under construction. The quaint flower market that Ahmed and I so fondly frequented was now an underground parking lot for a commercial building. The Arab Spring had blossomed in Morocco, and I was shocked to see Mohammed V University students protesting in the streets because of lack of employment opportunities. This was unheard of under the reign of King Hassan II.

Momma Habiba Zefri (also Zeffri or Zoufri) shed light on the intriguing family history. Given her age, her memory was phenomenal. Uncle Jamal, my dear brother-in-law, incessantly and patiently interpreted from Arabic to English and vice versa. Momma showed us her *Livret D'Identitié et D'État Civil*, an official government document written in French and Arabic that recorded personal events. It was comprehensive and contained her father's photograph, name, address, profession held, and birth and death information. The family tree was well documented. Momma has three brothers, Sadik, Ahmed, and Abdelbaki. At fourteen years old, she was married off to Mohamed Ben Ahmed Akahloun (1903–1961) who was forty-one. Momma's father, Abdesselam Ben Mohammed Zefri (1906–1974), and her late husband, Ahmed's father, were second cousins. We interrupted the oral history sessions halfway into our stay in Rabat, so Leila and I could play tourists and visit other areas of the country.

She and I went on a mesmerizing "Best of Morocco" bus tour from October 8 to October 16, 2010. We started in Casablanca, headed to Rabat, continued on to Meknes, and ended up in Fez—all in one day. Fez is a 1,200-year-old medieval city that is the spiritual and cultural center of Morocco. It is widely believed to have one of the oldest universities in the world. Over one million people live within the windowless walls of the ancient medina said to contain an estimated 9,500 alleyways. We were carefully shepherded through the labyrinthine of ever-forking lanes, so we didn't lose our way. There were no cars inside the medina. Goods were transported by donkeys, carriages, and motorbikes. It was intriguing.

Next we moved on to Ifrane, a winter ski resort in the Middle Atlas. The town surprisingly resembled a neat and orderly Swiss village with russet-tiled roof buildings. We passed through the cedar forest in the Azrou Valley and kept climbing. Making our way to Ouarzazate, we stopped at the Todra Gorge and the nearby scenic Dades Gorge, locally referred to as Morocco's little Grand Canyon. The drive was spectacular. There were hundreds of Kasbahs lining the route through stunning red and ochre desert landscapes, towns, and palm groves. The village of Kalaat M'Gouna is best known for its roses and its notorious secret prison destroyed by King Hassan II in the early nineties. Ouarzazate is the international film capital of Morocco. Movies such as *Lawrence of Arabia, Gladiator, Babel, The Bourne Ultimatum, Inception, and Son of God* were shot there at professional studios. We also saw dromedary camels, mingling with flocks of sheep. A young boy, wearing an oversized turban, looked after them.

From Erfoud we took a side trip to Merzouga, the edge of the Sahara Desert to ride camels and watch the sunset over the golden sand dunes. It was glorious and fulfilled yet another dream. Climbing on to the backs of these unpredictable animals was more involved than it looked. We were not forewarned, but we quickly learned a trick or two. One leans back when camels stand up; otherwise we can be tossed face forward. They straighten their back legs first and then the front legs catch up. Our camels moved with a jerky front-to-back and side-to-side motion, forcing us to hang on to the saddle for dear life. Our Berber guides walked in front of us, holding the reins. It was hilarious.

From Ouarzazate to Marrakech, we drove through the breathtaking Tizi n'Tichka pass in the High Atlas. The highest point was over 7,400 feet, and it is said there are 340 twisting bends along the way. During one tense moment, our bus met another one, approaching from the opposite direction. The drivers were both trying to make a hairpin turn. We waited precariously close to the edge of the road until the other bus safely passed. We drove through charming mountain villages, dense woods, and green fields and then reached Marrakech. Leila and I headed straight for our favorite spot, the Djemaa El Fna Square.

After two days of fun, we left the hypnotizing city and returned to Casablanca. The following day, we ate lunch near the port at Rick's Café named after the notorious place in the movie *Casablanca*. It had a tastefully decorated upstairs lounge where Humphrey Bogart's movie was being shown. By the way, we ordered, of all things, an "Obama Family Chili" dish that was excellent. That afternoon, we jumped on the train for Rabat, and later in the evening Momma continued to provide more details about her Moroccan ancestry.

On Leila's birthday, October 17, 2010, the family surprised her with lovely caftans, jewelry, and prepared a scrumptious meal. The next day, we journeyed to Tangier and visited Nozha Yemlahi, the wife of Ahmed's deceased brother Aziz, and her children. Her youngest child, who we were meeting for the first time, was named after my late husband. One of Momma Habiba's brothers, Abdelbaki Zefri, who moved to England several years ago, was in town. He shared some of his childhood memories with us. According to his best recollection, Momma and her mother were pregnant at the same time. It seems he and Ahmed was close in age and became playmates. After reliving the past with him, we did some exploring.

We ventured deep into the medina and found Momma Habiba's birthplace at 17 Rue Ourbah, Dar Baroud, which overlooked the Mediterranean Sea and the Straits of Gibraltar. The house was now the Moroccan headquarters for the *Coopération Pour Le Développement Des Pays Emergents* (COSPE), a French international organization that assists emerging countries with their development. By chance, we found a caretaker who showed us inside. The original blue door at the entrance, some of the tile work, the shutters, and the tiny bathroom were untouched. Although Uncle Jamal had visited the house fifty-three years ago, he recognized the neighborhood, especially the shops where he bought "sweets" as a youngster. He has an incredible memory.

At nightfall, we zigzagged our way through the medina and reached the old American Legation, the first diplomatic mission opened by the U.S. back in 1797. Today, the historical site houses the Tangier American Legation Institute for Moroccan Studies (TALIM), which serves as a cultural center, museum, conference center, and library. The building is unique, as it is the only U.S. National Historic Landmark outside America.

We retraced Ahmed's childhood footsteps by visiting his old primary school, *L'École des Fils de Notables* (attended by privileged children), and the old French hospital (now called *Kortobi*), where he was born. At the time, his family lived at 12 Rue de Shakespeare in the prosperous cosmopolitan community of M'Sallah. Today, the king's summer palace and the royal guesthouse are within walking distance. The house where Ahmed lived until age twelve is in ruins and practically covered over with bushes and trees. The view looking down on the Mediterranean Sea, however, is magnificent. Our excursion to Morocco was not long enough. We emotionally left the country on October 23, 2010, with a promise to return as soon as possible.

CHAPTER NINETEEN

TRACING SHIPWRECKS AND CAPE VERDEAN FOOTPRINTS

NORTH CAROLINA, SOUTH CAROLINA, AND GEORGIA

May 19–30, 2011

One retirement objective was to keep my thirst for travel well quenched. Recording my oral history and writing this memoir piqued my interest in retracing the steps of my forefathers. The more I delved into the story of the *Vera Cruz VII*, the vessel bringing my paternal grandfather to the U.S. in 1903, the more enthralling the odyssey became. Soon I found myself at Portsmouth Island in the Outer Banks of North Carolina.

Q: If this is similar to your other adventures, I am anxious to hear more.

AKAHLOUN: Through my research, I stumbled upon a group, the Friends of Portsmouth Island (FPI), which held biannual reunions on the island. As a granddaughter of one of the *Vera Cruz II* survivors, I felt strangely connected to the society and decided to contact Richard Meissner, the FPI President at the time. A gathering had already taken place, but I was invited to speak at the forthcoming annual spring meeting in Ocracoke Island, North Carolina. I was ecstatic, but there was one problem. In Virginia, my driving was limited to a twenty-five-mile radius. How could I possibly drive to the Outer Banks? A former

Foreign Service colleague, Mary Chin, was already planning a vacation to the Carolinas and Georgia and agreed to a side excursion to the Outer Banks. She was also willing to share the driving. We put our heads together and came up with an ambitious twelve-day itinerary.

On May 19, 2011, we set out by train from Union Station in Washington, D.C. Hours later, we reached the Rocky Mount station in North Carolina, and a prearranged taxi took us to a place called Faith Auto Body Shop. We picked up our rental vehicle, drove to Nags Head, and rested there. The next morning, we briefly visited the Wright Brothers National Memorial. I found it interesting that Orville and Wilbur Wright completed the world's first successful flight the same year my grandfather shipwrecked on the Outer Banks of North Carolina. We then drove to Cape Hatteras, took a ferry part of the way, and continued driving to Ocracoke Island. Ultimately, Mary navigated, and I did all the chauffeuring. Traveling on the exposed ocean front stretch of Highway 12 was intimidating, especially crossing the nearly three-mile long Herbert C. Bonner Bridge. I was completely out of my comfort zone but was relaxed because it felt as though some mysterious force was guiding me. We arrived at the quaint Sand Dollar Hotel late that afternoon.

The meeting was held the following day, May 21, 2011, at the former U.S. Coast Guard Station. The presenter before me displayed his Portsmouth Island paintings, one of which contained a beautiful monarch butterfly with deep orange-and-black wings. Ever since beginning my oral history project, these butterflies would periodically flutter around me while I was thinking about my grandfather. For instance, one sunny afternoon, I was looking at a library book on family history while waiting for the metro to the National Archives. Suddenly, a monarch landed near my hands on top of the page I was reading and rested there quite a long time. The butterfly only flew away when the train arrived. It was so strange that another passenger remarked, "Wow! That's unusual. Today is your lucky day." It turned out he was right as that afternoon some mysteries unraveled, and I made key discoveries about my grandfather's journey to America. I realized this was more than a coincidence.

A pattern was emerging, so I investigated and discovered monarch butterflies did have symbolic meaning. For example, in a certain area in Mexico, they are closely tied to the idea of spirits and are perceived to be returning souls of the deceased. Just prior to beginning my talk, I felt my grandfather's presence, encouraging and energizing me. My stage fright disappeared, and I began telling his story.

In my speech, I thanked Portsmouth for doing the right thing, embracing strangers in harm's way, sheltering the *Vera Cruz II* passengers for three days, and providing 2,540 meals. I stated that my grandfather fulfilled the American dream of owning property, educating his children, and becoming a U.S. citizen. As a result, four generations benefited from the kindness of the civic-minded islanders. I met several friendly descendants of the Portsmouth Island villagers, including James Carter who was related to Henry Pigott, one of the last individuals to live on the island. The atmosphere in the Outer Banks is very informal. Rudy Austin ferried fourteen of us to Portsmouth on his skiff. The reservation was not done by mail or through the Internet—we called him. Arrangements were made on the telephone. He simply wrote down my first name and said, "Okay, Penny. We'll hold two spots for you. Pay me later."

After the meeting of the Friends of Portsmouth Island ended, we sailed for the island. Travel to Portsmouth is contingent on the weather. On that particular day conditions were ideal—bright sun, temperature in the eighties, no wind, and a relatively calm sea. As soon as I caught sight of the U.S. Life Saving Station's watchtower, my heart started racing. At the dock, the infamous mosquitoes and biting flies swarmed around us. What is left of the village is now part of the Cape Lookout National Seashore.

Two individuals from the U.S. Park Service greeted us and said volunteers generally spend some time there performing caretaking tasks in the summer and fall. The Friends of Portsmouth Island also assist with restoring the place by raising money, repairing buildings, and doing whatever is necessary to keep interest alive in the abandoned village so as to prevent Portsmouth's legacy from fading away. There are no stores, food or freshwater to drink on the island. We carried plastic bags to deposit our waste material. I was driven by a gator-type vehicle to the very beach where the foot patrols walking along the shore spotted my grandfather's ship. The waves of the Atlantic were gently washing up onto the smooth white sandy beach and the temptation of dipping my feet into the inviting water was irresistible.

ELEANOR LOPES AKAHLOUN

The former U.S. Life Saving Station is now a museum. I climbed the ladder to the tower where night guards scanned the waters for endangered ships. I also peeked into the surf men's sleeping quarters and touched a replica of the monomoy, one of the surf boats used in the rescue of the *Vera Cruz VII* passengers. The incident is considered one of the most significant events in North Carolina's history. The boat, which comfortably held fourteen passengers, was twenty-six feet eight inches in overall length and weighed 2,100 pounds. When overloaded, these boats easily capsized. The exhibits told riveting stories of the rescues, the islanders' harsh lives, and the people's fierce love of Portsmouth village.

Only a few scattered historic buildings remain in the village, including the post office/general store, the Pigott residence, a tiny church, and a one-room schoolhouse with folding desks. As we left the island, Rudy Austin pointed out Dry Shoal Faint, where my grandfather's ship went aground. The sea has reclaimed the land and only a fast-disappearing sandbar marked the location. For me, the visit was a profound spiritual experience. Although the island is deserted, a spirit of the past seems to dwell there. It is a place that captures the soul and imagination.

Early the next morning, we left Ocracoke Island by ferry, arrived at Cedar Island three hours later, and drove to downtown New Bern, North Carolina, where we visited the historic St. Paul's Roman Catholic Church. It was located some sixty miles from the waterfront shed, which temporarily housed my grandfather and the other survivors. They worshipped at the church prior to departing by train for New Bedford, Massachusetts on May 17, 1903. At the time, St. Paul's was segregated: as downstairs was reserved for whites and upstairs for blacks. I was now praying at the main altar wondering if the Cape Verdean immigrants enjoyed the same privilege.

The following day we dropped off the rental car, boarded the train at Rocky Mount Station, and arrived seven hours later in Savannah, Georgia. The beautiful southern city was filled with historic architecture and public squares and parks. The huge live oak trees draped with Spanish moss were lovely. Three days later we went to Charleston, South Carolina, where I was introduced to the Gullah Geechee culture firsthand.

Interestingly enough, while assigned to Tunisia, I learned about this group of people from the Low Country and Sea Islands of the

Carolinas, Georgia, and Florida from my former supervisor, Barrington King. Because of my Cape Verdean roots, he thought there might be a connection. Many years later, I saw an attractive Smithsonian Museum exhibit of Mary Jane Manigault's sweet grass, coiled baskets. She was a 1984 National Endowment for the Arts (NEA) National Heritage Fellow. Now at Charleston's Old City Market, I had the pleasure of meeting her relatives and watching them make similar baskets. It is difficult to explain, but I felt an uncanny kinship with them. We had something in common—our West African origin.

Charleston Harbor was one of the most important places in North America for the transatlantic slave trade. Up to half of the enslaved Africans brought into the U.S. entered through this port. The Old Slave Mart Museum I visited was actually a showroom where selling and trading took place. The exhibits were overpowering. Sixty-year-old women in 1850 sold for $50. This struck a raw nerve. At sixty-eight, in terms of monetary value, I would be practically worthless. We took an overnight train back to Washington, and my desire to see the Cape Verde Islands was rekindled. A visit to the "the old country" was just around the corner.

ELEANOR LOPES AKAHLOUN

CHAPTER TWENTY

RETURNING TO MY AFRICAN ROOTS

CAPE VERDE ISLANDS

July 23–August 3, 2011

Laying eyes on the Cape Verde Islands satisfied a lifelong dream. The trip underscored how much roots nourish our lives and how essential they are in grounding us to earth. It was a precious gift to finally spend time in the land of my ancestors.

Q: So you have accomplished your goal. Was there a sensation of being home? Describe what you encountered. Were you traveling alone?

AKAHLOUN: Most Cape Verdeans of my generation long to visit the land their grandparents romanticized. The bond between the U.S. and Cape Verde Islands is indisputable. The chain of the nine inhabited volcanic islands—roughly the size of Rhode Island—is situated over 350 miles from the coast of West Africa. According to the State Department's "Background Notes," out of the more than one million people of Cape Verdean ancestry, fewer than half actually live on the islands. The largest concentration is in southeastern New England—primarily New Bedford and Providence. To this day, roughly 87 percent of the Cape Verdean Americans live in this area. Portugal, Netherlands, Italy, France, Brazil, and Senegal also have smaller communities.

Some moments give life a radiant glow. Arriving at the Praia International Airport in Santiago on July 23, 2011, was one of them. It was electrifying. The islanders greeted us with grace and warmth, and I definitely felt at home. Although we were unaware taking photographs of the aircraft was prohibited, there was no danger of being arrested. The security guards were forgiving and generous with their smiles. The day was sunny and hot, and the city seemed sparsely populated. Living conditions were harsh. Women walked in dry riverbeds with buckets balanced on their heads. The people were cheerful. The greeting *oi* (hi) was heard frequently. So was *tudu bon?* (Everything okay?), and other variations of the same response—*tudu dretu, tudu em forma* or *tudu sabi*. All these expressions nostalgically reminded me of sitting under my grandparents' grape arbor, listening to amusing Cape Verdean tales.

I went to the islands with a delegation of mostly Cape Verdean friends. Informally, we called ourselves "the Gate of Return." We were eleven—Vanessa Britto Henderson and husband Galen, Julius and Sandra Britto, Nancy Andrade, Frank Andrews, Francis Cabral (since deceased), Nancy Andrade Reid and husband Chuck, Karen Lamoureux, and myself. Some of us had done genealogical studies on our families and were now searching for missing links. Vanessa, a physician and director of Wellesley College's Health Services, organized the grand trip with the assistance of Henrique Pires, the brother of former President Pedro Pires, and Cultural Affairs Specialist Maria Brito Frederico at the American Embassy.

After checking into the comfortable hotel Pestana Trópico in Praia, which happily had its own generator, we began sightseeing Santiago, the largest island, the political center of Cape Verde, and the one which seems to have the strongest link to West Africa. In the countryside, chickens, goats, and cows roamed freely. Sometimes they blocked the road, forcing our van to stop. Some goats stretched out and relaxed on front porches next to their buckets of water.

In Assomba, we visited the house where Amilcar Lopes Cabral, a freedom fighter in West Africa and the father of modern African nationalism in Guinea-Bissau and the Cape Verde Islands, spent his informative years. We continued our journey to Tarrafal, a town where the former Portuguese concentration camp known as *Campo da Morte Lenta* (Slow Death Camp) is located. It was appalling. Between 1936 and 1954, Tarrafal was a political prison for Portuguese antifascists and during 1961 to 1974 anticolonial activists from Angola, Cape Verde, and Guinea-Bissau were incarcerated there.

Along the way, we passed a distinctive *rebelado* (rebel) community. This was quite a revelation. In the 1940s, former runaway slaves revolted against the Portuguese colonial administrators and Catholic priests who were reforming the church by eliminating native rituals that clashed with Christian doctrine. The group still practices its own religious and cultural traditions and lives in isolated communal fashion where they mostly shun television, radio, and other modern-day conveniences. However, the number of *rebelados* is decreasing. The older generation is dying off, and the youth are becoming more open to the outside world.

We also visited Fort Real de São Filipe, which overlooks the oldest settlement and Cape Verde's first capital city, Cidade Velha (formerly Ribeira Grande). The fort was built in 1590 to fend off attacks by the French and English but was later sacked in 1712 by pirates. Cidade Velha became an important port for trading slaves from Guinea-Bissau and Sierra Leone to Brazil and the Caribbean. The town's pillory— wooden framework on a post where disobedient slaves were chained up and humiliated—is a cruel and shameful reminder of the dark side of the island's colonial past. It was a depressing sight. Our guide, Francisco, who lived on the town's oldest street, Rua Banana, was steeped in Cape Verdean history. He stated with pride that Vasco de Gamma stopped at the Cape Verde Island on his way to India in 1497, and that Christopher Columbus, in 1498, while on his third voyage to the Americas, also visited the islands.

We strolled down the historical palm-lined street, turned a corner, and hiked up a hill to the church of *Nossa Senhora do Rosário*, dating from about the early sixteenth century. An accommodating caretaker, Rosalinda, escorted us inside and told us that Sunday masses were still being held there. Walking down the main aisle was creepy, because we were stepping on the tombstones of aristocrats buried under the church's floor.

Later, we had an inspiring conversation with Angelo Barbosa, a faculty member at the University of Cape Verde (UCV), the country's first public university. Vanessa and President Dana Mohler-Faria of Bridgewater State University in Massachusetts have established an exchange program with the university. Paulo Jorge Borges and Adilson Tavares are excellent examples of the merits of the program. After receiving their degrees, both young men returned home to teach full time in public schools.

One of the highlights of our visit to Santiago was a courtesy call on President Pedro Verona Rodrigues Pires who was stepping down at the end of his second term. In his presence, you detected a quiet, refined statesman filled with warmth, humility, honesty, and a love for his people. He emphasized the importance of young Cape Verdeans taking their historical responsibilities seriously, maintaining their self-esteem, and working diligently to unify and build the nation. The president also thanked us for returning to the islands and for our commitment of keeping the Cape Verdean heritage alive.

A few months later it came as no surprise when he won the Mo Ibrahim Prize for Achievement in African Leadership given to former African heads of state for good governance. The committee's chairperson said, "The Prize Committee has been greatly impressed by President Pedro Pires's vision in transforming Cape Verde into a model of democracy, stability, and increased prosperity." Under his leadership from 2001 to 2011, Cape Verde became the second African country to graduate from the UN list of least developed countries. Accepting the award, Pires modestly said, "Cape Verde began with close to nothing, but step-by-step, with the efforts of all Cape Verdeans, progress is being made."

The following day, July 27, was also exciting. We journeyed to Fogo, the island where my grandparents were born. Some of the cliffs rose straight up from the floor of the sea and caressed the low-lying clouds. The airport landing strip was sandwiched between the sides of a gray mountain and the ocean. There was virtually no room for pilot error. São Filipe, the capital, is a charming village with public squares and colorful terracotta-roofed houses with Bougainvillea plants growing on balconies. Cobblestone streets led down to sandy black beaches. The lovely hotel Xaguate faced the ocean. From my window, I could see a hazy outline of Brava, and it was difficult to curb my enthusiasm. In two days, we would be there—the very place where my grandfather's voyage to America started.

Meanwhile, we visited the church of São Lourenço (St. Lawrence) where my grandparents were married in 1909. I knelt down and prayed at the front entrance of the locked church. A white dove, symbolizing the Holy Spirit above the door frame, watched over me. The blue-painted church was decorated with a cluster of white rooftop crosses that were visible for miles. During a second visit, I found two ladies sitting outside the church. A young lady went to fetch the keys for me, while I chattered with her soft-spoken older companion. Evidently, they were already waiting for the priest for nearly two hours. The door was unlocked, and I stepped inside completely awestruck. The rustic church was well-maintained and very peaceful. I thanked the lady and gave her a red rosary. Frankie Andrews had a bag full of them. The same Onset group, Our Lady's Rosary Circle, that my mother belonged to and which Mary Rose founded thirty-two years ago, was still going strong. As we drove away, the women were still waiting. The lives of these islanders seemed to move at a snail's pace.

After this, we went to Curral Grande, my grandmother's birthplace, where we spotted an elderly man and two older women with pretty headscarves sitting on field stones. The scene was surreal. One of the sweet ladies actually resembled my grandmother, yet none of them knew anything about my relatives. The van climbed higher, and our ears began popping. Mist and fog hampered our visibility and forced us to turn around on a narrow piece of dirt road. My heart stood still; the slightest miscalculation by the driver would send us tumbling down the ravine.

On July 28, 2011, we drove to Mount Fogo, an active volcano approximately 9,280 feet high that last erupted in 1995. Toward the summit, the smooth highway became steep and curved around rocky lava cliffs. We drove through the *Chã das Caldeiras* (Plain of Craters) and ate lunch at the Tortuga, a bed-and-breakfast in the midst of the crater. It was a quiet, moonlike landscape and had the strangest sensation. Leaving the area, we encountered a procession of young and old mourners playing instruments, singing, and dancing in the back of trucks. They could easily have been en route to a pep rally. I believe a statement was being made in typical Cape Verdean fashion: "The environment might be inhospitable, the circumstances grim, but life is worth celebrating. We shall prevail." And there they were making the most of every precious moment.

We ran into several snags the next day. The route to Mosteiros was under construction and the heavy rains the previous night spelled trouble. At one point, big boulders in the middle of the road blocked traffic in both directions. We waited patiently until two men physically carried all the rocks way. After a while, the trip resumed. Later we ran into a mudslide that prevented us from climbing a hill. For better traction, we good-naturedly switched our seats and redistributed the load. At the third attempt, everyone moved to the back of the van. The strategy worked. We were in business again, and we merrily went on our way.

In a remote mountainous village called Relva, birthplace of Frankie Andrew's grandfather, construction workers were widening a gravel road that prevented us from advancing. He got out and struck up a conversation with a man he discovered commuted from Brockton, Massachusetts to the islands every year. Our dear Frankie had a knack for sniffing out Cape Verdean Americans living or visiting the islands.

At our hotel in Praia, Frankie was astonished to see Mary Montrond and her two daughters, who were friends from Warehem, Massachusetts. They were in the islands tracing their captivating family history. Their ancestry dates back to Duke François Louis Armand Montrond, a wealthy French man who made Fogo his home in the early 1870s. His background was in medicine and engineering. Some of his accomplishments included building roads and digging wells. He also singlehandedly increased the island's population. Nowadays, his descendants are scattered throughout the world. According to Mrs. Montrond, at least, three hundred of them alone live in the U.S. This was quite interesting.

Something else stunned me. After a while, Mrs. Montrond and I recognized each other, as she and my mother had collaborated on various community projects during my childhood. Meeting so many Cape Verdeans with connections to the U.S. was a familiar theme. Many of them returned to the island to work, to start businesses or simply to retire. Their educational background and skills, professional expertise, and income enriched the islands.

The following evening, July 29, 2011, we drove to the port area and waited for the *Kriola,* a newly operated catamaran passenger/cargo ferry that was transporting us to Brava Island, a stone's throw away from Fogo. The clear, dark night sky was studded with thousands of twinkling stars. A passenger terminal had not yet been built, and crowds of the young and unemployed milled around an improvised parking lot. It was rather chaotic. Because the ferry was delayed, we reached Furna, a tiny port in Brava built in an extinct volcano at the base of steep cliffs, after midnight.

ELEANOR LOPES AKAHLOUN

The ascent to Vila Nova Sintra, the capital, was nerve wrenching. The poorly maintained road was pitch-dark. As we coiled our way up the mountaintop and approached blind curves, the driver honked his horn. We were even more frazzled when we reached the hotel, which was in various stages of construction and devoid of any life. We slowly filed out of the van and carefully dodged the debris scattered on the ground. We waited at length for the door to open. Finally, someone stirred, briefly greeted us, and vanished. My room had no running water or towels. The lamps on the nightstand were not working, and the overhead fixture produced slightly more light than a candle. In another room, the toilet leaked and water seeped into the hallway. I flopped into bed at 2:30 a.m.

Less than four hours later, a crowing roster and blaring music from across the street woke me up. The view from the fifth floor room where we ate breakfast was delightful, but we were overrun by flies that entered via missing window panes. Nonetheless, I was thankful and grateful to be there, reliving family history. Brava is the smallest and the greenest of the Cape Verdean Islands and has a distinct history in that plantation slavery was not a dominant feature.

The morning's outing to Fajã de Água was filled with great anticipation. We ate lunch at Jose Andrade's *Pensão Sol na Baia*, overlooking the bay where my grandfather's 1903 odyssey began. Our host accompanied us to Tapum, a dreamy village with colorful houses. One of them was the birthplace of Nancy Andrade Reid's father. We were introduced to Jose's eighty-one-year-old friend, Mr. Da Silva, who instantly recognized Frankie Andrews. After residing in Wareham, Massachusetts for twenty-four years, he returned to the islands, remarried, and was now the proud father of a two-year-old. We were all flabbergasted. Jose D. A. Lopes, another hearty soul, informed us he had lived in America forty-six years. He was a former merchant marine who over the years painstakingly built his own vessel and boldly sailed it from New England to the Cape Verde Islands. The island's magnetism lured many people back regardless of how long they lived in the U.S.

We returned to Fajã de Água the next day, and I was still in a trance. At last, I was visiting Brava, the island considered the springboard for emigration of Cape Verdeans to America and the spot where American whaling ships stopped to recruit sailors and gather supplies. It was historic. I wanted to dip my feet in the Atlantic Ocean, but there were no beaches, just rocks and cliffs. I learned, however, there was a lagoon about two miles away where people swam. Nancy, Vanessa, and I decided to hike there. Along the way, we felt the spirit of our trailblazing mothers, Julia Andrade, Lena Britto and Rita Lopes, cheering us on. A short time later, I was standing in a clear blue pool of water under a bright sky watching waves crash against the rocks. I outstretched my arms and jubilantly shouted, "Mission accomplished!"

At the crack of dawn, August 1, 2011, we made our way back down to Furna. Our guide said the mountainous road contained at least ninety-five sharp turns. I lost count, but I was mindful of the van's squeaky, vibrating steering wheel, and the driver's struggle to control it. At the dock, two women balanced large red buckets on their heads that overflowed with fresh fish they were selling. Helpers carried portable scales and stools. The money collected was stashed away inside safety-pinned apron pockets.

Our ferry left Brava at 6:30 a.m. and arrived in Fogo about forty minutes later. That afternoon, we boarded the plane for Santiago, fastened our seat belts, and landed in Praia a few minutes later. The flight was that quick. The next evening, at a farewell dinner, I choked up when saying good-bye to Maria Brito. We were all touched by her generosity and humanity. She had played such a selfless role in organizing our extraordinary trip.

Unhappily, all good things come to an end. Two days' later, we departed the Cape Verde Islands. Inside the plane, my seat offered a stunning view of the blue sky. Three, odd-shaped white clouds captured my attention. I was immediately reminded of my mother and her friends and the many stories they shared with us of these very islands. At sunset, a big yellow ball with shades of purple, pink, orange, and red set the sky ablaze as the sun slowly began its descent and dipped beneath the horizon.

Q: In retrospect, what did you learn from your stay on the islands?

AKAHLOUN: Visiting the islands provided fresh new insights. It gave me a richer understanding of my ancestors in terms of their mixed heritage. While they traveled with Portuguese passports and considered themselves to be European, their cultural connection to mainland Africa was undeniable. The association is evident in the island's legacy of slavery, Cape Verdean food and diet, medicine, manners, and superstitions. I was able to internalize their desperation to flee their poor, drought-ridden society that promised little, if any, hope for advancement. Their rationale for signing up for long risky voyages chasing whales around the world, or crossing the turbulent Atlantic Ocean on unseaworthy schooners became crystal clear.

Q: *Now you have come full circle. What lessons can be derived from your Cape Verdean American experience?*

AKAHLOUN: My experience is distinct for a few reasons. To begin with, Cape Verdeans represent the first group of Americans from Africa to have made the transatlantic voyage voluntarily. They arrived in the U.S. long before other large racially mixed groups. Our society has a longstanding history of racial division. We tend to place people in rigid categories of black or white. The Cape Verdean population demonstrated that America's system of race classification is too narrow in scope. Ethnicity is not clear-cut. It is a complicated matter as physical features do not necessarily define a person's racial category.

Cape Verdeans, as well as similar groups, cannot be identified by the languages they speak, place of residence, or by profession. They live many different lives at the same time, and their identities are always changing and in flux. Their outlook and worldview is multiconfigurational. The Cape Verdean multiracial, multicultural society is a true illustration of cultural interweaving. While they accept and appreciate differences between people of all races, creed and color, whether red, brown, yellow, black or white, they are committed to their own way of life. This does not imply that Cape Verdeans are superior to others, as no culture is inherently better or worse than another. I was fortunate to have excellent role models. This ancestry subconsciously—but also quite consciously—shaped my love for travel and exploration and contributed to my ability to be flexible and adaptable to new communities and cultures.

CHAPTER TWENTY-ONE

A Pristine Wilderness Beyond Description

ANTARCTICA

January 2–11, 2014

There is a familiar expression that says, "Just when the caterpillar thought the world was over, it became a butterfly." After traveling to six continents and over fifty countries, I thought I had seen it all. That is until I experienced Antarctica. The very word stirs the imagination, but in reality, it impresses even more.

Q: Why venture to the far reaches of the globe to see penguins? They are plentiful at Sea World in Florida. And there you avoid frigid temperatures. Antarctica is one of the world's most remote, coldest, windiest, and driest continents. What influenced you?

AKAHLOUN: The idea came out of the blue. Prior to turning seventy and Omar thirty, Leila asked where we wanted to celebrate our respective birthdays. In particular, she wanted to know what places were on my bucket list. Spontaneously, I blurted out Antarctica. It was the only continent the children and I had not explored. Realizing how far-fetched this sounded, I quickly suggested more manageable destinations. Over time, I forgot about the conversation, but Leila has a long memory. She conspired with Omar. On April 6, my birthday, I was surprised with a complete tour package for a ten-day journey to the end of the earth—Antarctica!

For nearly a year, and with scant input from her brother and me, she meticulously planned the South Pole expedition. Omar flew from his home in Portland, Oregon; I traveled from Washington, D.C., and we met up in Atlanta, Georgia. After flying for nearly ten hours, our plane landed in Buenos Aires, Argentina. That night on December 30, 2013, Leila arrived from Johannesburg, South Africa, where she currently lives, and the anticipation of this lifetime venture began. We spent a few days in Buenos Aires before continuing our journey southward.

Our hotel was opposite the city's historic *Cementerio de Recoleta*, a splendid cemetery filled with the buried remains of past presidents, military heroes, noble prize winners, and the rich and famous. The resting place has more than 6,400 elaborate vaulted tombs and majestic mausoleums, some of which resembled chapels, Greek temples, pyramids, and miniature mansions. There was a good deal of traffic on the "street" leading to the simple crypt of Eva Peron, Argentina's most beloved and controversial First Lady. Healthy populations of cats also lived among the graves. It was a noteworthy, but somewhat melancholy, experience.

Adjacent to the cemetery is the beautiful *Basilica de Nuestra Señora del Pilar* that was built in 1732. The church with its ornate silver altar, tile work, and chapels is considered one of the best-preserved examples of Argentine colonial architecture. I attended mass there prior to and after our expedition to Antarctica. Dogs were welcomed. One barked during the service, but no one raised an eyebrow. Later, Leila arranged an outing at the Tango Porteno Theater. Omar and I were given lessons—my very first one. We ate dinner while watching a superb show. What a treat.

Buenos Aires was experiencing a prolonged, record-breaking heat wave that generated isolated power outages and water shortages across the city. Temperatures soared to at least 102 degrees Fahrenheit. The heat was unbearable, and there was considerable gridlock caused by various demonstrations. During New Year's Eve, we bought snacks from the sole kiosk that remained open until 6:30 p.m. We ushered in 2014 laughing and munching on our goodies at a deserted cafe outside our hotel. Upon landing in Ushuaia, Argentina, the following afternoon, the climate abruptly changed and seemed to be preparing us for the glacial winds heading our way.

Ushuaia, a charming place, is situated at the tail end of the Andes in the province of Tierra del Fuego. While the city is recognized as the southernmost settlement in the world, Puerto Williams on the Chilean side of the Beagle Channel technically holds this distinction. The town was primarily developed as a base, but as the military presence declined, tourism and scientific support activities grew and people began settling there permanently. Geographically, this village is closer to the South Pole than Ushuaia.

The following day, January 2, 2014, about 133 of us boarded buses at the pier that took us to the M/S Expedition, our mighty excursion vessel. It would serve both as our home and base camp for the next ten days as we explored the great white continent. I could hardly contain myself. The ship's crew and expedition staff greeted us with huge smiles and helped all of us settle into our cabins, where our luggage awaited us. After looking around the ship, we gathered in the Discovery Lounge for a mandatory lifeboat drill. Everything operated with clockwork precision. Shortly, we slipped out of the harbor and sailed east into the protected waters of the Beagle Channel. I was grateful to have my children at my side sharing this unique experience.

Before long it was dinnertime. During our delicious four-course meal, we chatted with likeminded travelers from all over the world and enjoyed the sweeping view of snow-clad mountains. Soon we steamed past the last outpost of civilization. The first night at sea we left the channel and entered the legendary Drake Passage. This five-hundred-mile-wide body of water separates Cape Horn, Chile, from Antarctica's South Shetland Islands, and connects the Atlantic Ocean with the Pacific Ocean. The warmer water of the north and the frigid Antarctic waters from the south converge here, but they do not readily mix. Under stormy conditions, the swells can reach a height of over thirty-three feet. The outer decks were closed as a safety precaution. To avoid seasickness, many people took pills, some wore patches behind their ears, and others required injections. I, fortunately, did not need any medication. I kept hydrated and practiced deep breathing exercises, which helped me to relax. By morning, the waves had settled somewhat although the ship was still rolling and pitching a bit.

In the afternoon of the second day, we saw a rainbow in the sky that formed a pretty arc over the ship's bow. I considered it a positive omen. Our orientation program was intense. We were fitted for our expedition jackets, tried on rubber boots in the mudroom where we would store our wet gear, listened to lifeboat drills, and learned how to safely get on and off Zodiacs. There was also a mandatory International Association of Antarctic Tour Operators (IAATO) briefing to ensure we followed environmental protocols. Later, we began bio security checks to make certain we did not carry any foreign flora and fauna, seeds, or bacteria onshore that might adversely impact the Antarctic ecosystem. We emptied our pockets and examined all hoods, cuffs, Velcro, and seams of garments we planned to take ashore. Waterproof pants, backpacks, camera bags, hats, mittens, and walking poles were also inspected.

The cruise organizers left nothing for the imagination. The resident ship photographer, Paul Teolis, held numerous workshops and successfully turned novices like me into budding professional photographers. Biologist Frank Todd, a recognized authority on penguins with some forty seasons of work in Antarctica, introduced us to the furry bird's charismatic world. It didn't take long to spot some remarkable seabirds following the ship. These included Wandering Albatrosses, which have the longest wingspan of any bird on the planet and Cape Petrels with their beautiful black-and-white speckled backs and upper wings. Depending on the condition of the sea, weather, wind, and ice, we hoped to land on Antarctic soil the following day.

During the night, we made our way down the Bransfied Strait into the Gerlache Strait and on to Paradise Bay. In the morning, Sunday, January 5, we were blessed with bright sunshine—a superb day for our first Zodiac ride. I braced for the cold but was pleasantly surprised at how relatively warm the outside temperature seemed, even surrounded by ice and snow. Four layers of polar grade clothing and ample supplies of hand and foot warmers worked like a charm. We landed at an unoccupied Argentine station, formerly known as Almirante Brown Base, in Paradise Bay. Along the rocky shore, lovable Gentoo penguins greeted us as Leila, Omar, and I ceremoniously stepped on our seventh continent together. It was exhilarating. Behind the abandoned station was a 164-foot slope that we hiked. We were warned to be careful climbing the steep, heavily crevassed area. Once we reached the top, there was a majestic view in every direction. Open blue sky, low clouds, and jagged snow-covered mountain peaks, immense glaciers flowing sometimes down to the sea or spilling into midair from an altitude of hundreds of feet. Everything was reflected in a mirror like sea.

Some of us slid down on our backside. It was frightening and thrilling at the same time. I literally flew down the hill at an incredibly high rate of speed but somehow managed to survive. Back in our Zodiac, we passed the same slope only to discover the back side dangerously plunged into the sea. We entered Skontorp Cove and explored the pristine bay. We got close views of the extraordinary icebergs broken off from the fast-moving glacier at the end of the bay. We weaved in and out of the dense ice flows and circled Wendell seals lounging on chunks of floating ice. High up on an exposed cliff there were Blue-eyed Shags feeding their young from the mud and rock nests. Our Zodiac driver cut the engine off so we could enjoy the tranquility and the breathtaking landscape. It was amazing!

After an appetizing lunch, we took a Zodiac ride to Port Lockroy, or Base A, on Goudier Island. This was the home of the U.K. Antarctic Heritage Trust's restored hut that contained a wonderful museum, gift shop, and the only public post office on the Antarctic Peninsula. In World War II, the British government was concerned about increased foreign activity in the Southern Ocean and as a result established this Port Lockroy station in 1944. The operation was taken over shortly afterward and used for scientific research purposes until 1962. Currently, the main building is designated as a historical site and is only staffed by a skeleton crew during part of the Southern Hemisphere austral summer (December, January, and February). The friendly colonies of penguins are more permanent residents.

The richness of Antarctica's Peninsula kept us in a constant state of awe. We never knew what the next day would bring. It was always different and stimulating. Monday, January 6, was another perfect day. Early in the morning, we sailed south for the Lemaire Channel, which runs between the mainland of the Antarctic Peninsular and Booth Island. The place is nicknamed "Kodak Alley," as it is regarded as one of the most scenic parts of the world and the most photographed section of the continent. The narrow passage is approximately seven miles long and clogs up at any time of the year. Ice conditions change daily, and danger is ever-present. We pushed pack ice out of the way and dodged icebergs as our ship slowly passed steep vertical cliffs falling straight into the sea on either side of us. The area's charm must be seen to be believed.

The afternoon was devoted to Zodiac cruising through a maze of spectacular icebergs and an unforgettable landing on Booth Island. The ice formations and the reflections on Pleneau Bay's clear water were remarkable. It is rare to see such powerful beauty, and we had a front row seat to view grounded bridges, giant cones, and long tubes of ice often strikingly blue, which are thousands of years old. Our boat circled a massive iceberg. Moments after photographing it, a huge chunk of ice crashed into the sea. Indeed, global warming is real and dangerous.

At another spot, we caught sight of a doe-eyed Crabeater and Leopard and Weddell seals sleeping on slabs of ice. Before long, we were walking among the penguins on Booth Island where many of them congregated. According to our guide, this was one of the few locations where all three long-tailed penguins—Gentoos, Chinstrap, and Adelie—nest together. Some of the adorable chicks were just hatching.

Despite all our activities, our day was only half over. It was time for the infamous polar plunge. Forty brave souls, including Leila and Omar, leapt off the ship into freezing water. I entertained the idea up until the last moment but then wisely opted to photograph the event instead. After this, it was time to bundle up and enjoy an Antarctic barbeque on the ship's windswept deck. It was quite a novelty.

The following day, we entered Cierva Cove, a seemingly make-believe world of floating ice from tiny fragments to large wind and wave sculpted blocks to enormous tabular icebergs. There were clusters of snow-capped icebergs some of which were filled with a bit of rock and grit. They were in stark contrast to the surrounding bright blue ice caves. The peninsula's glacier-lined mountains rose steeply against a partly sunny sky. The size, volume, and various shapes of ice were impressive and very symbolic of the unspoiled and rugged wilderness that is unique to Antarctica. It was so magical.

Crossing the Orleans Strait to the Palmer Archipelago, we encountered a pod of twenty-five blowing humpback whales feeding on krill. The captain maneuvered the ship toward them so we could better photograph their raised tail flukes as they prepared to dive underwater. We continued on to Mikkelsen Harbor on the south side of Trinity Island, where we experienced another Zodiac landing and toured the glacier-fringed harbor. Seals were stretching out on the beach next to a pile of whalebones and what remained of a boat. These were reminders of Antarctica's whaling days that began on a sizable scale during the early 1900s.

Our last day in Antarctica was January 8, 2014, and it was another fascinating experience. In the morning, we sailed through the narrow entrance of Telefon Bay in Deception Island into a large flooded caldera. Just then a seal was hauling itself out of the water on to a black sandy beach. It was another first for me. The weather was cold and windy. Snow flurries began falling but soon went away. We hiked up a steep slope to the rim of one of the many volcanic cones to view the massive crater formed during a relatively recent eruption. We identified at least six Crabeater seals relaxing on the beach surrounded by curious Chinstrap penguins.

The afternoon outing was at Greenwich Island's Yankee Harbor, where a young molting Elephant Seal was dosing onshore. But the Gentoos with their bright red-orange beaks, white stripes above the eye, and peach-colored feet were the highlight. We spent considerable time sitting and observing a colony of thousands of these nesting birds and their fluffy, bewildered chicks. At this point, they were like family to us. Steady streams of our social friends, ranging in height from twenty to thirty-five inches, were marching to and from the nests. Adults spend almost the entire day in the water hunting for food. Their fairly long tails stuck out from behind, sweeping from side to side, as they waddled awkwardly up and down the hill. Some were more sure-footed and hopped over boulders and the cracks between the rocks. Others stumbled on the ice or fell into the snow. It seemed difficult to fathom that they are the fastest bird in water and able to swim about twenty-two miles per hour. Lines of them were belly-flopping off ice and rocks into the ocean. Their boundless amusing antics were quite a spectacle.

Gentoo penguins often form long-lasting bonds and are highly nurturing. Male and female take an active role in raising their chicks. Most of the nesting penguins were feeding copious amounts of krill to their squeaking offspring, begging for food. Males gather the materials for the nest and are not above stealing stones from neighbors, which can lead to heated arguments. We witnessed some of this loud bickering, as well as some attempts at mating. Brown Skuas were circling above waiting to swoop down from the sky and steal eggs. The penguins threw back their heads, trumpeted loudly and fended off the attack. It was another brilliant day of excursions on the continent.

During the next two days, the Drake Passage was relatively peaceful. We had ample time for watching Southern Fulmars and other seabirds soaring in the sky. We also participated in various activities and attended

ELEANOR LOPES AKAHLOUN

excellent lectures. Our knowledgeable expedition leader, Alex Cowan, gave a thought-provoking talk on the increased levels of greenhouse gases and its impact on the planet. He explained it was potentially an enormous problem because if the global temperature rises to a level where it affects the Antarctic ice caps and glaciers, they could melt and the sea level worldwide would rise. Many cities located by water would be flooded. This would also be devastating for some countries that have coastal populations. Farmlands would be wiped out, and people would be homeless and incapable of feeding themselves. And some of the smaller island nations would simply disappear. These are only a few of the serious consequences.

Global warming is happening at an alarming rate. Fortunately, people are beginning to understand the risks involved and are realizing climate change affects all of us, every living thing. As a result, individuals, communities, government agencies, and organizations in the U.S. and internationally are trying to take constructive measures to slow down the damage being done to our planet. But, we don't have to wait for others to find a solution for this disastrous situation, each of us can take personal action. Little things can help, such as buying energy-efficient appliances, turning off lights when leaving the room, using compact fluorescent light bulbs (CFLs), running dishwashers or washing machines with full loads, car pooling, and writing elected officials and encouraging them to take a leadership role in addressing this complex problem of global warming.

Next, the ship's renowned biologist inspired us with his "Impossible Dream" presentation. Against tremendous odds, he created the famous Sea World Penguin Encounters. His pioneering work was responsible for the first environmentally controlled facility for breeding Adelie and Emperor penguins outside their native habitat. We also watched a marvelous documentary on Ernest Shackleton's 1914, long and daring Antarctic expedition.

At the captain's farewell, we met and thanked the outstanding crew that made our trip so enjoyable. We sailed pass Cape Horn, Chile, and spotted Peale's dolphins bow-riding along the ship. We then made our way to Ushuaia, where we disembarked Saturday morning on January 11. What a strange feeling it was to breathe warm air and watch people, instead of penguins, scurrying around. Sadly, the unimaginable beauty of remote glaciers and ice in all its myriad forms were left behind. The same day we flew to Buenos Aires. Before departing South America, we spent a lovely evening with Patricia Regules, a treasured family friend from our time in Uruguay.

Q: *There are few places on earth where there has never been war, where the environment is fully protected and where scientific research has priority. The whole of the Antarctic continent is like this. Why is that so?*

AKAHLOUN: The Antarctic Treaty System (ATS) is largely responsible. The main treaty officially went into force in 1961, and there are currently some fifty signatory nations agreeing to maintain the continent as a natural reserve: one devoted to peaceful purposes and scientific research. Military activity, nuclear tests, and the disposal of radioactive waste are banned.

Antarctica is the only continent without a permanent human population, but it is breathtakingly beautiful and almost unearthly. When we visit, we discover why we bothered to come to the South Pole. Our expectations are exceeded and our awareness of the planet's environmental issues is heightened. Its unspoiled wilderness is like nothing and nowhere else. Every aspect of Antarctica is enchanting and spellbinding. I felt like an intruder into another world.

Q: *I think you clearly explain why Antarctica should be on our bucket lists. Thank you, Penny, for reflecting on your life's experiences and for sticking with this oral history project. Your perseverance is remarkable. Before closing, do you want to touch on any other aspect of your extraordinary journey?*

AKAHLOUN: Yes. Thank you very much. Joining the Foreign Service was a rich, rewarding experience. For forty-three years, I served my country, traveled extensively, and met people from different ethnic, religious, geographic, and economic backgrounds. My work was enormously fulfilling. I loved it. Getting an up close view of history in the making was fascinating. I took pride in representing the U.S. and enjoyed empowering people and helping them resolve conflicts. I learned that despite physical or cultural differences we belong to one global family. We are interconnected and dependent on each other in many ways.

ELEANOR LOPES AKAHLOUN

Those who went before me showed me how to put one foot ahead of the other. They trained me to work extremely hard so as to improve my lot in life. Along the way, there were ups and downs, poor decisions and good ones, disappointments and delights, and failures as well as successes. And these setbacks made me stronger and wiser. Because of my ancestors, I learned to rise above, to respect all cultures, and to give back. They are gone now but not forgotten. Their valuable lessons are still with me.

If not for the loving encouragement of my children, family, the extended Cape Verdean community, my mentors and friends, this memoir could not have been written. As I look back over my life—born to Cape Verdean American parents, growing up in a sheltered community as a minority, moving to Boston to continue my studies, struggling to join the Foreign Service, marrying a person from a different faith and culture, wrestling with upward career mobility, being a single parent, retiring, and engaging in community affairs—I realize a higher power guided me. Faith, optimism, and determination paved the way. Only in America can this happen to an ordinary person such as me. Our land is rich in opportunity.

There was a much greater portion of joy than misery in my life. I learned early on that I am the source of my own happiness. Instead of seeking contentment through external forces, I generated the warm, fuzzy feeling internally, and this propelled me forward. When my carefully laid plans went astray, I didn't surrender. I fought harder and reminded myself failures were really successes in disguise. We are masters of our own thoughts. The decision to make them cheerful ones rests within us. And one final thought, age is not a complicating factor in pursuing one's treasured goals. I am moving from a good to better stage of life and have enough energy and ideas to fill another lifetime.

To the readers accompanying me on my voyage, the best of luck chasing your dreams and aspirations. Listen to your inner voice, which will lead you in the right direction. Don't give in to your fears. Everyone has the intrinsic strength and power to embark on a wondrous life's journey. Persevere when all seems lost, and eventually you will be rewarded.

BIOGRAPHY

Eleanor L. Akahloun, born in 1943, was raised in a small Cape Verdean community in Onset, Massachusetts. She is a retired diplomat with the U.S. State Department, where she served forty-three years initially as a Foreign Service secretary and ultimately as a human resources officer. She is a graduate of Chamberlayne Junior College and attended evening classes at Boston University.

She has traveled to over fifty countries and held assignments in the Philippines, Morocco, Kenya, Tunisia, Canada, Uruguay, China, Venezuela, and Washington, D.C. She has two children and currently resides outside of Washington, D.C., where she enjoys writing, traveling, practicing yoga, and engaging in volunteer work.

CPSIA information can be obtained at www.ICGtesting.com
Printed in the USA
BVOW04s1852041214

377597BV00001BA/9/P